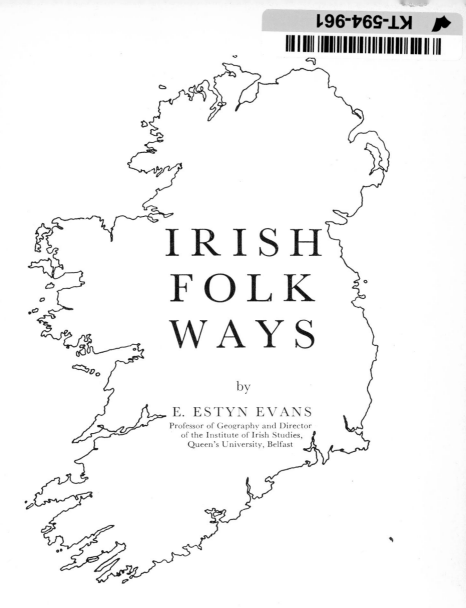

IRISH
FOLK
WAYS

by

E. ESTYN EVANS

Professor of Geography and Director
of the Institute of Irish Studies,
Queen's University, Belfast

Routledge & Kegan Paul

LONDON, BOSTON AND HENLEY

First published 1957
by Routledge & Kegan Paul Ltd
39 Store Street, London WC1E 7DD,
Broadway House, Newtown Road
Henley-on-Thames, Oxon RG9 1EN
and 9 Park Street,
Boston, Mass. 02108, U.S.A.

Printed in Great Britain by
Lowe & Brydone Printers Limited, Thetford, Norfolk

Second impression 1961
Third impression 1966
Fourth impression 1967
Fifth impression 1972
Sixth impression 1976
Seventh impression 1979

ISBN *0 7100 1344 2 (c)*
ISBN *0 7100 2888 1 (p)*

CONTENTS

LIST OF TEXT FIGURES

LIST OF TEXT FIGURES

LIST OF PLATES

Between pages 144–5

xi

PREFACE

The generous reception given to my *Irish Heritage*, published fifteen years ago, has encouraged me to go on collecting material on Irish folk life and to prepare this more comprehensive book on the subject. The earlier book was written, under difficult conditions, in the years 1939–41; it was an introductory study of an unexplored field, necessarily speculative and undocumented, and its main purpose was to arouse interest among Irish readers in the treasure-house of the past in which they live. It is hoped that IRISH FOLK WAYS will have a wider appeal. It is abundantly illustrated and fortified by references to a fairly full bibliography. Even so, parts of the text must be taken on trust, since some of the information was gathered from personal observation and conversations up and down Ireland. In the 'mountainy' corners of the country the past is ever-present, a ready topic of talk. I have checked the information where possible, for the inquirer must always be on guard against the countryman's facility of speech, his poetic licence and his fatal desire to please.

There is a great fascination in exploring the living past, but one cannot employ the strict methodology of the historical or natural sciences. The historian is handicapped in studying peasant peoples, not only because they leave no documents but also because their sense of time and values are not those of fully literate folk. The geographer, interested primarily in variations in space, makes an easier approach; yet he will miss much unless he has a concern for origins and a sense of the past. Without knowledge of the past he will not fully observe the present: it is the emotional shock which prints in the memory the first sight of some tool or custom which has survived from an earlier culture-layer. For the historian, on the other hand, the fact that it was described in the eighteenth century is more significant than that it occurs, unrecorded, in the twentieth.

xiii

However interesting we may find 'bygones' for their own sake—and most of us take a natural interest in the way our forefathers lived—there is need to know not only how these relics were made and used but also what beliefs were held about them. Wherever possible I have studied the techniques of making and using tools as well as their lore, and by assisting in the processes have learnt more than books can teach. There is a clear relationship between the ways in which men's basic needs are satisfied and the social organization. Nothing less than the whole of the past is needed to explain the present, and in this difficult task we cannot afford to neglect the unrecorded past. The crafts of arable farming, of animal husbandry and the home industries have done more to shape our instincts and thoughts than the trampling of armies or the wranglings of kings which fill the documents from which history is written.

The outstanding interest of Ireland for the student of European origins lies in the fact that in its historic literature, language and social organization, as well as in its folklore and folk customs, it illustrates the marginal survival of archaic elements of the Indo-European world. Myles Dillon has shown how the three classes of ancient Irish society—the learned class, the warriors and the peasantry—are closely paralleled in the three main castes of Hinduism: Brahman, Kshatriya and Vaisya. The ethnographer may be led even farther afield in discovering a skin boat, a rush charm or a wheel-less cart that will take him on a scientific trail to the ends of the earth. And geologists and botanists find a similar interest in the peripheral survival in Ireland of rock-formations and floras which in their day dominated a wider scene.

The decades of demographic instability which culminated in the Great Famine of 1845–7 brought radical changes in the economy and landscape of rural Ireland. A correspondent in *The Times* of May 19th, 1853, noted that 'all accounts describe the country and its inhabitants as assuming more of the half-picturesque, half-comfortable aspect, of an English landscape', no doubt because hedges and an orderly husbandry had transformed the naked famine-stricken scene. The famine, as we shall see, was a great social watershed and it marked the end of an era that might well be termed prehistoric. But it is the

xiv

changes which are taking place today, a hundred years later, that are finally extinguishing the prehistoric traditions. Mechanization and mass-production are invading the remotest glens, and things which were the commonplaces of fifty years ago are becoming as remote to the young as the Middle Ages. Knowledge of ways of life that have altered little for centuries is passing away; skills whose loss the practical countryman may have cause to regret are disappearing. The Irish Universities have a unique opportunity of fostering local studies and folk-lore-research, but only University College, Dublin, has seriously supported this work. The Government of Northern Ireland, however, is to be congratulated on having offered to help to finance an Ulster Folk Museum on the lines of St. Fagans in Wales and those of the Scandinavian countries.

Meanwhile the National Museum in Dublin, the Belfast Municipal Museum and the County Museum, Armagh, have been busy collecting and displaying the portable elements of material culture, and I have drawn freely on their exhibits for sketches of objects which it is now too late to find in everyday use. I wish to thank Mr. A. T. Lucas and Dr. J. Raftery, of the National Museum, Mr. W. A. Seaby of the Belfast Museum, and Mr. T. G. F. Paterson of Armagh for their assistance and encouragement. Among many other friends and colleagues whose help I cannot forget are Kevin Danaher and Sean O'Sullivan of the Irish Folklore Commission, Professor Michael Duignan, Professor M. J. O'Kelly, Professor Sean O'Riordain, H. G. Tempest, and Dr. A. E. J. Went; and among my former students R. H. Buchanan, Rosemary Harris, N. C. Mitchel, Dr. D. McCourt, Dr. J. M. Mogey, V. B. Proudfoot and G. B. Thompson. I have to thank the editors of the *Ulster Journal of Archaeology* and of *Ulster Folklife* and Mr. W. A. Seaby for the loan of blocks, and Mr. Seaby also for permission to use several photographs from the collection of the late R. J. Welch. Mr. W. A. Green, Miss H. E. Henry, Mr. Frank Scovell and Mr. C. E. F. Trench have kindly supplied me with photographs. Miss Eileen Duncan has prepared the four maps, and other acknowledgements appear under the text-figures. It is a pleasure also to acknowledge the help received, either orally or in correspondence, from numerous Irishmen in all parts of the country. Two books listed in the bibliography deserve special mention for their relevance to our theme: Sean O'Sullivan's *Handbook of Irish Folklore* and Wood-Martin's remarkable pioneer work on *The Elder Faiths of Ireland.*

Finally I would gratefully place on record the lasting benefits I have received from the teaching and example, at Aberystwyth, of Professor H. J. Fleure, who taught me to study regional social evolution as a continuous interaction between people and their environment. The deficiencies of this book, however, are my own.

Queen's University,   E. E. EVANS
  Belfast.
     January, 1957

I

IRELAND THE OUTPOST

THE charm of Ireland, north as well as south, lies as much in the colourful speech and old-fashioned ways of her people as in the beauty of her green fields and blue hills, the silver-glint of lake waters and the gold of the scented whins. The observant visitor cannot fail to be attracted by customs and turns of speech, by traditions and tools which are obsolescent if not archaic in England. He will occasionally see in use in field and farmyard implements which went out of fashion so long ago in most parts of Great Britain that one may truly speak of them as medieval. Thus the toothed sickle, the flail, the one-eared spade, the clod-breaking mallet and seed-rake, the up-right churn and the three-legged pot can all be closely matched in illustrations of English medieval rural life (Fig. 1). The boon-work which was an obligation owed by tenants to English landlords in the Middle Ages survives in the flax-pulling boons of Ulster, and the Anglo-Norman word for the lord's part of an estate, the demesne, is universally applied to the parklands of Ireland. The Irish baronies or kingdoms, as they are sometimes called, are similarly relics of the Middle Ages. The prevalence of the Roman Catholic religion, to which 76 per cent of the population of Ireland adheres—the figure is 94 per cent for the Republic of Ireland—reinforces this sense of the past; and the English dialects spoken in many districts, even if shot through with Gaelic-derived turns of phrase, are strikingly Elizabethan. A strong medieval flavour attaches to the feast-day gatherings and patterns, to strawboys, wrenboys and the Christmas mummers. Medieval too is the diversity of folk-customs and of locally-made tools, which will be found to vary from one

1

Fig. 1. 'The toothed sickle (1), the flail (2), the one-eared spade (4), the clod-breaking mallet (5), and seek-rake (7), the upright churn (6), and the three-legged pot (3), can all be closely matched in illustrations of English medieval rural life.'

district to another. The interest of these relics is enhanced when one discovers parallels among simple societies in distant parts of the world.

These ancient diversities are being ironed out at an increasing rate, and the opportunity of seeing and, what is more important, placing on record these age-old crafts and rites will soon pass. The wonder is that so many have persisted through the political, economic and social upheavals of the last 150 years. During that period the steady decline of the Gaelic language resulted in the loss of a great deal of information on local and regional life and of a vast store of oral literature, in which the lore of an ancient civilization was enshrined. The scientist must regard this loss as a tragedy comparable to that suffered by the historian in the disastrous burning of the Dublin Four Courts in

1922. Ireland is one of the last homes of the oral traditions of prehistoric and medieval Europe, which mirror the routine of rural life through the seasons, the contacts of peoples in war and in commerce, and the heroic deeds of half-legendary leaders. Luckily all is not lost: the devoted labours of the Irish Folklore Commission have rescued from the Gaeltacht and catalogued with scientific skill countless stories of the kind which enriched the literature of the medieval world. In Northern Ireland also belated efforts are being made to gather the harvest of lore and legend.

The study of both the material and spiritual folk-life cf Ireland and the oceanic fringes of Europe can throw light on the past and on the evolution of society in Britain and western Europe generally. English anthropologists and ethnographers have searched the farthest continents and enriched scientific literature with their findings, but they have neglected the little island across the Irish Sea. Irish scholars too, perhaps because they find it hard to detach themselves from what is familiar, have shown little interest until recently in the treasure-house of fact and fancy that lies about them. Some writers, indeed, appear to deplore the existence of the folk-customs I am describing in this book: they would conceal or even deny them. It has been learnedly argued, for instance, that the well-authenticated practice of 'ploughing by the tail'[1] was the lying invention of English propagandists, who passed an Act of Parliament prohibiting it, in 1635, merely to demonstrate how degraded the Irish must be! Those features of rural life which cannot be concealed or denied are regarded as due to the repressive hand of England, to penal laws, absenteeism and the poverty imposed by rack-rents and unscrupulous land-agents. Certainly there have been great abuses, and they have left the Irish suspicious and sensitive. It is unfortunate, therefore, that authoritative works recently published in England have needlessly exaggerated the tribal habits and pastoral nomadism of the ancient Irish. A writer in the *Cambridge Economic History*,[2] indeed, goes so far as to describe fifteenth-century Ireland as 'in great part, a

[1] *The Irish Book-lover* (May, 1943), 9.
[2] *The Cambridge Economic History of Europe*. Eds. J. H. Clapham and E. Power, 1 (1941), 161.

country of wandering pastoralists'. The Irishman cannot forget the wrongs that his country has suffered and he sees in such statements an echo of the calumnies which he finds in the majority of English descriptions of Ireland. Many of them were written with the preconceived idea of revealing 'a barbarous people devoted only to laziness . . . living on beasts only, and living like beasts . . . a filthy people, wallowing in vice' (to quote the earliest, Giraldus Cambrensis[1]). For several centuries his *Topographia Hiberniae* served as a guide and a gospel to those who sought to prove the Irish unworthy and incapable of self-government and to justify their conquest by England. Geoffrey Keating describes him as 'the bull of the herd for writing the false history of Ireland, wherefore they have no choice of guide'.[2] Gerald's picture of the 'mere Irish', as they came to be called, thus gained wide currency in England and was frequently copied. Between 1566 and 1606, for example, beginning with John Good's *A Description of the Manners and Customs of the Wild Irish*, a dozen colourful accounts were written, most of them little more than diatribes against Irish morals. (The Irish, be it said, retaliated by 'deriding and scoffing at such as lived civilly and after the English manner').[3]

It should be noticed, however, that with the deliberate colonization of Ireland that followed the sixteenth century wars a different note creeps in. The Irish people were still abused, but their country must be made to appear attractive to settlers. The first serious geographical account of the island had appeared in Camden's *Brittania* in 1586, when the Munster plantations were beginning. Detailed surveys and censuses were prepared for the Ulster plantations of the early seventeenth century, but it was left to Sir William Petty (1623–87) to make the most celebrated and exhaustive study of the island. His *Political Anatomy of Ireland*, in reality a human and economic geography, only serves to remind us what was lost when the maps and notes of his larger Down Survey perished in a fire in Dublin Castle in 1711. Petty aimed at a comprehensive survey which would

[1]Giraldus Cambrensis, *Topography of Ireland*. Trans. by J. J. O'Meara (1951), 85, 86, 90.
[2]G. Keating, *History of Ireland*. Irish Texts Society, I, 153.
[3]Sir George Carew, *Survey of Kerry and Desmond* (1617).

form the basis of a reconstructed Ireland. One of his proposals, perhaps the most original of all the varied suggestions for solving 'the Irish problem', was to import a further 200,000 English settlers so as to bring the total English population to half a million, and then to remove the 20,000 unmarried Irish girls and marry them off 'one in every English parish', replacing them by 20,000 English girls to be married to Irishmen. In this way the Irish language, food, clothing and customs would be replaced by English modes.[1] Petty's scientific approach was devoid of sentiment and left him without sympathy for the Irish past. Other seventeenth-century writers, however, interested themselves in the ancient forts and towers, and Sir James Ware, who published his *Irish Antiquities* in 1654, also collected Irish manuscripts. This antiquarianism was continued by the brothers Molyneux, whose essays were the first of countless misguided speculations on Danish Mounts and Round Towers.

The eighteenth century brought a more rational view of Ireland, thanks especially to Arthur Young, whose *Travels in Ireland* (1776–79) are justly renowned. There followed a spate of travellers throughout the nineteenth century, aided by improved communications and attracted, after 1845, by the grim spectacle of the Great Famine. Unfortunately most of the visitors, finding, in the words of the Earl of Bristol, 'nothing curious to engage admiration and nothing horrid enough to stare at', do not give us details such as contemporary travellers were eagerly gathering from remoter lands. Yet their accounts, vitiated as many of them are by prejudice and an assumption of moral superiority, do give us first-hand descriptions of conditions in rural Ireland before and after the famine. From the first decades of the nineteenth century we have valuable sources of information in the Ordnance Survey maps and letters, in the census returns and in the Statistical Surveys compiled for the Royal Dublin Society, covering nearly all the thirty-two counties of Ireland.

If we ask why so much of the past lives on in Ireland we must first notice the position of the island at the north-western extremity of the old world, the 'last outpost of Eurasia'.[2] Until

[1]Sir W. Petty, *The Political Anatomy of Ireland* (1691), 30.
[2]Grenville Cole, *Ireland the Outpost*, 9.

the way to the New World was opened up—a route the Irish were fated to follow in their millions—cultures and peoples moving across Europe found their last resting place in this Atlantic island. Here we need only pick out some of the most striking examples of such movements. Archaeologists have shown that the first Irishmen, who entered the island by the short sea-route from Scotland at a time, perhaps 7,000 or 8,000 years ago, when thanks to a lower sea-level it was even shorter than it is today, were the descendants of Old Stone Age man who sought refuge there. For nearly half the period that has since elapsed they were the only occupants of a heavily forested land which they shared with the beasts and the birds. As hunters, fishers and fowlers they spread slowly along the coasts and by tangled lakes and waterways south and south-west across Ireland. Their physical characters may be found in a small proportion of modern Irishmen, and certain of their habits, such as the building of lake-dwellings (crannogs) survived until a few centuries ago, while some of their skills— for example the skin boat or curragh—and their cults—the ancient rituals of fisherfolk and hunters—linger on to this day. The description, in the Irish legendary histories, of the first inhabitants of the land as fishers and fowlers may well be a genuine folk memory. In this oldest stratum, now almost submerged, Ireland preserves a sample of Palaeolithic Europe. Deep in this layer lie the roots of many superstitious customs, which depend for their efficacy on sympathetic magic such as is believed to have inspired the cave-artists of France and Spain.

The revolution in human economy and thought which is associated with food-production, the Neolithic revolution, began to affect Ireland about 4,000 years ago, carried by refugees and adventurers from Britain and also from France, Spain and the western Mediterranean lands. Thanks to an abundance of alluvial gold and copper the early metal age which followed was a period of increasing prosperity and industrial skill, when the products of Irish craftsmen found distant markets in Britain and on the continent. Throughout the Bronze Age the island was protected from the full force of the continental invasions which spent themselves in Britain: it was able to absorb such influences as trickled across the Irish Sea and to retain many of

6

its old habits, as is illustrated by the persistence of cremation rites from the earliest megalithic phase to the end of the Bronze Age, almost on the threshold of the Christian era.

At some stage towards the close of the Bronze Age the expanding Celtic culture, carried with the sword across western Europe, was able to gain a foothold in the north-east, whence in time it imposed itself and its language on the whole of Ireland and later, by way of Argyll, on Scotland too. But the price of this conquest was the loss of many elements of Celtic culture or their adaptation to the Irish environment and to long-established native tradition. The art of the Celtic overlords, for example, quickly develops forms and features which are insular and distinctively Irish. In other words there is more continuity of folk ways throughout the prehistoric period in Ireland than in Britain. And this Irish-Celtic civilization of the Early Iron Age was able, during the following period, to maintain itself through the centuries when the Roman Empire embraced nearly all western Europe. The spirit of its art and life was almost untouched by the mass-production and standardization of imperial Rome. It survived long enough to be caught up and revitalized in the late Celtic phase by the fervour of a Christian faith whose adaptation to Celtic tradition is illustrated in Saint Columba's famous phrase: 'Christ is my druid'. It was a time of great missionary enterprise, but at home its greatest achievement was the taming of the damp lowland forests which earlier peoples had shunned. Legendary history, now receiving confirmation from archaeological research, tells of technological advances and increasing population and settlement from about the seventh century onwards.

Irish Christianity grew up within the forms of Irish life: the church claimed no martyrs and there is little evidence of conflict with older beliefs, which clearly were absorbed. The Celtic church was peculiar in that the centres of its life were the great monasteries: there were no cities to form the seats of powerful bishops. Instead, the founders' kin retained the ownership of the monasteries, and the Celtic tradition survived in administration as in art and architecture. It was only after the ravages of the Vikings and the reassertion of pagan cults that the Irish Church was reformed by Saint Malachy, who established

7

a system of dioceses and raised St. Patrick's Church at Armagh to the primacy in the eleventh century.

But it was the Norsemen who established the first port-cities of Ireland—Dublin, Wexford, Waterford, Cork and Limerick—and provided the Anglo-Normans with bases from which to attempt their conquest. It was the fate of these newcomers, as of earlier invaders, to be absorbed, but the towns which they and their successors established became the instruments of Anglicization. Yet outside the nine south-eastern counties where the Anglo-Norman influence was strongest, there are few towns which are older than the sixteenth and seventeenth centuries, and as late as 1841 less than 15 per cent of the Irish population was urban. It is significant that even today no inland Irish town has a population reaching 20,000: in the Republic, indeed, only one or two exceed 10,000, and that barely. It is the immemorial peasant tradition which dominates the heart of Ireland. In some inland counties the rural population is still as much as 90 per cent of the total: for the Republic of Ireland as a whole it amounts to 62 per cent, and the figure for the more industrialized counties of Northern Ireland is only slightly under 50 per cent. In Ulster the plantation of English and especially of Scots Presbyterian settlers in the seventeenth century was at last successful in maintaining its identity, though as we shall see the material culture is strongly moulded to its Irish environment. Partly because this region of entry has received through the centuries almost every culture-layer that has been deposited in Ireland, there is perhaps a greater variety of survivals in Ulster than in any other part of Ireland. In some ways this most British part of Ireland is also the most Irish.

Although the tribal nomadism of medieval Ireland has been exaggerated, there can be no doubt that the pastoral tradition has dominated Irish life through the ages. Cultivation was certainly practised from Neolithic times, but the older crops, wheat and barley, were in course of time supplemented and in many parts replaced by oats, which became the corn of Ireland as of Scotland, food for men as well as animals. For half the year the arable land was under stubble, pastured and manured by grazing stock, so that the favoured acres around the settlement—the infield—might produce grain year after year. The rough grazing beyond—the outfield—was broken up periodically in temporary enclosures, and it may be assumed that such a system had developed from the shifting agriculture of prehistoric times. Relics of outfield cultivation, usually in association with family-communes, can be traced in many regions of difficulty throughout Western Europe, both in the mountains of the centre and along the oceanic fringe from Spain to Norway. 'If we knew medieval England completely', states Sir John Clapham, 'we should find plenty of it.'[1] In most lowland areas of good soil throughout western Europe, however, it was replaced by a system involving large open fields, normally three in number, each of which was used in rotation for autumn sown corn, usually wheat, followed by spring corn and fallow. This scheme called for considerable organization and a large variety of tools and implements: it came to be governed by complex regulations and controlled by the lord of the manor, and it is significant that the feudal system and in due course the nation-state evolved in areas where the openfield economy was practised. There was more freedom and flexibility in the smaller and simpler outfield system, and in Ireland the feudal order was successfully established only in the English Pale, where the three-field system was introduced by Anglo-Norman settlers. Elsewhere the tribal system prevailed, and for the study of folk-customs the important unit within that system was the family commune living in clustered house-groups, hamlets or clachans. The prevailing cattle-economy called for a minimum of equipment, the subordinate cultivation little more than spades or light ploughs and hand-operated tools. Even the lowliest members of society had some interest in the land and its cultivation was not beyond their means. Possession of a cow, a horse, a pig or a few sheep demanded even less in the way of equipment and tools. The simple arts and crafts of prehistoric times proved adequate, and the poorest man was able to play his part in the community and stand on his own feet. A democratic

[1] H. J. Clapham, *A Concise Economic History of Britain* (1949), 48, Similarly Gilbert Slater, *The English Peasantry and the Enclosure of Common Fields* (1907) regards what he terms the Celtic system 'as influencing to varying degrees the type of village community in England.'

way of life was fostered by the ease with which the humbler members of the community could compete with others in arts demanding not wealth but personal qualities, in poetry, oratory, song and physical prowess. Down to our own day the small size of the average farm has encouraged the survival of simple tools and limited the acquisition of machines. Subdivision of farms and the depressing effects of short leases and absenteeism were contributory factors. Subdivision of holdings was prohibited under an Act of 1881, but like so many other prohibited practices it did not cease.

The retention of many of the attributes of a peasant society is the key to the survival of the folk ways with which we are concerned in the following chapters. Even the Great Famine which marks a grim watershed in social and economic history did not entirely obliterate them, though it had such far-reaching effects that it might be regarded as the end of prehistoric times in Ireland. First in importance is the strength of blood-ties in extended family groups, still maintained even in many urban communities. During the air raids on Belfast, for example, the problem of finding billets for evacuated homeless was complicated by the refusal of large groups of related families to be separated from each other. In remote rural areas the blood-tie is a dominant force, governing economic as well as social relationships,[1] its loyalties overriding the impartial administration of justice. A relative is a 'friend', even if 'far-out'—that is, remotely connected—and friendship is a matter of blood relationship. A peasant community is concerned first and foremost with the maintenance and continuity of society: it does not judge—and cannot be judged—purely by economic standards. Immemorially peasant families have been large, and childbearing is widely regarded as part of the ritual necessary to bring success with the stock and the crops. In rural Ireland barrenness in a wife still tends to be regarded as an unnatural and disgraceful thing, and many superstitious cures for 'the sterile curse' are recorded. This is but one example of a widespread attitude towards life, to which comparative anthropology offers many parallels. Sympathetic magic, or the performance

[1] C. M. Arensberg and S. T. Kimball, *Family and Community in Ireland* (1940), Ch. 13.

of certain acts in the hope of inducing success in similar fields of action, provides an explanation of many of the folk-practices with which we are concerned.

Pushed too far, however, the observance of such antiquated practices in the end defeated its purpose and threatened the extinction of traditional life. A clue to much of the paradox in Irish culture is to be found in the reaction which follows an adherence to custom carried beyond the breaking-point. Spade-labour for example has reluctantly given way to the plough, but once the plough is generally accepted the spade becomes a despised implement so that a vegetable garden is a rare thing, at best a tiny plot left to the care of the women. In another field, the substitution of the vilest American films for the traditional ceilidhe gathering is a sad change. The crisis of the Great Famine was a major turning-point, and there followed a general reaction against everything associated with it. This was particularly true of the Irish peasants who sought refuge across the Atlantic: the American immigrants, driven from the land by extreme poverty, were determined to have nothing more to do with it and became almost invariably town-dwellers. The donkey and the goat, symbols of poverty, are neglected and despised in many parts of Ireland. A Donegal crofter once told me he dare not keep a donkey for fear of being unable to marry off his daughters: instead he kept a horse, though he could ill afford one, for its prestige value. The dangerously monotonous diet of Irish countryfolk, also, can be explained in the light of the famine. So bitter is the folk-memory of these times that useful wild sources of food are now neglected and despised; for example, wild berries of all kinds, the ubiquitous eel, hare and rabbit; the cresses and the edible seaweeds and fungi. It should be added, however, that some of these foods were apparently tabu—the rabbit, an Anglo-Norman invader, was rarely eaten—and that the potato had played its part in debasing diet in the period before the famine.[1]

Perhaps the most striking example of reaction is to be found in the expressed desire of most country people to have an isolated dwelling-house. The clachan or hamlet, once the centre of communal life and tradition, is despised, a symbol of squabbling

[1] R. N. Salaman, *The History and Social Influence of the Potato* (1949), Ch.15.

11

poverty, and it is the wish of nearly everyone to have a house where he cannot be overlooked. What is surprising in the light of these physical changes is the extent to which old customs and habits of mind survive to this day. As the late R. A. S. Macalister wrote in his last book, perhaps not entirely without malice: 'The importance of Ireland is that, thanks to the 'time-lag', it has rendered to Anthropology the unique, inestimable, indispensable service of carrying a primitive European *Precivilization* down into late historic times, and there holding it up for our observation and instruction.'[1]

Finally we should notice how the physical diversity of the country conspired with its remoteness to permit the survival through the centuries of indigenous peoples and customs. 'Mountainy men', in the picturesque Irish phrase, keep their foothold in every corner of the land, for mountain refuges lie all around the coast. Even the broad central lowland is diversified by several isolated ranges, still more by extensive bogs where movement has always been difficult. Before forest clearance and drainage were effected, woods, lakes and bogs were widespread, and the English made every effort to destroy the forest remnants because they sheltered the native 'wood-kernes'. So it had been in Norman England; where the land became difficult, through mountain or forest, or where water filled large spaces, the pikesman or bowman could hold his own against the man on horseback, and a democratic flavour was in the air.

[1] R. A. S. Macalister, *The Archaeology of Ireland* (1949), x.

II

FROM FOREST TO FARMLAND

THE tools and traits we are describing in this book have persisted through the centuries because of their close adaptation to the Irish environment, physical and social. They have gathered around them, in that environment, associations of usage and ritual without which they are meaningless, so that transplanted into another land they would be museum-pieces, as indeed they are rapidly becoming in many parts of Ireland. To understand them, therefore, we should consider them not in isolation but as part and parcel of a particular environment. To a large extent a culture owes its specific peculiarities to its geographical setting, and that is why our first chapters will be concerned with the face of the land and with the fields, farms and houses in which generations of Irish countryfolk have lived and worked.

It was from a forest environment that the cultural landscape slowly emerged. The destruction of the native forests was virtually complete by the seventeenth century. Thereafter constructional timber had to be imported, and the rural population turned to the fossil oak and pine of the bogs. In the eighteenth century landlords planted their lowland demesnes with exotic species of trees, but only in our own day, under government schemes of reafforestation, are the hill lands here and there being planted and abandoned fields being put back into forest. With the passing of the oak forests a wealth of woodcraft and tree lore perished and a wide range of skills declined, of which we get tantalizing glimpses from archaeological discoveries and legendary tales. Instead of the almost unbroken forest cover which once existed a 'closed association' of farms and fenced fields

13

now stretches from coast to coast. So much of the scene is fashioned by man that it requires an effort of the imagination as well as the findings of scientific research to picture the landscape as it was before his coming. Palaeo-botanists, from their studies of plant-remains and pollen-grains preserved in the peats (Chapter XIV), are slowly reconstructing the post-glacial succession of forests as arctic willow, birch, hazel, pine, alder and oak spread in turn over the face of the land. The dwarf vegetation of the early post-glacial period, with its scattered birchwoods, was too thin to form peat, but with the warmer climate of the Boreal phase (beginning about 7000 B.C.) pine and hazel, followed by oak and elm, spread across the country, and both fen-peat and wood-peat began to form in the undrained hollows of the lowlands. The growth of forest and peats was accelerated as the warm seas of the succeeding Atlantic period flooded the coasts at a time of rising sea-level, between 5000 and 2500 B.C. During this phase the alder flourished and the high humidity brought the rapid growth of sphagnum moss on the bogs.

It was during the following sub-Boreal period (2500–500 B.C.) that the Irish forests reached their greatest development, covering even the exposed seaward slopes of the western mountains where today not a single tree can be found growing. During this period, among the thinning forests of rocky hill-slopes, man made his first clearings for cultivation and turned the mountain winds to profit in drying and harvesting his crops. Thus the distribution of mountain masses gives a clue to the nuclear regions of Irish civilization, though it should be noticed that there are parts of the Central Lowland where thin dry gravel or limestone soils gave a more kindly foothold. As compared with the broad upland masses of Great Britain, the mountains of Ireland are broken into many fragments which lie scattered around the coasts. They fall, however, into four major divisions which are broadly distinguished by age and structure: those of the north (Ulster) the west (Connacht) the south-west (Munster) and the south-east (Leinster) (Fig. 2).

Geologically the northern mountains are of immense antiquity, and rocks younger than the coal-measures, apart from the ubiquitous glacial deposits, are everywhere rare except in

14

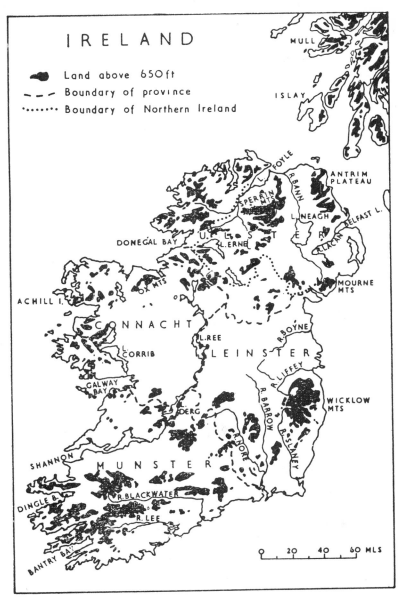

IRELAND

- ◣ Land above 650 ft
- ‒ ‒ ‒ Boundary of province
- •••••• Boundary of Northern Ireland

MULL

ISLAY

FOYLE

R.BANN

ANTRIM
PLATEAU

SPERRIN
MTS

L.NEAGH

BELFAST L.

DONEGAL BAY

U. L. S. T. E. R.

L.ERNE

R.LAGAN

MOURNE
MTS

OX MTS

ACHILL I.

C O N N A C H T

L.REE

R.BOYNE

L.CORRIB

L E I N S T E R

R.LIFFEY

GALWAY
BAY

WICKLOW
MTS

L.DERG

R.BARROW

R.SLANEY

SHANNON

R.NORE

M U N S T E R

DINGLE B.

R.BLACKWATER

R.LEE

BANTRY BAY

0   20   40   60 MLS

Fig. 2. The Provinces of Ireland.

15

the extreme north-east, where granites and lavas of Tertiary age are outliers of the Scoto-Icelandic igneous province. In Co. Antrim the basaltic lavas have covered and preserved with their armour-plating both red Triassic sandstone and white Cretaceous limestone (chalk) to give sea cliffs of strangely contrasted colours facing the North Channel. The western mountains are also of great age: the monotony of their bog-strewn schists is relieved only by lines of great quartzite peaks which break into the ocean at Croaghaun and Slievemore in Achill Island. In the south-west the parallel folds of Old Red Sandstone finger out to the Atlantic between Dingle Head and Mizen Head, and here again the highest summits are all in sight of the sea. The granite core of the Wicklow Mountains dominates the south-east in the most massive and continuous high ground in the country, and touches the sea on the outskirts of Dublin. Similarly in the north-east Slieve Donard, the highest summit of the Mourne Mountains, raises its great dome to 2,796 ft. only 1½ miles from the Irish Sea.

Only on the east coast, between the Wicklow Chain and the Carlingford Mountains, is the highland rim broken wide open in a 50-mile gateway giving access to the interior. Floored by well-drained glacial soils and favoured by a low rainfall of less than thirty inches in the year, this strip of coast has been for 1,000 years Ireland's metropolitan region. In fact, long before Dublin was founded by the Vikings, Tara claimed to be the capital of all Ireland, and not far away the island's most spec-tacular prehistoric monuments—the corbelled chamber tombs of the Boyne Valley—take us back to the early Bronze Age. The dark age Middle Kingdom of Meath, based on Tara and the Boyne Valley, looks backward to the glories of the Bronze Age and forward to the English Pale which was the first conquest and the final refuge of the Anglo-Norman planters. Its land-scape and character are distinctive to this day. What the Middle Kingdom and the Pale both lacked was a natural frontier to the west comparable to the Border Hills of Scotland or to the upland edge of the Welsh Marches.

The other four kingdoms, which have survived as the four provinces, broadly correspond to the four areas—north, west, south-west and south-east—which have upland massifs as their

nuclei. We may think of the four kingdoms as slowly crystalliz-
ing throughout prehistoric times around areas of primary
settlement among the hills. The political organization of these
areas had to await the coming of Celtic conquerors, but fundamental in their differentiation are the divergencies in megalithic
practice. The penetration of megalithic culture to all parts of
the island is one of the most striking facts in the prehistory of
Ireland. Again and again, in seeking for the origins of persistent
customs we find ourselves led back to the megalith builders
and their monumental preoccupation with death and the after-
world. The domination of the megalithic cult was much more
complete in the western isle than in Britain, where it took root
mainly in the uplands facing the Irish Sea.

All around the Irish coasts the megalith builders found hill
masses where shallow soils and thinning forests gave them a
foothold and ice-carried boulders provided the material for their
gigantic tombs and ritual circles. It is significant that the
megaliths appear to fall into four major regional groups—five
if we include the Boyne area—which correspond with the
historic provinces. This has been most clearly demonstrated
for Ulster where the distribution of 'horned cairns' has been
shown to correspond closely with the upland areas north of the
Dundalk-Sligo line.[1] Similarly Meath, Dublin and Louth contain
the finest passage-graves, of which New Grange on the Boyne
is the supreme example. I have no doubt that the ground
pattern of regional differentiation in Ireland was established
in the megalithic era during the first half of the second millennium B.C.

It remains to say something of the lowland heart of Ireland
where the four provinces meet along the line of the middle
Shannon north and south of Lough Ree, which is the geometrical
centre both of the lowlands and of the whole island. Near-by
Athlone, therefore, serves as the centre of Eire's broadcasting
system, but in no terrestrial sense is this bog-strewn central
lowland a dominant cultural region. Its function has been largely
negative, for it has served as a refuge area remote from the
contacts of the coastal fringe and the urban forces which radiate

[1] O. Davies and E. E. Evans, 'The Horned Cairns of Ulster', *U.J.A.* 6 (1943),
7–23.

17

from it. The Gaelic conquest of the Irish Midlands was not completed until the sixth century A.D., and down to the Anglo-Norman invasions the distinction between free and tributary tribes remained.[1] The counties bordering the middle Shannon—Leitrim, Roscommon, Longford and the western parts of West-meath and Offaly—are probably as full of survivals as any in Ireland. This is the land of the loy and the steeveen (Chapter X) and the last home of many an ancient custom. The lowland of which it is the centre is floored with limestone levelled off at about 200 ft. but diversified by occasional low hills, by intricate solution lakes and by glacial eskers and drifts among which lie countless small lakes and bogs (Fig. 3). It is hard to realize the isolation from which this area suffered before the introduction of improved wheeled vehicles and the coming of the canal and the railway.[2]

Let us now look at the cultural landscape which the hand of man has fitted to the physical frame of the island. Although man has been in this country for only a fraction of the time he has occupied South England and the continent, his mark is everywhere. Wander where you will through the length and breadth of the island, and through the dozens of lesser isles around its shores, and you will never fail to see traces of human activity, past or present, even in the most empty and inaccessible spots. Apart from the more or less datable remains of church and rath, castle and cairn, the land is covered with the marks of man's toil. The history of rural Ireland could be read out of doors, had we the skill, from the scrawlings made by men in the field boundaries of successive periods. In them the unlettered countryman wrote his runes on the land. The student of historical geography has been greatly assisted in the task of interpreting this palimpsest by the new tool of air-photography which, given suitable conditions, will pick out all man-made marks on the face of the earth.

The sturdy field walls and hedged banks which give the countryside its intimate character are by no means as immutable

---

[1] T. F. O'Rahilly, *Early Irish History and Mythology* (1946), 204.

[2] Improvements in public transport were initiated by the Italian, Bianconi, who, profiting from the cavalry horses thrown on the market after the Napoleonic wars, began his famous fleet of 'cars' in Tipperary in 1815.

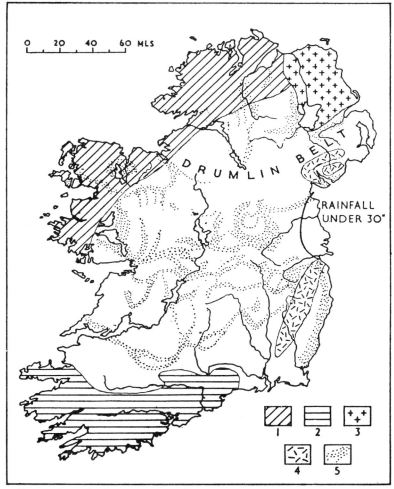

FIG. 3. Some landscape features. (1) Caledonian Highlands, (2) Armorican ridge and valley, (3) North-eastern basalts, (4) Eastern granites, (5) Glacial sands and gravels (eskers) (after J. K. Charlesworth). Drumlins are little hills composed of glacial drift. See Pl. 5, 1.

as they appear. The pattern they make has changed with the centuries in response to new needs and new tools. At present we are in a period of fairly rapid change, for the tractor calls for larger and more regular fields than those made by the spade

19

and the horse-plough, and old hedges are being grubbed up to give the machine elbow-room. This in turn leads to a demand for larger farms, for the small holdings which are characteristic of Ireland (one half of the farms are between fifteen and fifty acres) have customarily just so many fields as will give a proper balance between pasture and plough, and where two or three tiny fields are knocked into one the balance is upset. In the same way earlier technological advances, though on a smaller scale, have changed the cultural landscape at different periods. Demographic crises have had similar effects. Before the Great Famine, for example, 80 per cent of all Irish farms were under fifteen acres.

From the earliest times, it seems, Ireland was a land of small holdings and small field-plots. Yet the actual pattern of small hedged fields as we know it today is of no great antiquity. For the most part it is a consequence of the agrarian revolution which affected the country, at various dates in different parts, between about 1750 and 1850. It was the planting of thorn hedgerows and the building of stone walls that fixed what had previously been ill-defined and temporary field boundaries, associated with the openfield or rundale system of land use. With permanent enclosure went the consolidation of holdings into compact independent blocks, though in some districts independence was achieved without grouping the fields to- gether so that properties consist of scattered hedged fields which reflect the disposition of plots under the earlier openfield system. The hedge in fact has had a hard struggle for survival in the poorer districts. Both the thorns and the gates which enclosure brought with it were frequently hacked down for firewood, and to this day a wooden gate is a rarity in the countryside: the field gates are almost invariably of iron. There are many districts where the thorn hedge itself is almost un- known, where low earthen mounds half overgrown with bramble and whin (gorse) give us a glimpse of a stage between per- manent enclosures and the openfields which they replaced. In Donegal gangs of villagers threw down the landlords' fences as quickly as they were erected,[1] and in some parts of the county they are still kept in repair for the summer months only.

[1]Lord George Hill, *Gweedore*, 41.

Little attention has been given to the Irish openfield system.[1] It has escaped the notice of historians because the revolution which broke it down was a prolonged and silent one, involving no Enclosure Acts such as those which record the disappearance of the English openfields. Under the Irish system it was the practice, in some areas at least, for the plots to change hands periodically among co-partners by the casting of lots. Thus the transition to consolidated holdings was easier than under the English system, where the scattered plough strips were apparently permanently held. It is important to examine the openfield system more closely than might seem to be warranted by its almost complete disappearance from the modern scene, because it was against this background that many of the tools and customs we shall discuss were evolved. Just as in lowland England the English village was inseparable from its openfields, so in Ireland hamlets or 'clachans' accompanied the old form of land utilization. They will crop up again and again in the chapters which follow. But today and for the last century or so the isolated farm has characterized the Irish rural scene (Fig. 4). From some elevated viewpoint in the mountainy parts one may count hundreds of small whitewashed homesteads dotted among the fields, each nestling behind a handful of wind-bent trees and approached by its own access-road—the loaning or borheen beloved of the sentimental song writers. Every farmstead has the air of a fortress, an independent unit within its jealously guarded boundary fences, defended by a heavy iron gate hung between stout stone gate-pillars (Fig. 5) and claiming rights of way whose protection keeps the town solicitors profitably engaged. The degree of independence has been notably strengthened by the Land Acts (1869–1925) under which former tenants have become their own landlords. Peasant-proprietorship is an established fact throughout the country, though it has by no means solved Ireland's problem's as some politician-prophets claimed it would.

The truth is that, taking the country as a whole, most of the farms are too small to be truly independent of their neighbours. Bitter experience and the traditional land-hunger of a community

[1]E. E. Evans, *Geography*, 24 (1939), 24–36; D. McCourt, *Economic History Review*, 7, 369–76.

where the land has been almost the sole available resource go far to explain the jealousy with which established rights are maintained, but there are deeper needs and bonds in

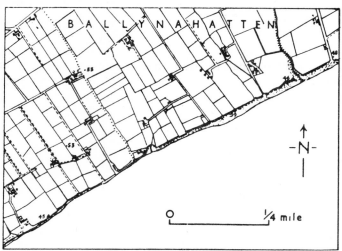

FIG. 4. Map of scattered farms on the Co. Down coast, showing seaweed-roads. (Based upon the Ordnance map with the sanction of the Controller, H.M.S.O.)

FIG. 5. 'Defended by a heavy iron gate hung between stout stone gate-pillars:' an Ulster farm.

the rural community. It is convenient for the farmer to live among his fields near his stock—to look after the calving cow—and for the farmer's wife to keep a close watch on her poultry. (Not long ago, as we shall see, it was quite common for the cows to share the kitchen, and the cow-byre and dwelling house are still often under the same roof.) But for jobs requiring traction-implements or expensive tools the help of neighbours is necessary. The small family-farm can support only one horse, and thus there is a good deal of co-operation, perforce, among neighbours in tilling the ground, in harvest work and other operations. Both seed-time and harvest are, in the Irish climate, seasons of heavy pressure, when the work must be got through speedily, and nothing is so conducive to speed as a 'gathering' of neighbours among whom a spirit of rivalry acts as a spur. These relics of former communal habits are becoming less frequent with mechanization, but in many districts not less than a quarter of the small farmers possess only one horse, so that 'joining' or 'cooring' to make up a two-horse team is usual. In all such cases no money payments are made. A fairly common practice, however, is for the small farmer to buy a second horse at the February fairs and sell it in May after the spring work is finished.

In this and other ways the isolated houses are bound by ties of neighbourhood and friendship so that one may think of them as forming close-knit communities lacking only the physical nucleation of former times. The improving planners, eager to confer urban amenities on the countryside, would have 'housing schemes' and planned villages in place of scattered houses, but nothing could be less suitable under existing conditions. Physical independence is the price paid for good neighbourliness. The old clachans, necessary so long as the infield-outfield or rundale method of land-use was practised, became a hopeless anachronism when new tools and new crops brought with them a rotational system and hedged fields.

We have little knowledge of the nature of rural settlement in sixteenth and seventeenth century Ireland, but since partner-ship farming, presumably with clachans and rundale, is well attested in ancient Ireland and is known to have been widespread in the eighteenth century it is safe to suppose that there was a

23

continuous tradition of partnership. Rundale, as we find it in decay in the nineteenth century, was a diseased system that had outlived its purpose. A few examples will serve to illustrate the appalling conditions to which it led when the removal of traditional checks and the adoption of the potato had allowed the population to expand recklessly within the framework of an inherited system of land use and settlement.

Our first example comes from the present century, and from Co. Mayo. The clachan of Rathlackan, when the Congested Districts Board tried to disperse it in 1918, was occupied by fifty-six families whose land was scattered in 1,500 fragments, some of them no more than a dozen square yards in area (Fig. 6). A two-acre holding was split into eighteen tiny plots, and on the average twenty-seven lots were held by each farm. Such was the confusion that it was not until 1942 that the process of re-distribution and consolidation of holdings was completed, with the result that 'fairly compact holdings' were provided for thirty-two families.[1]

The following quotations are from the pamphlets of an 'improving landlord' in Donegal, and refer to a period about a hundred years earlier, in the 1840s.

'We suppose it would not be believed that in this district, until very lately, fences were altogether unknown. In some instances a tenant having any part of a townland (no matter how small), had his proportion in thirty or forty different places, and without fences between them. One poor man who had his inheritance in thirty-two different places, abandoned them in utter despair of ever being able to make them out . . . The rundale system was a complete bar to any attempt at improvement; as, on a certain day, all the cattle belonging to the townland were brought from the mountains and allowed to run indiscriminately over the arable land. And in spring no individual occupier would set or sow, or labour in the fields, before a certain day, when the cattle were again sent to the hills, until after harvest. In one instance a small field of about half an acre was held by twenty-six people.'[2]

---

[1] *The Irish Times* (12th Jan., 1943). This was achieved only at the cost of the physical collapse of one land-officer and the mental breakdown of another.

[2] Lord George Hill, *Gweedore*, 22, 46.

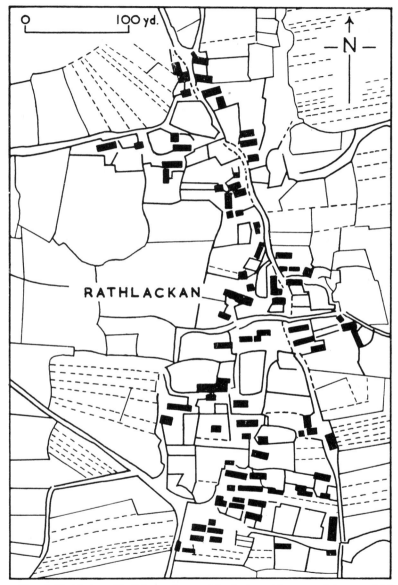

RATHLACKAN

FIG. 6. Rathlackan, Co. Mayo: the rundale cluster with some of the openfield strips as they were before reorganization began in 1918.

In Connacht conditions were even worse, as may be judged by the persistence of the Rathlackan cluster down to 1942. So swollen were some of these settlements that one of them, Menlough near Galway, now consisting of a dozen farms set among the ruins of others, is said to have had 2,000 inhabitants in 1845, while lacking 'head or centre, market, church, chapel or school'.[1]

In Ulster there are many examples of small clusters which have persisted because they did not become swollen to disastrous proportions. They were characteristic, for instance, of flax-growing areas and were occupied by farmer-weavers who depended on each others' services at harvest-time, and they survived the crisis of the great famine although many decayed with the decline of hand-loom weaving soon afterwards. Despite all the disadvantages of life in these clachans, their inhabitants were reluctant to leave them. It was stated in evidence before the Devon Commission that even if they were moving only half a mile away 'they were crying as if they were going to America'. It was in fact from such decaying house-clusters that a great number of the emigrants to the United States set out across the seas in the second half of last century.

[1] T. C. Foster, *Letters*, 293.

III

BALLY AND BOOLEY

BAILE (bally) is the Gaelic word for the home-place or townland,[1] Ireland's smallest administrative unit; buaile (booley) the name of the summer milking-place or shieling where in times past the flocks and their tenders spent the summer months. I believe that seasonal nomadism (transhumance) between bally and booley is an important and neglected aspect of Irish social history, and one which goes far to explain many features of traditional life. It is significant that the Irish word for a boy (buachaill) originally meant a herdsman. The charge of nomadism, using the word in its worst connotation, which English writers made against the Irish, finds some justification in the prevalence of a pastoral economy which was, in fact, more comparable to that of the Swiss peasants or the Norwegian milk-girls. Wherever transhumance is or has been practised, it is associated with difficult environments and marginal conditions, where it has provided opportunities for escape from authority and served as a means of preserving and transmitting ancient traditions. This is well illustrated in the example of the Carpathian shepherds of Roumania.

It is clear from the Irish laws and from the findings of archaeology that farming practice had permitted some degree of permanent settlement long before the dawn of the Middle Ages, probably by early Celtic times. Of all the administrative units

---

[1] I have discussed the townland unit in my *Mourne Country*, Ch. 11. My colleague Mr. J. B. Arthurs thinks that the word *baile* may be a very old pre-Goidelic word, and that where 'ballys' are numerous the indigenous peoples had been left mainly undisturbed by Goidelic expansion.

of different sizes and various origins into which rural Ireland
is divided—townland, parish, barony, diocese, rural district and
so on—it is the townland which most closely touches the daily
life and social relations of the countryman. The townland is his
postal address, for individual farms preserve their historic communal anonymity: they still belong to the townland though
they have become separate units since the 'town' or cluster has
broken up. The farms rarely carry any names other than those of
their owner (Mulligan's place, Thomson's farm or merely
O'Brien's) and since there may be a dozen O'Briens in a
particular townland various nicknames[1] and patronymics are
used to distinguish between them. Thus one farm may be
Kilty O'Brien's (from its left-handed owner), another Patsy
Kate O'Brien's (from the owner's mother), and a third Yank
O'Brien's (a returned emigrant, this). Similarly, the public
house takes its title not from the brewers who supply it or from
heraldic beasts such as the Red Lion but from the Mooneys or
the Murnaghans who own it. Shops in country towns, too,
carry personal names, and the nucleus of their trade is built up
among blood relations.

The townland names, involving so many land holdings, are
legal titles, and their Gaelic names, however erroneously spelt
on the Ordnance Survey maps, are fossilized in their current
forms. Only an Act of Parliament can alter them. A glance at
any six-inch Ordnance map will reveal the strange names that
Gaelic imagination contrived and English scribes corrupted.
Here are a few which I have come across in Ulster: Ballywillwill,
Ballymunterhiggin, Aghayeevoge, Treantaghmucklagh. In all
Ireland there are no less than 5,000 townlands beginning with
'Bally', forty-five of them named Ballybeg (little town). Some
2,000 townlands begin with Knock (a hill); there are sixty
called Tully and there are eleven Edens. The degree of repeti-
tion shows that these names have come down from a time when
life was organized on a local basis. There are between 60,000
and 70,000 townlands in Ireland, averaging 325 acres or
½ sq. mile, and the average townland population in the rural
areas is perhaps fifty. In fact their size varies considerably,

[1] Writing in 1682 (*West-Meath*, 113), Sir Henry Piers noticed their prevalence
in that county '. . . so as no man whatever can escape a nickname.'

since they were based on the fertility of the land rather than its acreage, and it seems that many moorland tracts were not divided until fairly recent times, for they were formerly shared as common summer pasturage by the people of a whole parish or barony, covering 100 sq. miles or more. In such hilly areas the townlands may be as much as 2,000 acres: on the other hand in thickly-settled lowlands they are frequently less than 100 acres, and some anomalous fragments of an acre or two are designated townlands. This diversity also reflects cultural differences both between regions and between various classes from the kings and chiefs down to the humblest of bondmen. The first Ordnance Survey (1830–42) suppressed many of the local names for subdivisions and applied the term townland universally. Though the townland appears to have been equated with an agricultural unit, the ploughland or *seisrach*, it is clear that in many parts of the country 'the cow's grass' was the effective unit of measurement. Of Donegal about 1840 we read: 'The land is never let, sold or devised by the acre, but by 'a cow's grass'. This is a complement of land well understood by the people, being in fact the general standard; and they judge of the dimensions of a holding by its being to the extent, as the case may be, of one, two or three 'cows' grass'. They have divided not only into the fourth part of a cow's grass, called a 'foot', but into the eighth part of a cow's grass, or half a foot, denominated 'a cleet'.'[1] In Bantry, Co. Cork, land was let 'in the wilder parts by what is termed the gneeve, which is the twelfth part of a townland, and therefore of very undefined acreage'.[2]

To judge from surviving examples of clachans and openfields, it was customary for each house in the cluster to have a small enclosure or 'gort' (garden) adjacent to it, their high walls lining a maze of narrow lanes winding haphazard among the houses (Fig. 6). These settlements were characterized by an extreme disorder, as though the houses, in the words of one writer, had fallen 'in a shower from the sky'.[3] Linear villages, it is true, are not uncommon along the western seaboard,

[1]Lord George Hill, *Gweedore*, 26.
[2]*Parliamentary Gazetteer* (1844), s.v. Bantry.
[3]Caesar Otway, *A Tour in Connaught* (1839), 353.

arranged in some semblance of order along a road, but they are likely to be late colonies or the result of land re-distribution. As a visitor during the famine years wrote: 'The villages in which the greater portion of the people (of western Ireland) reside . . . consist of collections of hovels . . . grouped without regularity, formed of clay, or loose stone with green sods stuffed into the interstices'.[1] A little earlier, in 1839, the people of Achill Island are described as 'living in little cabins built in loose clusters varying from twenty to eighty in a cluster: these clusters or villages are sixteen in number'.[2] Still earlier, in 1802, Donegal is said to have had about 500 'villages', which were, however, 'dispersing daily into separate habitations and holdings'.[3]

The absence of any discernible plan as compared with many English or German villages has led visiting critics to regard the clachan as a reflection of the disordered Irish mentality. The word that best fits the untidy house cluster is one often heard in Ireland—'throughother'—which is properly applied and probably owes its origin to the scattered plots of the openfield (Fig. 6). Despite this apparently casual disorder the selection of a house-site was a matter for the most careful deliberation. Shelter from the prevailing winds was a prime need, so that the houses seem to snuggle together, generally located in a hollow or on a lee slope. To this end a man might throw his hat into the air on a day of wild winds and mark its falling place. But it seems it was at all costs necessary to avoid giving offence to the fairies by building across one of their 'pads'. In Tyrone it is said that 'no man would build a house till he had stuck a new spade into the earth'. If the fairies had not removed it overnight the site was safe.[4] In Cavan I was told that a small line of stones was first built on the site: if it was intact next morning the fairies were not displeased. The ill-luck which dogged the person who had inadvertently built his house across a fairy pad is one of the many themes which crop up in the stories one hears throughout the country.

[1]J. Pim, *The Condition and Prospects of Ireland* (1848), 116.
[2]Edward Newman in *The Magazine of Natural History* (1839), 569–77.
[3]James McParlan, *Statistical Survey of the County of Donegal* (1802), 64.
[4]Rose Shaw, *Carleton's Country* (1930), 15.

These clachans, while some had their speciality such as weaving or thatching, were concerned primarily and almost exclusively with agriculture and attracted none of the elements of the true village, whether church, inn or shops. Itinerant 'tinkers and tailors' paid periodic visits and with the pedlars and beggars brought news of other districts, but the economic and social needs of the hamlet were met by periodic visits to the fairs and by seasonal gatherings of various kinds. Within the group the bonds of kinship were close and strong, and ties of marriage carrying reciprocal responsibilities linked one clachan with another within small neighbourhood units consisting of perhaps half a dozen townlands. With the close kinship bonds went corresponding rivalries with adjacent neighbourhoods which provided social motive force by acting as incentives. These rivalries broke out characteristically into feuds and blood-letting at fairs and gatherings. But in later days, at any rate, internal rivalries and squabbles were more conspicuous and found more opportunities within overgrown kinship groups which had become too complicated to function smoothly. A few illustrations will suffice.

One visitor explained the presence of the back-doors on clustered houses, for which we shall offer other explanations in the following chapter, by the fact that the women needed an escape when too hotly engaged in rows with neighbours.[1] Joint ownership sometimes extended to single animals with strange results. For example: 'three men were concerned in one horse; but the poor brute was rendered useless, as the unfortunate foot of the supernumerary leg remained unshod . . . and accordingly it became quite lame.[2] We are reminded of the difficulties arising from the joint ownership of fruit trees in some Mediterranean countries. It was in Donegal too that I heard of a ram which died of exposure when it was part-shorn by one of its joint owners. In the same district a man wishing to build a wall around one of his fields but unable to get his neighbour to agree, deliberately erected it a yard or two on his own side of the boundary so that the neighbour would still be forced to herd or tether his cow to prevent it trespassing on the

[1]Isaac Weld, *Statistical Survey of Roscommon* (1832), 475.
[2]Lord George Hill, *Gweedore*, 23.

narrow strip between the boundary and the wall. 'Fights, trespasses, confusion, disputes and assaults, were the natural and
unavoidable consequences of the rundale system.'[1] On the other
hand we must recall the extreme reluctance with which the
system was at last abandoned, the social benefits it conferred
on members of the kin. The reforming landlord, Lord George
Hill, comments that 'the pleasure the people feel in assembling
and chatting together, made them consider the removal of the
houses, from the clusters or hamlets in which they were
generally built to the separate farms, a great grievance.'[2]
Another writer gives as the basis of the tenants' grievance,
'the recollection of nights of social concourse, of aid in sickness,
of sympathy in joy and sorrow, of combined operations of
defence against bailiff or gauger'.[3] There were ceilidhes and
spinning parties, and many a clachan had its shanachie (story-
teller) and its fiddler or piper—usually a maimed or simple
person—who accompanied with folk-tunes. Folk-songs, occu-
pational airs and legendary tales were kept alive in this way.
Apart from the co-operation implicit in the openfield system
there was a good deal of sharing in other ways. Thus there
would be a communal corn-kiln for drying the grain before
grinding, a knocking stone for pounding barley, and in some
districts a corbelled stone sweat-house which took the place
of the village doctor in treating rheumatic pains.

The openfield which lay around the cluster, normally on the
down-hill side so that the vital manure could be 'sliped' down-
slope (see Chapter XIII), seems to have been kept in cultivation
in some areas at least year after year. This was the infield, in
contrast to the outfield, the outlying rough pasture bits of
which were temporarily reclaimed and then left to rest for long
periods. We shall return to the plough and spade and methods
of cultivation in another place but may refer here to the allotment of the holdings in the common fields. Although in many
parts of the country the holdings, by the end of the eighteenth
century, had become fixed in their scattered parcels on the
several qualities of land in the openfield, there is abundant

[1]Lord George Hill, *Gweedore*, 22.
[2]ibid., 42.
[3]W. R. Wilde, *Dublin University Magazine*, 41 (1853), 20.

evidence that periodic re-allotment had been a general practice. It continued well into last century in some parts of the country, for example Antrim, Cork, Kerry, Mayo, Galway and Kilkenny. The casting of lots, annually[1] or triennially[2] was the occasion for much display of feeling, and was regulated by a headman or 'king' who also made arrangements for the summer pasturing.[3] In Kilkenny[4] the lots were cast by means of marked stones wrapped in clay. The ritual was prolonged. 'They sometimes play at it to try their luck before they will cast lots in good earnest. Even then they must sometimes make a new division if too many are dissatisfied.'[5]

To understand the openfield system in full working order we should see it in its total geographical setting, the booley with the bally. Here in the hilly fringes of Europe, towards the ocean, even moderately fertile land is limited in extent: soils derived from barren rocks and heavily leached by excessive rains are subject to waterlogging, acidity and the accumulation of peat. Spring is the only season without excessive rain, and ploughing or digging in autumn or winter even if possible is unprofitable. Winter wheat is a risky crop in most parts, and the emphasis is on spring corn, especially oats. This meant that the arable land was free of crops from October to April, and it allowed pasturing and manuring by livestock for rather more than half the year. So deep-rooted is this communal pasturing that there are districts in Donegal where to this day the livestock of the whole townland has the run of all the farms through the winter. And elsewhere, as I know to my cost, having tried for many years to cultivate a garden in the Mountains of Mourne, one's neighbours have a lingering habit of ignoring the fences at that season, when food for livestock is scarce.

Manuring and treading of the infield by cattle and sheep were supplemented in spring by quantities of manure taken from the cabins, 'some houses having . . . from ten to fifteen

[1]Antrim: Ordnance Survey Memoirs, Rathlin Island (1830); Cork and Kerry: Lord Dufferin, *Irish Emigration* (1867), 349.

[2]P. Knight, *Erris in the Irish Highlands* (1836), 47.

[3]ibid. For Norwegian parallels see *The Scandinavian Economic History Review*, 4 (1956), 17–81, 77.

[4]W. Tighe, *Statistical Observations, County of Kilkenny* (1802), 419.

[5]Sir Henry Piers, *West-Meath*, 117.

tons weight of dung, and only cleaned out once a year!'[1] Sea
wrack and shell sand were carted up to thirty miles inland from
the coast.[2] In the absence of permanent fences the majority of
the cattle must be moved away during the summer and those
remaining carefully herded or tethered on the outfield, or put
in temporary enclosures to manure that part of the outfield
which was due for cultivation.[3] In its origins and full development the rundale system depended on the movement of most
of the livestock to summer booleys situated some distance
away. Here the widely distributed uplands and boglands played
their part in the traditional economy. Although late survivals
of the booleying system are hard to find, little of it managing
to outlive the crisis of the Great Famine, we are beginning to
track down its history and significance. The Irish texts are as
disappointing and vague as they are in many matters touching
the common people, but folk-memory comes to our aid. There
are stories, and place-name evidence, from most parts of the
country, and regional variants of the practice are being studied
and mapped.[4]

We give first some quotations from the few discerning observers who drew attention to the practice. Edmund Spenser's
enlightened spirit of inquiry is shown in his remark: 'Have you
ever heard what was the occasion and first beginning of this
custom? for it is good to know the same.' He writes, in 1595,
'There is one use amongst them, to keep their cattle and to
live themselves the most part of the year in boolies, pasturing
upon the mountain and waste wild places.'[5] His objections to
the system, however, reveal his Englishry: the booleys hid
outlaws and loose people, and the wandering life made the Irish
barbarous. The following brief reference comes from O'Flaherty's famous account of West Connacht: 'In summertime
they drive their cattle to the mountains, where such as look to
the cattle live in small cabins for that season.'[6] In the eighteenth

---

[1] Lord George Hill, *Gweedore*, 17.
[2] E. E. Evans, *Mourne Country* (1951), 141.
[3] W. Harris, *The Ancient and Present State of the County of Down* (1744), 131.
[4] J. M. Graham, 'Transhumance in Ireland', in *The Advancement of Science*, 37 (1953), 74–9.
[5] Quoted in H. Morley, *Ireland Under Elizabeth and James I* (1890), 67.
[6] R. O'Flaherty, *H'Iar Connaught* (1684), 17.

century we find a description from Ulster: 'In the bosom of the
Mourne Mountains there is a place called the Deers' Meadow
to which great numbers of poor people resort in the summer
months to graze their cattle. They bring with them their wives,
children and little wretched furniture, erect huts, and there
live . . . and often cut their turf.'[1] A century later a fuller
account of a more complicated transhumance, reminiscent of
the Norwegian seaboard, comes from Donegal: 'It often happens
that a man has three dwellings—one in the mountains, another
upon the shore, and the third upon an island, he and his family
flitting from one to another of these habitations . . . This
change usually takes place upon a fixed day, the junior branches
of the family generally perform the land journey on the top
of the household goods with which the pony may often be seen
so loaded, and at the same time so obscured, that little more
than the head can be observed; and thus the chair or two, the
creels, and the iron pot, the piggin, and the various selected
et cetera . . . creep along the roads.'[2] The author goes on to
comment on the restrictions imposed on the comfort and possessions of the peasants by their 'Arab mode of life'. In Achill
Island too the movements were complicated, involving the
entire population which, having moved to the summer pastures
and sowed their corn, returned to the permanent coastal village
for the high summer to fish and went back to gather the harvest
at the booley in the autumn.[3]

For the most part we are dependent on folk tradition for
details of booleying. The Ordnance Survey Letters written in
the 1830s contain valuable material from Counties Antrim and
Londonderry, and the following extract relates to the parish of
Dunaghy: 'Some of the very old men of the country recollect
seeing the boliehouses inhabited. They were built of sods upon
a foundation of earth and stones and were thatched with heath.
Many of the poorer sort lived here in summer grazing the cattle
upon land that nobody appears to have claimed and supporting
themselves upon their milk and blood which they took from

[1]W. Harris, *The Ancient and Present State of the County of Down* (1744), 125.
[2]Lord George Hill, *Gweedore*, 24.
[3]An account by Sir William Wilde, written in 1836, is contained in Wood-
Martin, *The Rude Stone Monuments of Ireland* (1888), 238.

them occasionally. To render the latter more palatable they are said to have mixed it with the leaves of the wild sorrel.'

In Achill a few old people still nostalgically accompany their cows to the old booleying grounds, but everywhere else the system has died out completely. Many hilly districts, however, are open runs for summering stock which are visited periodically or placed in charge of a herd. This system was prevalent in the early nineteenth century and is thus described in the Ordnance Survey Letters for County Londonderry, parish of Upper Cumber. 'Herds are partially employed, males and females indiscriminately, who tend the cattle in the summer on the moors and mountain farms. They are from ten to sixteen years old and are paid for that half year from 15s. to 21s. In winter they return to their parents, who are burdened with their support from November to May.' In theory the total number of grazing units in a commonage is calculated and the units allotted to each landholder in proportion to the size of his farm—originally to his share in the openfield. The unit is known as a collop (in Ulster and Mayo a sum—the Scottish equivalent) and is the amount of pasturage that will support a cow. The sums may be taken up by other animals, and a scale which varies slightly from one district to another gives the equation. Thus a sum equals three parts of a horse, four sheep, eight goats or twenty geese. With the decline in the utilization of the hill-pastures and the general breakdown of traditional practices, grazing rights on commonages are neglected and stinting is rarely operative.

The observant walker in the hills will notice in sheltered hollows by the banks of streams clusters of grassy mounds set in a green sward, or it may be small piles of stones under some rocky outcrop. These are the only tangible relics of the booley houses, and in most parts of Ireland they were deserted so long ago that the shepherd will tell you they are the remains of Danes' houses.

Only where the huts were stone-built are the remains easily recognizable. In Achill Island they are oval in shape, or rectangular with rounded corners, and many have the opposite doorways which are still characteristic of the winter dwellings. In some bogland areas where place-names and traditions tell of booleying there are no discernible traces, for the flimsy constructions in such sites, built without stones, have been buried under the peat. Frequently the huts were built into a sloping bank of peat or gravel, and the roofs were constructed of bog timbers covered by long strips of sod and thatched with heather secured with ropes. We shall see that long roofing-sods are typical of traditional peasant dwellings to this day, and their use may go back to pastoral origins. It was observed

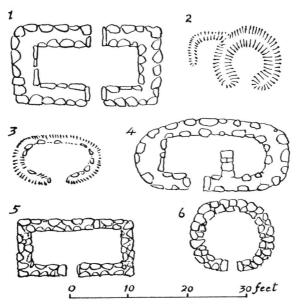

FIG. 7. Plans of booley houses. Nos. 1, 4, 5, Achill Island; Nos. 2 and 3, Mourne Mountains, Co. Down; No. 6, Co. Mayo.

near Newry in 1690 that the cabins were built so conveniently of hurdles and long turf 'that they can remove them in summer towards the mountains, and bring them down to the valleys in winter.'[1] Circular hut-foundations are also found, some built of stones, others of sods, and the former may well have had corbelled stone roofs. The huts are generally in groups of

[1]George Story, *An Impartial History of the Wars of Ireland* (1691), 2nd ed. (1693), 16.

from five to twenty, either clustered or spaced within calling distance of each other. They are nearly always located near running water, usually near the headwaters of mountain streams, where patches of bright green grass and such characteristic flowers as tormentil may reveal their sites even when almost all trace has gone (Fig. 7).

IV

THE THATCHED HOUSE

VISITORS to Ireland have not failed to comment on the
wide gap which separates the splendid if often dilapidated
mansions of the landed gentry from the humble dwellings
of the mass of the rural population. This is a characteristic
dichotomy which runs through Irish life and goes deep into the
Irish past: it was foreshadowed in the distinction between the
Gaelic overlords and the tributary tribes who were still in an
inferior position at the time of the Anglo-Norman conquest.
By English standards the Irish farmer is a small-holder. Substantial farmhouses with some pretensions to architectural
dignity are in general restricted to the planted areas and they
are few in number compared with the traditional single-storied
thatched cabins of the peasantry. These have so frequently
been condemned as artless and insanitary that it might be
supposed nothing could be said in their favour. Their disadvantages indeed are obvious, and they have given way in many
districts to slated houses of cement-blocks or bricks and are
doomed to vanish entirely under a wave of thin-walled boxes
with garish red roofs. But it is not only sentimentalists who
deplore their disappearance. With their passing, writes Robin
Flower, something of the old world passes away, 'for the older
type of house was in a right harmony with its surroundings,
while these high and bare constructions stand in a perpetual
contradiction of the whole environment of hill and sea and sky
in which they are so violently set down.'[1]

In fact a good deal more could be said in favour of the old
styles, at their best providing homes of character, comfort and

[1]Robin Flower, *The Western Isle* (1944), 46.

beauty which vary subtly from one region to another in response to local climates, conditions and contacts. The use of local building materials meant that they fitted into landscapes of which they were literally a part, their clay or stone walls gathered from the earth on the spot, their timbers dug from the bogs, their thatch harvested from the fields. A Swedish ethnographer writes that 'the best Irish thatching gives the finest peasant roof in Europe.'[1] The result of an unbroken tradition was a fine simplicity of style and proportions, with nothing of the vulgar obtrusiveness of the new fashions in country houses, based too often on urban styles and red-brick respectability. Before the famine, houses in the market towns also were very largely of traditional local style save in the central square. Isaac Weld, describing Roscommon in 1832, states that out of its 517 houses no less than 462 were thatched.[2]

Our concern is with the old-style house as a shelter for man and beast and as the vehicle of family lore and regional tradition. In the crowded clachans limitations of space and the fact that diarying was mainly practised in the summer booleys go far to explain the absence of separate byres or dairies. Sanitation was of the crudest and closets unknown. It is these aspects of Irish rural life that have most readily aroused the amused indignation of the critics and the defensive wrath of Irish patriots. As we read in an earlier description of the Western Isle:[3]

> At one of th' ends he kept his cows,
> At th'other end he kept his spouse.

The custom of housing man and beast together has been very general among pastoral peoples in regions of difficult climate, whether in Highland Britain or the European mountain zone. Parts of Ireland, however, have long had a different type of house giving more family privacy: in the lowland parts of Leinster, East Munster and South Ulster the house with central chimney and fireside partition did not easily allow of the keeping of livestock in the house, and one is inclined to regard

[1] Åke Campbell, *Folk-Liv.* (1937), 228.
[2] Isaac Weld, *Roscommon* (1832), 307.
[3] W(illiam) M(offatt), *A Description of the Western Isle*, Dublin (1724), Canto 2.

this style as an improvement introduced by English settlers. This central-chimney house with its 'jamb-wall' hearth will be described in the following chapter. In any event, although stray hens, a pet lamb or a farrowing pig may occasionally join the cats and dogs in an Irish kitchen, the keeping of cattle in the house is a thing of the past. Yet it was so recently practised, especially along the Atlantic seaboard, that many existing houses are not far removed from kitchen-byres, a cross partition conveniently converting the byre into a bedroom, store or dairy.

Moreover the shape and internal arrangements of the prevailing pattern of traditional rural dwelling are conditioned by these antecedents. The long rectangular shape was sanctioned by custom and preserved by superstition; a house, to be 'lucky', must not be more than one room wide (Fig. 8). 'Widen the house', I have heard it said in Donegal, 'and the family will get smaller'. The hearth gable of the house was, where possible, dug into the slope of rising ground, so that it would have been difficult to enlarge the house by widening it: it could grow more easily in length. The long shape is also characteristic of humble dwellings in the small straggling Irish towns. Their streets are lined by whitewashed cabins strung end to end interminably; in the 'cabin suburbs' one rarely sees a house that is not aligned along the road. Describing Ballymoney in Co. Antrim about 1830 the Ordnance Survey Letters state that many houses facing the main street had no access to the byres and stables behind, so that cows and horses had to be taken in and out through the house. In parts of western Ireland cows were brought into single-roomed houses within living memory. In Clare Island, Co. Mayo, there were at the turn of the century only five or six houses out of the total of 120 into which the cattle and pigs were not taken at night.[1] Writing of the village of Kilgever near Westport in 1880 an observer states: 'It is a terrible thought that these huge heaps (of manure about the doorsteps) had all been taken from the single rooms, each of which formed a common stye for men, women, children, horses, cows, pigs and poultry.[2]' It is still characteristic of many small farms that the manure heap is not far from the

[1] C. R. Browne, *Clare Island and Inishturk.*
[2] J. H. Tuke, *A Visit to Donegal and Connaught in the Spring of 1880* (1888), 54.

front door, for the cows are kept in a byre which is a continuation of the dwelling house, an obvious convenience though there is not, as in the longhouse of Wales and Dartmoor, direct access from kitchen to feeding-walk.

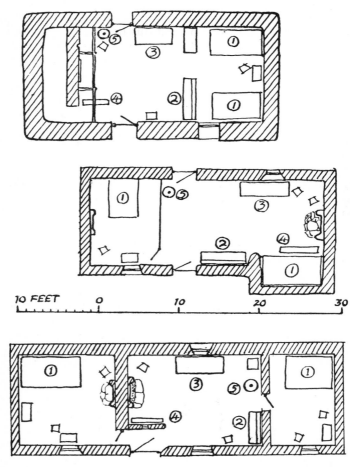

FIG. 8. House plans. *Above:* hipped-roof house, Co. Galway (compare Fig. 13, 2). *Centre:* house with outshot, Co. Donegal (compare Fig. 12, 3). *Below:* house with jamb-wall, Co. Down. (1) bed, (2) dresser, (3) table, (4) bench, (5) churn.

Poverty and rack-renting undoubtedly contributed to the long survival of such conditions, but they ultimately derive from cultural forces of wide distribution and high antiquity. It used to be said in defence of the custom of sharing the house with the cow that she helped to keep the house warm and that in turn the cow yielded more milk. Inquire further and you will find that it was thought to be unlucky if the cow was not able to get a glimpse of the fire. Behind this belief there lies faith in the power of the fire to dispel evil spirits. The end of the house farthest from the hearth is commonly referred to as the 'bottom-end', a relic of the time when it housed the cattle, for it was obviously wise to have the floor sloping down towards the byre. Many cabins and huts were constructed as lean-tos against a bog-face or an old fence (ditch). Hence the saying applied, for example, to the Cappagh district of Co. Armagh, that 'you can't cross a ditch or you'll fall down a chimney'. It should be recalled that in Ireland the tenants built and repaired their own houses with, normally, no assistance from the landlord, and there was little inducement to build houses to last longer than the lease of say twenty-one years. Only in Ulster under the custom of tenant right could outgoing tenants claim recompense from the new tenants for improvements made.

The simple rectangular shape is a feature of west European house-types from prehistoric times and has characterized some houses of Neolithic age excavated in Ireland. Such houses were usually built of timber, clay or sods (scraws). Circular or oval houses are of similar antiquity, whether made of stone or of wattles, but although a few round-ended rectangular houses survive, the round hut of corbelled stone slabs is used today only as a store place or animal house (Chapter IX). The houses of Achill Island are described by several writers about 1840 as circular or oval in shape, built of boulders without mortar and having the thatched roof continuous with the walls. They had neither chimneys nor windows, and the single door was sometimes not more than four feet high. None of these houses is now inhabited though their ruins can be seen. The round or oval house, however, has probably contributed to certain features of the traditional rectangular-house in some areas, for example the central hearth and the hipped roof which is proper to a round-ended house. But there are many missing links in the evolution of the Irish house, which archaeological excavation will hope to find some day. Interpretative studies of Dark-Age texts are also needed.[1]

Clues to old methods of house building may also be found in forms of construction used for outbuildings or in childrens' games. There is, for example, a Hallowe'en spell or divination game known as 'building the house' in which twelve couples of holly twigs are arranged in a circle, pushed into the ground and tied together at the apex. A live turf representing the fire is placed in the centre. The coupled twigs are named after the boys and girls present, and the pair which first catches fire indicates which boy and girl will first be coupled in marriage.[2] Compare with this a description of Irish houses in the early seventeenth century: 'the baser cottages are built of underwood, called wattles, and covered with thatch . . . of a round form and without chimneys, and in my imagination resemble so many hives of bees about a country farm.'[3]

Today nearly all Irish farm-houses are a simple rectangle in ground plan, anything from ten to twenty feet in width and of varying length according to the number of rooms they comprise, each room being the full width of the house. The normal developed house has three rooms, consisting of a central kitchen with a bedroom at the bottom end and another— the best room, called simply 'the room'—behind the chimney, which helps to warm it (Fig. 8). This, in the Gaeltacht, is the 'west room', reserved for family mementoes, for the old people and especially for the dead. Here the body is placed during wakes, and a wealth of superstition gathers around this room.[4] Arensberg may have been mistaken in translating the Gaelic *iarthar* as 'west', for the word also means 'back', but there are old beliefs about the orientation of the dwelling house, and it is possible that there was an association between death and the direction of the setting sun. The confusion between 'west' and 'back' is amusingly illustrated in the story of the Irish boy who,

[1]Angus Graham, 'Archaeological Gleanings from Dark Age Records', *P.S.A. Scot.* (1950–51), 64–91.
[2]Lady Wilde, *Ancient Legends of Ireland* (1888), 111.
[3]Luke Gernon, *A Discourse of Ireland, Anno 1620.*
[4]C. M. Arensberg, *The Irish Countryman* (1937), Ch. 1.

when asked why he had not washed behind his ears, replied "'twas too far west!' Death within the year is said to be the fate in Mayo of the man who lengthens a house by adding to the west end.[1] In the old style, as we shall see in the next chapter, houses of more than one storey are rare, though half-lofts or sleeping lofts in the roof lit by a small gable window are fairly common.

A very general feature throughout the north and west is the presence of two doors in the kitchen, one opposite the other (Fig. 8). Only one—the front door—is in regular use: the back door is reserved for days when the wind 'blows contrairy'. Around it more superstition is gathered. A stranger must not be allowed to leave the house by the back door lest he take the luck of the house with him. In the Aran Islands a corpse was always carried out to the graveyard through the back door, and the front door of all houses in the clachan was closed as the funeral procession passed by.[2] The usual explanation of the opposite doors is that they made it possible to regulate the draught for the open fire. This arrangement is characteristic of pastoral areas in western and southern Europe, such as Andalusia and the Roman Campagna. A seventeenth century visitor to Ireland writes: 'the hearth is placed in the middle of the room. The smoke goes through no particular place, but breaks through every part between the sods and wattles of the house, which commonly is no bigger than an overgrown pigstye, to which they have two doors, one always shut on that side where the winds blow'.[3] When chimney flues were added the dispersal of the smoke was facilitated so that the back door tended to go out of use. Nowadays it is often blocked or converted into a window or wall-cupboard. In the traditional kitchen-byre the flagged passage between the doors served as a path for livestock, and the cow was driven out through the back door after milking. I found an interesting relic of this in Co. Armagh, in the custom of taking every new calf, and also any animals purchased at the fair, through the house for luck. In Kerry, 'down to the present day, some houses are the scene of the

[1]C. R. Browne, *The Mullet*.
[2]A. C. Haddon and C. R. Browne, *The Aran Islands*.
[3]'A Tour in Ireland in 1672–74', *J.C.H.A. Soc.*, 10 (1904), 96.

morning—and evening—milking of the cows', each animal being driven in turn, in at the front door and out at the back door.[1]

The Census of 1841 estimated that nearly half the families of the rural population of Ireland, then some 85 per cent of the total, were living in the lowest state, in one-roomed mud cabins. In Co. Kerry the percentage was as high as 67 per cent, and in Bear barony in Co. Cork it reached 81 per cent. Although mud houses are now in a minority, many substantial examples remain as well as innumerable decayed specimens. Over many parts of the bog-strewn Central Lowland, where stone is not readily available and transport of materials is difficult, the clay-walled house remains typical. Formerly many single-roomed cabins were made of sods (scraws), especially in boggy country. In Tipperary they were said to be the commonest type about 1780.[2] A few survive. I have seen one in Co. Antrim partly cut out of a bog-bank, housing a large healthy family; and they have been described from other parts of Ireland. Booley houses, we have seen, were frequently built of sods. At its best the mud-walled house can be both durable and comfortable, and many observers warn us not to assume the poverty of their builders. As Arthur Young remarks: 'Before we can attribute such deficiencies to absolute poverty we must take into account the customs and inclinations of the people.'[3]

Mud walls were built up with a fork in layers twelve to eighteen inches deep of a mixture of damp clay and cut rushes which had been left to sour. A stone foundation layer sunk into the ground was usually built first, and sometimes the gable ends, especially if a chimney flue was to be included, were built entirely of stone. They were afterwards trimmed with a sharp spade to a thickness which averages about twenty inches but may be as much as thirty. They had to be of massive construction for stability, and the doors which were cut out subsequently were kept narrow. Similarly the window openings were narrow and placed high in the walls, coming directly under the thatch, so that they resemble eyes glinting below shaggy eye-

---

[1] Åke Campbell, 'Irish Fields and Houses', *Béaloideas*, 5 (1935), 57–74, 70.
[2] (Thomas Campbell), *A Philosophical Survey of the South of Ireland* (1778), 145.
[3] A. Young, *Tour*, 2, part 2, 37.

brows. Thick coats of limewash renewed annually gave protection from the weather and it was essential that the thatch
should overhang at the eaves. The roof is typically thatched
at the gable, that is, hipped, for it was difficult to build the
walls above about six feet high. Alternatively the gables above
this height were often finished with turf or sods (Fig. 9). The
overhang of the thatch makes the mud-walled house unsuited to
the windy coasts of the north and west where the thatch is
securely tied down with ropes and trimmed flush with the eaves.
Close observation will show the most intimate relationship

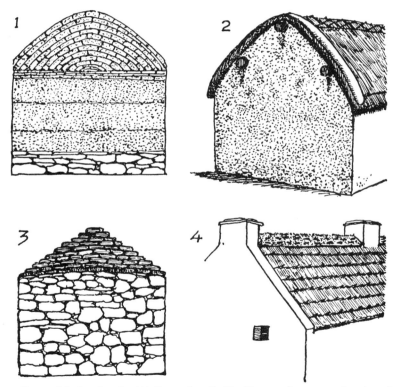

Fig. 9. Mud and sods. (1) Internal wall, Co. Down, of stone, mud and mud
bricks, (2) projecting purlin ends of mud house, Co. Armagh: mud coping, (3)
internal wall, Co. Meath, with sod top, (4) thatch secured with pegged fir-ropes
and ridge of pegged sods, north Antrim.

between building materials and techniques and types of thatch, and when slates or tiles are adopted for roofing it will be found that old roof patterns are faithfully followed by local builders. An interesting variant of the mud house occurs around Lough Neagh, where the main weight of the roof is carried on three massive purlins the ends of which can be seen projecting outside the upright gables (Fig. 9). I suspect these houses were built to take tall looms, for the use of purlins means that there are no couple-ties crossing the room, but the distinction between the purlin and the coupled-rafter roof may be fundamental. The purlin-roof may go back to the log house with which it is associated, for example, in Scandinavia. One advantage of the upright gable over the hipped roof is that it made the extension of the house by the addition of further rooms much simpler. It could have been copied from medieval churches or planters' houses.

For constructional reasons, and also because window glass was long a luxury, the windows of the traditional cabin were few and small and placed for preference on the side away from the prevailing winds. Many of the surviving houses, moreover, were built in the early nineteenth century, when tax was levied on the number of windows. The ever-open door, its lower part closed with the additional half-door, admitted most of the light. The half-door is often regarded as peculiarly Irish, but in fact it is an old-fashioned feature which has lived on longer in the western isle than in Great Britain. It is found in parts of the north of England, for example in miners' cottages in Co. Durham, and it is said to be characteristic of Chinese houses. In Ireland the half-door serves to let in the light while keeping out unwanted animals, and it makes a convenient arm-rest for purposes of conversation or contemplation. This is how a countryman justified it to me: 'A man standing at the open door would be wasting time, but leaning on the half-door he is just passing time'. To give maximum efficiency, the window openings widen internally, an arrangement behind which there may be a lingering tradition of defence against unwelcome strangers. At any rate most of the light came from the doorway, and thus one sees the force of the picturesque phrase referring to the unwanted visitor as one who 'darkens the door'. A wattle frame, a handful of straw or a dried sheep-skin served as a substitute for glass, and it is remembered in Co. Fermanagh that a mare's cleanings (the placenta) best served the purpose. My informant added significantly: 'No bayonet would go through it'! In one Donegal parish in 1837, according to a petition sent by the school teacher to the Lord Lieutenant of Ireland, there was 'not more than ten square feet of glass in windows in the whole (some 1,500 houses) with the exception of the chapel, the school house, the priest's house, Mr. Dombrain's house and the constabulary barrack'.[1]

Fig. 10. A coupled roof of bog-oak, Co. Donegal, the ridge rounded against the wind (compare Fig. 12, 3).

Details of the roof-frame of the long house show many minor variations from place to place, but as a general rule it is composed of coupled rafters traditionally of bog-oak chosen for its strength as well as from the scarcity of live oak trees (Fig. 10). A house is measured, not in feet, but by the number of bays it contains, a bay being the distance between the couples, which is standard in any one district. There is some evidence that the

[1]Lord George Hill, *Gweedore*, 16.

coupled roof was borrowed from the frame-house introduced by English planters: it may, however, have evolved from the wattled house if this was supported, as seems likely, by crucks. The coupled rafters are joined by one or two cross-ties secured by wooden pins, and pegs driven into the rafters hold in place the long purlins which support a layer of branches or thin laths of bog-fir. On these rests a warm blanket of carefully fitted sods (scraws), an essential element of the traditional roof, keeping out cold and damp and serving as a hold for the rods (scollops) with which the thatch, over the greater part of the country, is secured (Fig. 11). The sod undercoat is an

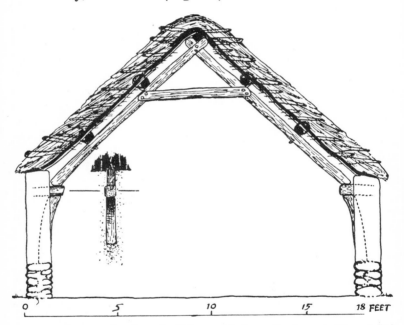

FIG. 11. Cross-section through old house, Maghery, Co. Armagh. The coupled rafters are supported on uprights set in the mud walls. The scraws are sewn to the purlins with fir-ropes. Successive layers of thatch are secured with rods pinned down with hair-pin scollops.

archaic element which overrides all differences in house and roof construction and must be of high antiquity. It has been taken over from an old culture-layer—it finds parallels in

Norway and other sub-arctic regions—and from an economy where straw was not available. We have already noticed that cattle-herders in the early seventeenth century built their booley houses of boughs coated with long strips of green turf. The long sods made a portable roof which could be slung on a pole between two pack-horses.

The sods were cut in strips from carefully selected spots where a close-grazed sward gave a thick mat of grass-roots. They measure two to three feet wide and about one and a half inches thick, and as they were cut they were rolled on to a stick and carried like a carpet. Their roofing sods, wrote Thomas Campbell in 1778, 'they call scraws (they are rolled up like scrolls) but they would be better called hides, for they are flayed off the earth.'[1] In the north, where the flachter or breast-plough was used for paring sods (Chapter X), the scraws might be as much as twelve or fourteen feet long, though short turves were also used. They were carried on to the roof up two ladders and laid on grass upwards, overlapping at the ridge on the side away from the wind. They overlapped laterally also, the scraw on the windward side running over its neighbour on the lee (Fig. 14). In many such details careful attention was paid to the wind and the rain, for example the strongest purlins were put on the side whence driving rain was most to be expected. Similarly the stoutest couples were placed at the weather end of the house, and they were sometimes given a slight inclination towards the wind. A seemingly artless cabin may thus be found to show the most careful adaptation to local conditions.

The first thin layer of thatch was, in some parts of the country, sewn on to the purlins with a thatching needle—the older pattern has a large eye to take hay-rope (Fig. 15)—and the roof might then be finished in one of several regional styles. In the eastern part of Co. Down, and sporadically elsewhere, the straw is laid on in specially prepared bundles or stapples[2] (Gaelic *Stapull*) and the thatch is plastered down at eaves, gable and ridge with clay or mud. A few scollops are added at ridge and eaves. This is probably a very ancient method,

[1] Thomas Campbell, *A Philosophical Survey*, 146.
[2] K. Danaher, *Béaloideas* (1948), 203–17.

designed for temporary habitations, for it results, after repeated additions of straw and mud, in an extremely thick and heavy roof. Yet its distribution on the east coast seems to point to introduction from overseas, and in Co. Down it is known as English thatch. One would like to know more about old thatching techniques in other parts of north-western Europe. In Galway a house with mud-sealed thatch is known as a 'shaken house'.[1]

Another way of securing the thatch, which has a limited distribution chiefly along the Antrim coast, we may term the pegged method. Horizontal two-ply ropes made of sally, heather, or the tough fibres of bog-fir roots are laid along the roof parallel to the eaves at intervals of a foot or so and pegged to the scraw with wooden pins which are pushed in upwards so as not to lead water through the roof. A row of scraws is pegged to the rather sharp ridge (Fig. 9, 4). I have observed this style of thatch in south-west Lancashire. Much more widely distributed is the thatch which is found along the north and west coasts from east Ulster round to Kerry, but comes into its own particularly in Donegal, where it gives some of the most attractive roofs in north-western Europe. In Donegal they are rounded at the ridge to throw off the winds, the supporting couples being designed to this end with short cross-pieces breaking the angle of the ridge (Fig. 10). In some districts the ropes, formerly of twisted straw or bog fir but now generally ready-made of sisal, run in both directions to make a complete network; in others the horizontal ropes are omitted because of the obstructing gable-ends which, rising above the thatch, protect it from the winds. The ropes are secured to the walls by means of a row of stone-pegs below each eave. This method of tying is found also in north Mayo, most typically in areas known to have been settled from Donegal in the seventeenth century.[2] Here the horizontal ropes are carried over the gable in steps left for the purpose (Fig. 12, 2). Such roofs are said to be 'stitched': a close mesh may require up to a mile's length of roping. The older method of securing the ropes, from Mayo to Kerry, is to fasten the ends to small boulders

[1] C. R. Browne, *Inishbofin and Inishshark.*
[2] C. R. Browne, *Ballycroy.*

FIG. 12. Roped thatch, western seaboard. (1) Dingle, Co. Kerry. (2) Achill Island, Co. Mayo. (3) Teelin, Co. Donegal.

53

which rest on the thatch directly over the eaves (Fig. 12, 1). This method has an extremely primitive air but it has the advantage over the pinned ropes in that it is simpler to keep the ropes taut. A still older method, frequently seen on thatched stacks and rarely on buildings, is to let the weighted ropes hang from the eaves. In Donegal a century ago boulders weighing fifty or sixty pounds are stated to have been suspended on hay ropes.[1] This very primitive mode is found also in the Inner Hebrides.[2] Roped thatch in general seems to be characteristic of the Atlantic seaboard of Europe and areas around the North Sea.

The most widely distributed mode of thatching is by means of scollops, or sally rods (sometimes hazel, briar or bog-fir), which pin down the thatch. In well-finished work the rods are hidden, for if exposed they tend to let water seep through the scraw, but it is customary to leave a row exposed at the eaves and ridge and against the gables, where the outer layer of straw should lie snugly. The exposed scollops are often arranged in lattice patterns, and the expert thatcher delights in showing his skill and leaving his grace-mark in finishes of various designs which are practical as well as decorative, serving for example to distribute the rain and prevent 'guttering'. Thus twists of straw (bobbins) at the gables carry the drips evenly to the ground. When the ridge—and sometimes the eaves as well— is also adorned with a row of bobbins the scollop-thatched roof can be most attractive (Fig. 13, 1). A thatched chimney occasionally adds the last finishing touch. The word scollop is derived from the Gaelic, and it is natural to assume that this most widely distributed of all styles—from north Antrim through the heart of the Irish midlands to south Cork—is indigenous. But rod-thatching is widespread in England and on the continent, and it may have reached Ireland with the Celts. There are various ways of pushing in the scollops: they may be thrust in at each end (Fig. 14) or bent into wooden staples resembling large hairpins, which secure the ends of horizontal rods (Fig. 13, 1). The scolloped thatch is perhaps best suited to, and is almost universal on, roofs which are

[1] *Dub. Univ. Mag.* 41 (1853), 715.
[2] Colin Sinclair, *Thatched Houses* (1953), 36.

Fig. 13. Scollop thatch. *Above:* Co. Cavan, with ridge of bobbins. *Centre:* Co. Galway, with thatched chimney. *Below:* Co. Tipperary (after R. H. Buchanan).

55

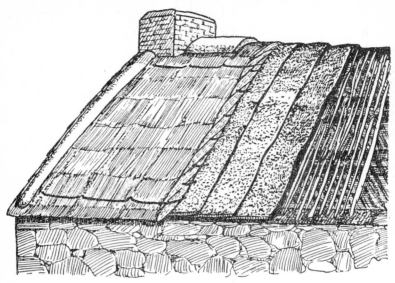

Fig. 14. Detail of scollop thatch, Co. Armagh, showing roof construction, sods and mud coping (after R. H. Buchanan).

hipped. The best work is seen on houses of the jamb-wall type.

Oat-straw, despite its poor lasting qualities, is employed for thatching in some districts, because it is the only available material. Being pliable it is widely used for patching. In the old days outfield straw was preferred for thatching because it was tougher than that grown on the infield. Wheat or rye is much more durable than oat straw and rye is specially grown for its straw in parts of Donegal, where I have known flax also cultivated to provide thatching material. Reeds are fairly commonly employed in the south-west and locally elsewhere if no straw is available. I have seen heather used in north Donegal, and in other areas marram grass, rushes and 'mountain grass' (probably *molinea*). The expert thatcher prefers his straw to be cut with a sickle and thrashed by hand and he scorns machine-thrashed straw. Best of all is straw from which the corn has been removed by hand-scutching or 'lashing' over a stick or stone, the 'barrel' of the straw being thus unbroken (Chapter XV). Nowadays a thatched roof is becoming a mark of sophistication, and among the farming population a new roof is hardly ever covered with thatch. The country thatcher finds employment in patching, not thatching.

The erection of such simple houses as I have described did not call for the services of specialists. When the need arose the collective skills of a whole community were available, and one can readily see how prescribed methods were handed down in any particular area. 'The custom on such occasions', wrote Lord George Hill[1]—he is speaking of Donegal in the years before the Great Famine—'is for the person who has the work

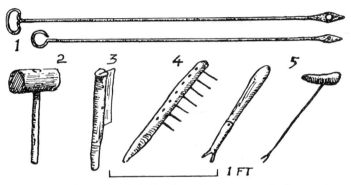

Fig. 15. Thatching tools. (1) Needles, the upper one for hay or fir ropes. (2) Mallet. (3) Trimming knife. (4) Rake. (5) Spurtles for stappling and patching. All from Co. Down except the last, from Co. Meath.

to be done to hire a fiddler, upon which all the neighbours joyously assemble and carry, in an incredibly short time, the stones and timber upon their backs to the site, men, women and children alternately dancing and singing while daylight lasts, when they adjourn to some dwelling where they finish the night, often prolonging the dance to dawn of day'. Like all work done in common, the thatching too was regarded as a sort of festival. In the Aran Islands 'from the moment a roof is taken in hand there is a whirl of laughter and talk till it is ended, and, as the man whose house is being covered is a host instead of an employer, he lays himself out to please the men who work with

[1]Lord George Hill, *Gweedore*, 40.

him'.[1] Synge goes on to remark that much of the intelligence and charm of the islanders is due to the absence of a division of labour and to the wide development of each individual. Truly it may be said that with the disappearance of the thatched house something more than a picturesque archaism passes from the land.

[1]J. M. Synge, *The Aran Islands*, 156.

V

HEARTH AND HOME

THE kitchen and the hearth are the very core of the Irish house, and the turf fire burning continuously day and night, throughout the year, is the symbol both of family continuity and of hospitality towards the stranger. When it goes out, it has been said, the soul goes out of the people of the house. The fire serves not only to prepare food and dry clothes, to bring warmth and comfort to the family and to ailing animals, but also to keep the thatch dry and preserve the roof timbers, so that 'when the smoke dies out of a house, it does soon be falling down'. This is one reason for the persistence of single-storey houses open to the roof, where the turf smoke could circulate among the rafters and keep the scraws and under-thatch dry. A 'smoke', in the seventeenth century inventories and to this day among country folk, means a house. In the days before chimneys were adopted the cabins were described as oozing smoke through the thatch so that they resembled 'reeking dunghills'. It should be remembered that the brick or stone chimney flue is a relative newcomer and, as we are constantly being reminded in these days of fuel shortage, a great waster of heat. The chimneyless open fire was much more effective as a house-warmer. The turf smoke, it is true, despite the draught-regulating mechanism of the double doors, must often have been troublesome, but as we shall see the furniture was designed to keep heads low.

Dry peat burns too quickly if the draught is strong, and the fire does best at floor level, glowing on a great stone slab or on a cobbled hearth set in the mud floor. The area immediately around the fire is also paved, but the rest of the old-style

59

kitchen is generally floored with puddled clay which takes a surprisingly well-wearing surface. The housewife will tell you that such a floor raises less dust than one of concrete, and if it tends to wear unevenly this matters little since the cooking pots and some of the furniture which is not built-in has three legs instead of four and will therefore stand firmly on an uneven floor. The rocking chair, despite New England's claim to have invented it, was surely first devised for such a floor. Lime, cowdung or ashes were sometimes added to the floor when it was being prepared, and mud scraped off the road, already well puddled, was considered an excellent floor material.[1] In Armagh, we are told, floors were made by simply digging up the ground and trampling it: 'They sometimes have a dance for that purpose, and many a match comes out of a thing of the sort.'[2] Another method was to keep a flock of sheep moving about the newly spread floor for some hours until it was well puddled. The bottom byre-end of the old-style one-roomed farm house was cobbled, and a flagged walk led from door to door. Devices for tying up the cows were secured to or built into the bottom gable: a variety of stone and wooden fasteners may still be seen in the deserted houses of Slievemore on Achill Island. One writer humorously observes of Co. Galway that the cow had to be tethered lest she should eat the bed-straw, but that pigs and poultry were free to roam.[3] The hens spent the night on a rope or pole hung across the kitchen from eave to eave, and laid their eggs in handsome nesting-baskets of woven straw (Fig. 16). Here we may notice a curious bit of folklore which suggests that hens were carefully looked after for superstitious reasons, as well as for their economic value and for the cockerels' time-keeping. It is said that every night the hens, when they argue among themselves before settling down, are plotting to leave Ireland and fly back to Norway, but in the end they decide to postpone the trip for another day! In Co. Limerick elaborate three-tier wooden hen-coops are sometimes seen in the kitchen, and in Co. Down I have found the sitting

[1] J. Binns, *The Miseries and Beauties of Ireland* (1837), 1, 112.
[2] ibid., 186.
[3] T. A. Finlay, 'The Economics of Carna', in *The New Ireland Review* (April, 1898).

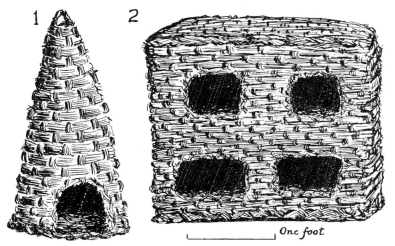

FIG. 16. Straw hens' nests. (1) Co. Clare. (2) Co. Leitrim.

hen warmly ensconced in a stone-box alongside the fire. In the mud floor one may sometimes see large 'pot-holes', hollows in which the heavy iron pot is placed when the boiled potatoes are pounded for pig-food (Fig. 19). The wooden or iron 'beetles' with which the pounding is done are as varied in shape and size as they are indispensable (Fig. 17). Sometimes

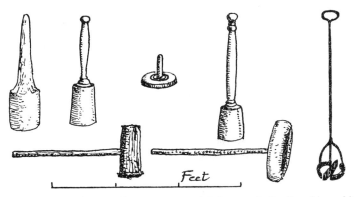

FIG. 17. Beetles, for pounding potatoes and, below, mells for 'knocking whins', Co. Antrim. Beetles similar to the first example were formerly used also for washing clothes and for breaking flax before hand-scutching.

a wooden plank is set in the floor as a footing for the pot, or to give the spinning wheel a firm base. The upright churn also needs a firm footing and in the Mourne Mountains a movable granite flag was kept for this purpose. I have seen a mud floor in Co. Down with several round holes in which milk was poured for each 'member of a family of cats. In the Bronze-Age Orkney village of Skara Brae every hut had stone-lined holes sunk in the floor, which were thought to have been used to store limpets.[1] In archaeological excavations near Belfast I have found holes which were presumably used for storing milk-products sunk in the clay floor of an 'earth-house' (souterrain) of the Dark Ages.[2] In some old houses there is a hole near the fire, either in front or let into the wall alongside, which is used to store the ashes.

In nearly every example of prehistoric and early historic houses which have been excavated, the hearth occupies a central position, and cooking pots would have been suspended either from the roof timbers or from specially constructed supports. We know from English travellers that this continued into recent centuries. Thus Fynes Moryson: 'the chief men in their houses make fires in the midst of the room, the smoke whereof goeth out at a hole in the top thereof.'[3] He goes on to say that the humbler clay or wattled cabins also had their fires in the middle, and in the early nineteenth century we read of houses in West Antrim where the fire, though not in the centre of the room, was 'advanced some feet from the gable wall so that the persons of the family can readily sit round it.'[4] The description given by Charles Lever of the little cabin of Owen Joyce on one of the Brannocks Islands off the west coast, even if fictional, is worth quoting because Lever was probably drawing on tradition. It reads: 'It was built in a circular form, the chimney in the middle. Certain low partitions sub-divided the space into different chambers, making the centre the common apartment of the family, where they cooked, and ate, and chatted.'[5] In the course of time, however, the fire has come to

[1] V. G. Childe, *Skara Brae*, 17.
[2] E. E. Evans, *U.J.A.*, 13 (1950), 5–27.
[3] Fynes Moryson, *The Description of Ireland*, 231.
[4] G. V. Sampson, *Memoir*, 275.
[5] Charles Lever, *The Martins of Cro' Martin* (1864), 2, ch. 31.

be placed against the gable or, in the central chimney house, against a partition-wall, and one cannot doubt that the general adoption of chimney flues has been the deciding factor. This innovation, slowly adopted from about the sixteenth century onwards, gave rise in time to many regional styles of chimney breast in brick and stone. I suspect that the wattled smoke canopy (Fig. 18) was the native response to the novelty of chimney flues, but I cannot find that it was adopted outside the areas of strong English influence. The substitution of peat for

FIG. 18. Hearth with jamb-wall and wattled smoke-canopy, Co. Armagh. Meal-bin and settle-bed on left.

wood seems to have made little difference to the architecture of the hearth. When coal came to be burnt, however, the fire had to be lifted off the floor, or the hearth fire given a stronger draught by installing a built-in 'fan bellows' which forced air through a tube into the floor of the fire.

The wattled smoke canopy or brace (? breast) is still fairly common in houses with central chimney and fireside partitions, mainly in the south and east. The front of the canopy rests on a strong horizontal beam, the brace-tree, which may extend right across the kitchen from wall to wall, four or five feet out from the fire and five or six feet from the ground. Or one end of the beam may rest on a supporting jamb set under one corner of the canopy. In that case—and invariably where the front door is adjacent—there may be a draught screen of wood mud or stone —the jamb-wall—built out from the fireside and terminating in the jamb, so as to partition off the fireside. This curtain-wall is pierced by a small window known as the entry or spy-hole, through which an approaching visitor can be spied from the fireside through the open door (Fig. 18). I have seen a few jamb-wall houses of this type in Co. Armagh where the brace-tree nevertheless continued to the side-wall, so that the visitor had to stoop under it on entering the house. If a door is swung on the jamb-post a small hall or internal porch is readily pro-vided. This is characteristic of developed houses of traditional style in the Lagan Valley near Belfast, and a further refinement is to hang a mirror over the jamb-window, a looking glass replacing the plain glass of the peep hole and reflecting chang-ing fashions. The jamb-wall, called also in Ulster the hollan-wall, is well-known under that name in the south of Scotland and the north of England and may thence have reached eastern Ireland in plantation times. In Cumberland it was termed the sconce and in Lancashire the speer, which was the name of the screen which crossed the end of the halls in the Oxford colleges. James Walton tells me that in north Yorkshire the jamb post, called the witch post, is occasionally found to be covered with designs intended to protect the hearth from evil spirits. Sprigs of rowan are tied to its top for the same purpose. The partitioned hearth is characteristic of eastern and southern Ireland: it extends into the Central Lowlands but it is almost entirely lacking in the west and in the north-western province of the outshot-house to be described below. Dr. Desmond McCourt tells me that he knows of two or three hybrids— having both the outshot and the partitioned hearth—in the foothills of the Sperrin Mountains, where two cultural pro-vinces meet.

The smoke canopy varies in shape and method of construction from one region to another. The commonest type is made of

laths and wattles (willow, hazel or briar), plastered with a
mixture of clay and cowdung or ashes and coated with limewash.
In parts of the south hay or straw ropes soaked in mud (putogs)
were used, twisted between a frame of horizontal rungs and
plastered over with mud or limewash. In Co. Armagh one
occasionally sees a heron's wing hung on the brace: it is used
for dusting the hearth. The jamb-walls—and internal walls in
general—were traditionally constructed of wattle and daub, or
of mud or wood. The wattle and daub construction is undoubtedly an old technique which, in the days of plentiful timber, was
much more generally used in house-building. Internal partitions carried up to the roof, however, probably followed the
adoption of the chimney flue, and if so this innovation must be
reckoned as a contribution to privacy as well as to comfort.
We note in passing that wattlework found its last traditional
use in house construction in the wicker doors of the west, and
in the windbreaks of the north, bundles of hazel or birch branches
(wassocks) set up on the windward side of the door. The stone-
built external porch must be regarded as a relatively novel
addition to the traditional house style.

Wooden or stone seats are often built in near the hearth,
and the wall behind the fire, protected by a flagstone or a
built-up hob, usually has a keeping hole on each side of the
fire (Fig. 19). Known as boles in Antrim and coves in Cavan,
these may be elaborated in Achill Island, for example, into two-
or three-tier wall-dressers whose ancestry lies in the stone house
tradition of the mountain country. There is an old belief that
the left-hand keeping hole belongs to the woman and the right-
hand one to the man of the house. Here you may see in safe
keeping, on one side the woman's knitting, on the other the
man's clay pipe. Stone dressers were a characteristic feature of
the huts at Skara Brae,[1] where also Professor Childe found
evidence that the women occupied the left side of the fire and
the men the right. In the Hebridean black-houses the left-hand
side of the fire was the woman's quarter.[2] Similarly in the old
turf houses of the Highlands, 'the women were invariably
ranged around the central fire on one side, the men on the

[1] V. G. Childe, *Skara Brae*, 15.
[2] A. Mitchell, *The Past in the Present*, 52.

Fig. 19. A Donegal hearth, with crane, creepie and bread-iron. Pot and pot-hole on right.

other'.[1] It is interesting to notice that it is the Mongol usage to allot the right side of the yurt to men and the left side to women.[2] We are surely dealing with a very ancient tradition related perhaps to the ordered routine of a pastoral nomadic life. For the Mongols the right and left sides were symbolized respectively by horse and cow. In the humblest Irish farms, which lack sanitary conveniences of any kind, it is customary for the women to use the byre and the men the stable.

If we now turn to the methods of suspending cooking pots over the fire we shall see how the woman's functions are best carried out on the left side. Besides the convenience of this for a normal right-handed person, there lies behind it the notion that for good luck significant actions involving the food supply—such as ploughing, casting a net or taking a pot off the fire—should follow the direction of the sun's movement in the sky. Thus the crane on which the pots are hung is almost

[1]Hugh Miller, *My Schools and Schoolmasters* (1857), 96
[2]E. D. Chapple and C. S. Coon, *Anthropology* (1946), 539.

invariably pivoted on the left side of the fire so that it swings out with the sun. The iron crane is more characteristic of stone fireplaces than of those with wattled braces, which tend to preserve older methods of hanging. Some of them, indeed, have a large crane or 'gallows' of bog-oak with a long arm pivoting on a massive heel six feet high: I have come across several in Co. Armagh (Fig. 20). One may guess that well-appointed houses of the central-hearth style had some such appliance in early times, turning, perhaps, as do similar hanging-devices in the Roumanian shepherds' wooden *stanas*, on an upright post pivoted in the tie beam of the rafters. Framed within the white-

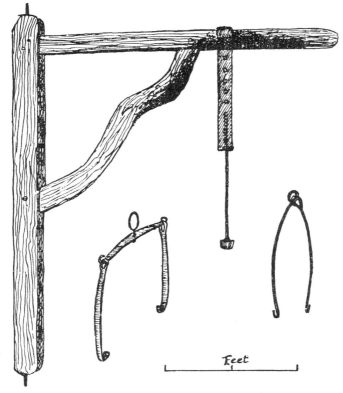

Fig. 20. Bog-oak crane and adjustable pot-hanger, Co. Armagh, with fittings for hanging griddle and pots.

67

washed jambs of a stone chimney (Fig. 19) the simple wrought-iron crane has the simple beauty of fitness to purpose which most hand-made things possess. The smith rarely attempted the decorative scrolls which were more suited to light objects such as oatcake toasters. From the cranes must hang the mighty iron pots, some with a capacity of 25 gallons, to hold food for man and beast. One hears of examples which were literally 'cranes', fitted with a windlass and chain to lift pots on and off the fire. Such capacious vessels could not have come into use had the fire not been at floor level.

The adjustable pot-hanger which hooks on to the arm of the crane is a simple but effective device for adjusting the height of the hanging pot (Fig. 20). Like so many of the culture-elements we are describing in this book, it apparently belongs to the Atlantic fringes of Europe. While it could be a medieval or later introduction to Ireland, research may show that it is a Celtic trait (fire-irons are a ritual feature of early Celtic cultures) which has found its last refuge in the open hearths of the west. The crane and other fire-irons and the very soot that clings to them have been regarded with superstitious reverence by virtue of their association with fire. Soot carried in the pocket, for example, gave protection on a journey. More ancient in origin than the crane is the hanging chain suspended from a crook-stick and terminating in a movable pot-hook (crook). From existing examples one could work out a plausible evolutionary sequence of hangings from the roof-suspension which can still be seen in the black-houses of the Hebrides. The sequence begins with a wooden peg stuck high in the back wall of the fire, giving way to a transverse bar set parallel to the wall in the smoke canopy, which might in turn become the arm of the crane. These crook-sticks are said to have been made of holly. The long chain of the first example certainly gives more 'play' than the short suspension from a chimney bar, but the peg is more inaccessible and this supports the contention that it is a survival of the long hanging from the roof-timbers over a chimneyless central hearth.

Pots and pans and other hearth-gear we shall discuss in the next chapter, but here we should notice some further architectural fittings of the partitioned fireside. On one side of the canopy, sometimes on both, resting on the brace-tree is a wattled shelf or loft which goes under various names such as, in Ulster, skeagh, hurdle or flake. The double loft in the fireside from Co. Cavan illustrated in Fig. 21 is slatted and floored with reed matting, the reeds being bound together with split briar after the manner of a bee-skep. As the term hurdle would imply, these lofts are frequently made of wattle. The heat could rise through them and keep everything above bone-dry, and this was the allocated place for storing various treasured possessions as well as a great deal of 'trumpery'. Here the rushes were dried in the preparation of rush lights, and here the horse-collar was stored when not in use, a reminder that it was made partly or wholly of straw and must be kept dry.

If we are right in supposing that the wattled chimney canopy is a relatively late feature it follows that we cannot regard the chimney loft as an old element in the Irish house. Yet the loft is a traditional fitting for which there seems to be some evidence in early literature, and the need for storage-space must have led to the utilization of part of the roof space. It seems that the loft over the kitchen which nowadays has often become a bedroom in the roof—lit by a small gable window and entered by a steep stairway or even a ladder—began as a half-loft over the bottom end. This survived in Clare Island into the present century and was used to store tools and dried fish. In Fermanagh the half-loft was the hens' roosting-place, serving to protect the cows from droppings and now transferred with them to the byre. By tradition the loft is the sleeping-place of the children, and the man and woman of the house have their bed near the fire, either in the kitchen or in the bedroom behind the chimney flue.

Nowhere is the relationship between the parental bed and the fire better defined than in the traditional house of the north-west, where a small bed-wing—the outshot or *cailleach*—projects out from one of the side-walls at the chimney-end of the kitchen (Fig. 8; Fig. 12, 3). The distribution of this type of house, north of a line from Cushendun in Co. Antrim to south-western Galway, corresponds with many other north-western cultural distributions, and the area is curiously coincident with that of the oldest rocks in the country, the infertile schists and

69

FIG. 21. Fireside with quern, Belturbet, Co. Cavan.

quartzites. The bed-wing gives a narrow room additional width where it is most needed, near the fire. It may be that sufficiently long timbers for sizeable rafters were not easily procured in these mountain regions of poor soil. We may be dealing, however, with a feature which has died out in other regions and which has lived on in difficult country. The built-in wall-bed— the half-neuk—is known in the Orkneys, the Faroes and in the Hebridean black-houses and is characteristic of humble societies in other parts of the world. It is possible that in Ireland the wall-bed attests contacts with western Scotland which have repeatedly influenced that part of the country running south-westwards from Co. Antrim following the 'Caledonian grain' to Connacht. In any case the wall-bed appears to be restricted to the extreme north-western fringes of Europe.

The open hearth with all its associations is truly the heart and centre of house and home. The fire is, with her children, the 'care' of the woman of the house. 'A woman can never go to the fire', runs an Irish saying, 'without tampering with it.' The manifold duties of the housewife keep her moving about the hearth, tethered to it for most of the day. Her last duty at night is to 'smoor' it, burying a live turf in the ashes to retain a spark which can be fanned into a blaze next morning. This custom was fortified by the belief that the good folk, the fairies, would be displeased if there were no fire for them through the night. I have sat at fires which, it was claimed, had not been allowed to go out for over a century, or for as far back as family memory could go. It is to the fireside seat that the visitor is invited, for this is the place of honour, and it is around the fire that tales of old time are told. The magic of the open fire, playing upon the fancies of generations who have gathered round it, has engendered a host of beliefs and portents. The fire can give warning of wind and weather, of lucky and unlucky visitors, of marriage and death. Above all, it is a shrine to which ancestral spirits return, a link with the living past.[1]

[1]Since this chapter was written A. T. Lucas has published (in *Arctica*, 11, 16–35) an account of Wattle and Straw Mat Doors in Ireland. See page 65.

VI

POTS AND PANS

STORIES of 'the crock of gold' remind us of the superstitions which have gathered around the humble unglazed vessels of baked clay used in prehistoric times for domestic and funerary purposes. The novel art of pot-making—the magic transformation of soft clay into indestructible pottery —must have made a deep impression on the native mind when introduced into Atlantic Europe from the Mediterranean region some forty centuries ago. It symbolized, too, a new way of life, for it accompanied the revolutionary arts of food-production and the establishment of settlements which were more or less permanently fixed to the soil. The possession of pottery greatly facilitates cooking and boiling and marks the beginning of the long line of peasant soups, stews and porridges. But primitive pottery does not stand up to hard use and the wastage was great—to the delight of archaeologists. For prolonged stewing metal vessels were preferable, and in Ireland 'the pot', in recent centuries, invariably refers to the three-legged iron cooking pot. Life revolves about the fire and the pot, and it was remarked during famine years that victims 'clung to the pot when all else had gone'.

For the archaeologist potsherds are an invaluable guide to changes of culture. Clay vessels had religious as well as domestic significance, and we know that as the Bronze Age advanced through the second millennium B.C. the domestic food vessel was adopted as a cinerary urn, and the deposition of cremated bones in urns continued in Ireland into the Christian era. Earlier, some of the megalithic cults had involved the offering to the dead of enormous quantities of broken pots. In a late Neolithic burial cairn at Lyles Hill near Belfast I found tens of thousands of potsherds which had been collected from domestic refuse and thrown into the cairn during the course of its erection.[1] The broken plates which may be seen exposed on the graves in some old burial-grounds in Co. Mayo are probably placed there in continuation of ancient practice. The breaking of pots is one of the elements in Hallowe'en pranks— one might almost say rites—and again we notice the association with the dead, for All-Hallows is the time when the dead are believed to return to their homes.

It would appear that by breaking a pot you broke its spirit; and by transference the power of the dead to do harm. Readers will recall the significant lines from *Hamlet*, referring to the suicide of Ophelia: 'Her death was doubtful . . . for charitable prayers, shards, flints and pebbles should be thrown on her.'[2] In some places in south-west England potsherds figure in the 'lent crocking' rites at Easter: like Easter eggs they are symbols of fertility. The association of fertility and decay, of life and death, comedy and tragedy, is clearly displayed in the wake games which are described in Chapter XX. This association, we note in passing, is ever-present in the mind of the Irish countryman, and the juxtaposition gives dramatic quality to the work of many Anglo-Irish playwrights.

This is not the place to enlarge on the technology of early pot-making, but it may be observed that the designs, fabric and finish of the Neolithic family of pottery in Ireland were far superior to those of succeeding periods: indeed it was not until wheel-made pots found local markets in the medieval towns that technically superio~ vessels were made in this country. In late prehistoric and early historic times the wealthy were able to import fine wares in small quantities from the continent, but the peasant homes over most of Ireland apparently did without pottery—the Gaelic word for potter is a loan-word—and vessels of wood, metal or leather did duty for the now universal imported 'delph'. The Dutchman, Gerard Boate, writing in 1645, said that 'the use of earthen vessels hath been very rare among them, and to the most part unknown even

[1] E. E. Evans, *Lyles Hill: a late Neolithic site in Co. Antrim*, H.M.S.O. (1953).
[2] *Hamlet*, Act V, Sc. 1.

until these very last times, although a great number of English potters have set up their trade'.[1] No tradition of hand-made pottery survived in Ireland as it did in the Barvas ware of Lewis in the Hebrides. On the other hand another ancient craft of prehistoric origins persisted into living memory in the making of wooden noggins in which milk and porridge were taken. They are small stave-built vessels of oak, having one stave projecting

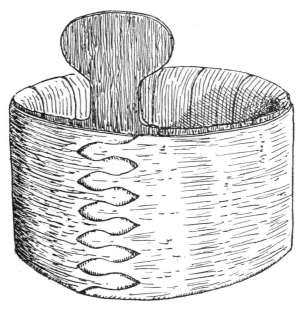

Fig. 22. Wooden noggin, Co. Down. Height of rim, 3 in.

to serve as a handle. The staves are held together and the single-piece base kept in place by a thin band of ash joined by inter-locking tongues (Fig. 22). This method of fastening the wooden band is found on the similar 'piggins' of parts of Britain, also in Scandinavia and throughout the Asiatic Arctic region, and it may well derive in these islands from an ancient circum-polar culture. The noggins were made by skilled craftsmen who

[1]Gerard Boate, *Ireland's Natural History* (1652), 159.

were known as noggin weavers. Cheap delph has now taken the place of the noggin, but the word survives in a phrase I have heard applied to a child who is thriving on his food: 'he wants a stave out of his noggin'.

The art of pot-making declined and in many parts of the country almost disappeared after the late Bronze Age, when bronze cauldrons came in to provide serviceable cooking-vessels. Some archaeologists have related this decline to the climatic deterioration of the Late Bronze Age, but it is more reasonable to associate it with an increase of pastoral pursuits and a diet of whitemeats. The bronze cauldrons were highly prized: from Gaelic literature we know that they were the special property of the head of the house and they seem to have taken on something of the magic of the early pots. They were sometimes credited with strange virtues such as the ability to yield to each guest the piece of flesh to which his rank or occupation entitled him, and they occupy a prominent place in folk-lore and legend.

It is interesting to notice that the bulk of the earliest pre-historic pots in Ireland are of plain brown burnished earthen-ware, faithful copies of the leather prototypes proper to a pastoral people. This western European Neolithic pottery is one of the indications of a common substratum in the early civilizations of Atlantic Europe. The round-bottomed vessels simulated round-bellied leather containers, which may well have continued to be used for cooking into historic times. We know that whole cow-hides were employed for the purpose in Elizabethan times. This is undoubtedly a survival of older custom: we find it among hunting peoples, for example the Indians of Labrador are in the habit of preparing broth in a vessel made from the belly of a caribou. A relic of the substitu-tion of pots for skins may perhaps be seen in the persistent Irish belief that the money obtained from the sale of a cow-hide should be used for the purchase of a metal vessel. The Scots, as Froissart and Burt tell us, cooked their beef in skins stretched on four stakes. Fynes Moryson says of the Irish: 'Flesh they seethe in a hollow tree lapped in a raw cow's hide, and so set over the fire.'[1] From prehistoric times we have many ancient

[1] Fynes Moryson, *The Description of Ireland*, 228.

cooking places, which have been popularly known to Irish-speakers as *fulachta fiadha* (deer roasts), consisting of mounds of burnt stones usually set in marshy places. Excavations have shown that they contain dug-out trunks or plank-lined pits sunk in peat where water was heated by hot stones. Hundreds of these mounds are known in Cos. Cork and Kilkenny and they occur sporadically in other parts of the country, as also in Wales and more rarely in England and Scotland. Some Irish examples have been dated to the Bronze Age, though it is believed that their construction continued into the Middle Ages.[1] They are interpreted as the bivouacs of summer hunting parties, and would represent an archaic tradition preserved by the privileged classes, but they have their humble counterparts in the stone-lined pits filled with hot turf, in which, I have been told, peasants would cook their potatoes when working some distance from home.

FIG. 23. Cooking pots: round-bottomed suspension vessels through 4,000 years: Neolithic (earthenware); late Bronze Age (bronze); medieval (bronze); and modern (cast iron).

The essential continuity of form and function is strikingly demonstrated by a series of Irish cooking pots such as is illustrated in Fig. 23, from the round-bottomed Neolithic bowl with its suspension holes to the present-day globular iron pot with its twin lugs and its three stubby legs—a concession to a hard uneven floor. The three-legged pot is the countrywife's maid-of-all-work and it is only slowly giving way to flat-bottomed pans and kettles. The oven-pot also, a kind of Dutch oven, is widely utilized, and the pot-roasts which it cooks to perfection have replaced spit-roasted meat. It is said to get its other name, the bastible, from the fact that it was first made at

[1]M. J. O'Kelly, *J.R.S.A.I.*, 84 (1954), 105-55.

Barnstaple in Devon. The oven-pot may be suspended over the fire but in the south rests on a trivet: the lid is dished so that live turves may be placed on top. It is used also for bread-baking, though the griddle is most commonly employed for this purpose (Fig. 24).

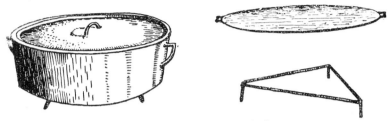

FIG. 24. Oven-pot, griddle and trivet.

Here we come to a fundamental fact in the geography of the Irish hearth—the absence of the built-in oven. The one exception which proves the rule is its occurrence in the extreme south-east, where, in Co. Wexford, the baronies of Bargy and Forth have retained many features dating from their English settlement in medieval times. Over most of Ireland even when a cooking-range is installed in the hearth, the oven is not used for bread-baking, for oven-bread is not a native food. In central Europe on the other hand the bread-oven, originally of clay, is of great antiquity and the stone or metal oven has come to dominate the fireplace. The difference in bread-types is related on the one hand to environment and economic organization and on the other hand to a whole set of eating habits and ethical values.

Thin bread, or bread in cakes, made without yeast, has been from early times the common bread in most parts of Atlantic Europe, from North Scandinavia to the Basque Country, including Highland Britain and Ireland. Farther afield it is typical of many Mediterranean areas and parts of Asia. In north-western Europe it is closely linked with the cultivation of oats, though home-baked wheaten bread is made in the same way and mixtures with maize and with potatoes are similarly prepared. Potato bread (fadge), a mixture of wheat flour and boiled potatoes, is a popular food which surely had its origins in difficult times.

77

As throughout Highland Britain it was the dramatic fall in the price of wheat in the 1880s, thanks to imports from America, that changed the eating habits of the people and led to a decline in the consumption of oaten and barley bread. The commercial baking of oven-bread from imported wheat is thus a fairly recent development virtually confined to the large towns, especially the milling ports, and its distribution through the rural areas explains the ubiquitous bread-vans of the country roads. We should probably make an exception of the English-settled parts of the east coast in the Pale as well as in Bargy. Dublin and Drogheda have a rare advantage in Ireland in that, thanks to their relatively dry climate, grain need not be kiln-dried before milling. The town bakeries cater for country tastes by providing an extraordinary variety of cakes and farls as well as standard loaves. One of the big Belfast bakeries turns out some seventy varieties of plain and fancy bread which are distributed over several Ulster counties. In the Scottish Highlands, similarly, most of the bread consumed comes from a Glasgow factory: home-made, even locally-made, yeast-bread is almost unknown. 'The van' is therefore one of the necessities of life: its forerunner was the tea-van, famous for its fast high-stepping horses, once a familiar sight in the Irish countryside.

The baking of thin bread has steadily declined under this urban competition. White bread and stewed tea are woefully inadequate as a staple diet but there were perhaps greater gastric evils in indigestible soda bread made with unboiled water from surface wells. The use of buttermilk and above all a large consumption of butter were, however, traditional. On balance the housewife has profited, for she was truly the slave of the fire. Thin bread has the disadvantage of going stale quickly, and a good housewife was expected always to have fresh bread ready. Labourers have been known to refuse to work on farms where there was not a daily baking of bread. The baking board or trough hung ready to hand on the wall, and the meal was stored near the fire to keep it dry (Figs. 18 and 21). Old people have told me how, when they were children, they were called on periodically to tramp the meal in its wooden chest or ark, treading it down with bare feet to drive out the air and lessen the risk of its going musty. In Wales the meal-chest was considered to be the best place to store a well-dried ham.

Originally the flat round oatcakes were baked on a flat stone, and such flagstone griddles continued to be used in the nineteenth century in parts of Co. Kerry. A late seventeenth-century traveller wrote: 'Their general food is a thin oatcake which they bake upon a broad flat stone made hot, a little sheep's milk cheese, or goat's milk, boiled leeks and some roots.'[1] In Yorkshire the flagstone was built-in over a separate fire and gave way slowly to the iron 'bakestone'. The bread was hardened in front of the fire, resting against a three-legged 'bread-stick' of the type shown in Fig. 25. Representations of bread on the sculptured high crosses of the Early Middle Ages show just such round discs. The traditional form of thin bread, however, is the farl (fardel), shaped like a quarter-circle. The large circular cake is marked with a cross so that it can be readily broken into quarters (farls) after baking and hardening. The 'harning' is done on a wrought iron 'harnen stand' or toaster which has taken the place of the simple bread-stick. It is worth noticing that the Beltane cakes, formerly eaten at the fires which were lit on hill-tops on May Eve, were baked, in Scotland at any rate, before the fire without touching iron.[2] I have seen a few examples of carved stone breadstands which were designed to bake the bread in front of the fire, and no doubt rough stones were originally used for this purpose. The baking stones are elaborately carved and often carry dates ranging, in Scottish examples, from 1674 to 1791.[3] Irish examples seem to be confined to Ulster and they probably represent one of the many culture traits introduced from Scotland (Fig. 25, 6). The wrought iron toasters are tastefully designed and exhibit a great variety of ornament. Specimens from north Ulster and from Scotland display an almost Spanish exuberance in the intricacies of their spiral terminals, and one would like to know if they have their counterparts along the Atlantic coasts of Europe. They are now for the most part museum pieces, for one rarely sees them in use and great numbers have found their way to the scrap heap in the last half century.

[1]'A Tour in Ireland in 1672–74', *J.C.H.A. Soc.* x (1904), 96.
[2]J. M. McPherson, *Primitive Beliefs in the North-east of Scotland* (1929).
[3]A. Mitchell, *The Past in the Present* (1880), 239.

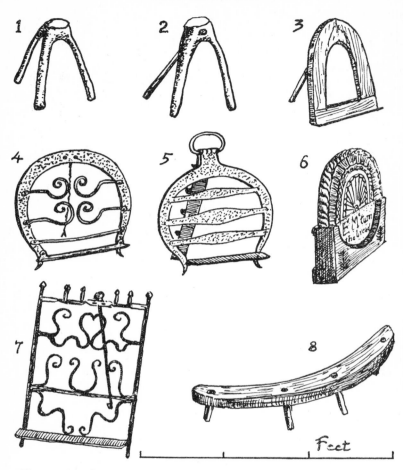

FIG. 25. Oatcake toasters (harnen stands). The first three 'bread-sticks' make an evolutionary series. They are from Armagh, Galway and Clare. Nos. 4 and 5 are bread-irons from Derry and Down; the latter is fitted with a spit-rack. No. 6 (from Fermanagh) is in stone. No. 7 is an unusual type from Armagh. No. 8 is a toasting fender from Antrim.

Among food gatherers such as the Californian Indians we find that wild oats are parched before they are ground in a mortar. A similar custom, known as 'burning the corn in the ear', survived until recent times in Ireland and met with as much scorn from English observers as did 'ploughing by the tail' and other archaic customs. In fact it seems to have been associated with tail-ploughing and certain other practices and would thus represent a very ancient cultural substratum which it was once fashionable to call Pictish. It was sufficiently prevalent in the seventeenth century to justify the passing of an Act of Parliament forbidding it, in 1635. 'The wild Irish', writes Fynes Moryson, 'do not thresh their oats, but burn them from the straw and so make cakes thereof.'[1] A fuller description comes from Martin Martin's famous account of the Western Isles: 'The ancient way of dressing corn . . . is called Graddan, from the Irish word Grad, which signifies quick. A woman sitting down, takes a handful of corn, holding it by the stalks in her left hand, and then sets fire to the ears, which are presently in a flame; she has a stick in her right hand . . . beating off the grain at the very instant when the husk is quite burnt, for if she miss of that, she must use the kiln. The corn may be so dressed, winnowed, ground, and baked within an hour after reaping from the ground.'[2] Graddan bread was esteemed for its sweetness. Burstin is the Shetland name for corn dried in this way, or by rolling hot stones among it, or sometimes by deliberately roasting the grain in a kettle.

The taste for butter which makes the Irish consumption per head one of the highest in the world recalls the traditional place of 'whitemeats' in the diet. The Foreign Agricultural Circular of the U.S. Department of Agriculture (October 1955) giving the *per capita* consumption of dairy products for various countries in 1954, shows that the Republic of Ireland is second only to New Zealand in butter consumption, but on the basis of milk and milk products Ireland comes first, with a *per capita* consumption of 1,425 lb. The explanation is to be found not in a large consumption of milk—here Ireland ranks eighth—but in the low average fat content of Irish milk. Nevertheless the *per capita* consumption of butter is extremely high, 41 lb. per annum, as compared with 14 lb. in the United Kingdom and 9 lb. in the U.S.A. Butter spread thickly on fresh bread is a tasty if simple food, and one suspects that in pre-famine times

[1]Fynes Moryson, *The Description of Ireland*, 229.
[2]Martin Martin, *The Western Isles* (1703), (1934 ed., 244).

the staple was butter and oatcake rather than oatcake and butter. When bread was made from gritty quern-ground flour the butter would have served as a lubricant to assist the swallowing process. 'They swallow lumps of butter mixed with oatmeal', wrote Fynes Moryson about the year 1600, 'and love no meat more than sour milk curdled.'[1] When food was left out for the fairies it was generally oatmeal and butter: needless to say, particularly when accompanied by whiskey, it disappeared during the night. In the very high present-day Irish consumption of milk products we notice once more the survival of ancient custom, for milk products were the staple food of medieval times in all parts of the British Isles.[2] The Irish laws distinguish between summer and winter food, and the consumption of meat was almost confined to the winter months. Pork was the most highly esteemed meat, but no doubt deer and other products of the chase augmented the fare for the upper classes. Surplus cattle were presumably killed off at Martinmas and salted as 'marts', but among the peasantry the emphasis was on milch cows, and cow's meat was fit only for stews. Butter—and whiskey also—was preserved in bogs to be available in the lean days of spring (Chapter XIV). On the other hand there is little evidence of cheese-making apart from soft cheese, including that made from sheep's milk, and the Irish consumption of cheese is today probably the lowest in Europe. The making of hard cheese is a comparatively late development everywhere, so that Ireland may be said once more to have remained faithful to ancient practice. With a *per capita* consumption of 2·7 lb. in 1954, the Irish republic comes last in the fifteen countries for which figures are given in the U.S. Foreign Agricultural Circular quoted above; the highest is Norway with 19 lb. per head. I may add that I have found no record or tradition of the milking of sows which occurs in parts of Spain and which, it is suggested, may have been a Celtic custom.[3] It is said in Ireland that if a man drinks sow's milk he can see the wind for ever after.

[1] Fynes Moryson, *The Manners and Customs of Ireland*, 321.
[2] J. C. Drummond and A. Wilbraham, *The Englishman's Food* (1939), 51.
[3] R. U. Sayce, 'Milking and Dairying', *Montgomeryshire Collections*, 51 (1951–52), 120–54.

Despite certain conservative elements it must be recognized that very great changes have taken place in the Irishman's diet in recent centuries. Tea and the potato, invaders from east and west, have largely replaced whitemeats, although another more recent pair of intruders, maize-meal and rice, distributed by the British government during the famine, have made no such conquest. Dr. Salaman has fully discussed the depressing effects of the potato on diet and culture.[1] Unless one has seen a peasant family sitting down to a meal of boiled potatoes it is hardly possible to credit the consumption figures. It used to be reckoned that a stone a day was the allowance for a labourer, and it was 'by no means uncommon, in times of plenty, for a labourer to eat 14 lb. of potatoes at a meal'.[2] An average consumption of 8 lb. per day for each member of a family is well authenticated. It is not surprising that there was a general craving for 'kitchen', tasty relishes such as strong butter when this bulky, starchy and monotonous food came to dominate the Irish diet. There seems to have been an expansion of sea fishing to keep pace with the demand for 'kitchen'. Down to recent times salt fish were hawked through the autumn countryside by noisy 'cadgers', and the careful housewife would have a barrel or two of salt herrings put by for the winter. One is reminded of the 'relishes' with which many African peoples relieve the monotony of a diet of mealies.

One of the many Irish customs which the English found revolting was the bleeding of cattle. Fynes Moryson wrote: 'they often let their cows' blood, eating the congealed blood with butter'.[3] Arthur Young notes that in Wicklow 'they bleed their horses and cows, and mix the blood with meal for food'.[4] In Ulster cattle were bled 'in a smooth place, the coagulating blood being strewn with salt until a little mound was formed. This was cut up into squares and 'laid by for use as food in the scarce time of the year'.[5] Unfortunately few details of the bleeding operation have come down to us though I have been told that it was customary to close the wound with a cloven stick.

[1] R. N. Salaman, *The History and Social Influence of the Potato* (1949), chs. 11–18.
[2] I. Weld, *Roscommon* (1832), 429.
[3] Fynes Moryson, *The Manners and Customs of Ireland*, 321.
[4] A. Young, *Tour*, 2, 62.
[5] C. Otway, *Sketches in Erris and Tyrawly* (1841), 333.

In some parts of the country the blood was made into puddings. Sheep's blood, in this case caught at the slaughtering, is used for making blood puddings in parts of the south, and black puddings made from pig's blood are popular in other parts of the country. I believe one might divide Ireland into two regions according to the popularity of black and white puddings, but I would hesitate to demarcate the border!

A great deal of information could be collected on local and festive foods and on food substitutes which were resorted to in famine years. The traditional times and names of meals also offer a fruitful field of investigation and they should be listed before new fashions entirely replace them. In many parts of the country only two meals were taken, at morning and evening, a fact to be remembered when considering the colossal quantities of food that were consumed at a meal, but it should be added that there were times when little food of any kind was available to the poorer people.

VII

FURNITURE AND FITTINGS

GOOD craftsmanship in wood is so rarely seen in the Irish peasant house that one easily notices a piece of quality furniture. The chances are that it has come out of 'the big house' or, near the coast, from a wrecked ship. Very little oak furniture has survived from the days before the famine, and what there is is likely to be of bog-oak, that is timber dug out of the bogs. The truth seems to be that by the time improved styles of furniture and settled conditions of life had come about, in the second half of the seventeenth century, the native oak-woods had been almost everywhere destroyed, and the common furniture came to be made of bog wood or imported soft woods. The gentry favoured mahogany. Already in the early seventeenth century Ireland was importing pine wood from western Scotland,[1] and during the eighteenth century it was the returning timber ships from Newfoundland and Nova Scotia that initiated Southern Irish emigration to the New World.

No doubt this lack of good quality peasant furniture may be partly attributed to poverty, and to the recurrent famines, of fuel as well as food, which brought despair and led to the burning of furniture. But it also reflects the weak tradition of built-up furniture among a people predominantly pastoral and to some extent nomadic. Certainly degrading poverty and insecure tenancies did not provide the means of support for skilled craftsmen: yet in Wales, where conditions under an

---

[1]H. G. Graham, *The Social Life of Scotland in the 18th Century*, 4th ed. (1937), 196. On bog timber see A. T. Lucas in *Béaloideas*, 33, 71–134.

often oppressive landlordism were not dissimilar, a strong tradition of good quality oak furniture was standardized in the eighteenth century and has remained a source of inspiration and pride ever since. The destruction of the native oak woods and the stronger pastoral strain in Ireland were perhaps the dominant factors, but once more we note the exceptional position of the barony of Bargy and Forth, where Gabriel Beranger commented in 1780 on the good-quality, well-kept furniture: 'I have seen in these cabins bureaus of oak so clean that they shone like polished mahogany.'[1]

Sturdiness rather than elegance was the characteristic feature of Irish peasant furniture, and many small household and dairy fittings were hand-cut from the solid or lathe-turned. Yet there was no lack of care taken in the proper arrangement of the furniture in the house. Its disposition was fixed by long custom and varied little throughout the country. One is reminded of the careful division of the limited floor-space of the nomads' tent among the Lapps or Mongols. In fact only by adhering to a strict formula could the family and all their belongings be fitted into a single room which was traditionally also a byre. Invariably the centre of the room, and the whole space in front of the fire, was kept open. This was, for the bulk of the peasant population down to the eighteenth century, the family sleeping-place. According to an account of Mayo in 1799, they slept naked with their feet to the fire, lying on rushes, with a covering of blankets or day-clothes.[2] An earlier account of the Rosses of Donegal, relating to the middle of the eighteenth century, gives us more details: 'All the family lay together in one bed, and, if any visitors came in the evening, they too slept with them; for they set no bounds to their hospitality . . . heath or bent bushes were spread across the floor, to a length sufficient for the number present, and in breadth about six feet; over this litter, the mistress of the house laid part of a long plaid or blanket, on which the others, having stripped off their clothes, lay down as fast as they could; men and women together, all naked: then the mistress having drawn the rest of the blanket over them, lay down herself, naked also. This they call a

[1] Lady Wilde, 'Memoir of Gabriel Beranger', *J.R.S.A.I.* (1876), 132.
[2] In C. Otway, *Sketches in Erris and Tyrawly* (1841), 28, 32.

Thorough-bed.'[1] The Poor Law Commissioners reported in 1836 that nearly three-quarters of the 10,000 inhabitants of one parish were sleeping on the floor, though they add that this was because the bedsteads had been burnt to boil potatoes. Even after 1850 the custom of sleeping 'in stradogue' as it was called, was not unknown in the west.[2] In Ulster, too, though the master and mistress of the house would have slept in their wall-bed, the young children, where there was only one room, must have slept on the floor. Long custom as well as wretched poverty explains the statement made by Patrick McKye of a Donegal parish in 1837: 'Nor can many of them afford a second bed, but whole families of sons and daughters of mature age indiscriminately lie together . . . and all in the bare buff.'[3] The wall-bed was a wooden frame built into the outshot which has been described earlier. It had its own wooden covering or tester to give protection from roof drips, and originally, to judge by the Hebridean black-houses, the covering was of sods. In Donegal, bog timber supplied the bed frame, and the mattress was made of wattles or of ropes twisted from the root fibres of bog-fir. That fir-rope mattresses were once standard fittings is shown by the specification for the beds to be supplied to the Belfast Charitable Association in 1774.[4] But some of the wall-beds in parts of Connacht were until recently mere stone benches covered with dried bracken. Half-ruined examples may be seen in the deserted houses of Slievemore on Achill Island.

In the house with fireside partition the kitchen bed often takes the form of a settle-bed, a seat by day and a bed by night. The front and seat are in one piece, hinged at the bottom so that the whole can be folded down to make a low bed (Fig. 18). In bachelor homes, where the settle-bed has been retained, I have been offered a seat on one which had been closed a moment before by bundling in the mattress and bedclothes. Placed against one of the side walls near the fire, the settle-bed

---

[1] J. C. Walker, *Historical Memoirs of the Irish Bards*, 2nd ed. (1818), Appendix 1, 196–204.
[2] *The Saxon in Ireland* (1851), 192.
[3] Lord George Hill, *Gweedore*, 16.
[4] R. W. M. Strain, *The Ulster Medical Journal*, 22 (1953), 37.

admirably illustrates the economy of space and function characteristic of Irish kitchen fittings, but I doubt whether this rather
complicated piece of furniture is of any great antiquity: it was
probably introduced by planters or adapted from a settle fitted
with a coffer seat.

The black-houses, as described in the nineteenth century,
had no table, and there are still to be seen, in Donegal for
instance, houses where there is no kitchen table. At meal-times
the family sit around a shallow potato basket resting on the
circle of knees. The origin of the tripod tray-table of south-
eastern Europe and south-western Asia is surely to be sought in
a similar custom. In fact the Blasket Island table was described as
a tripod to which was fitted a board which hung on the wall
when not in use.[1] The little round table is known from many
parts of western Europe. There is, for example, the three-
legged 'cricket' table of Wales, which has a special place in the
affections of the family. Placed near the fire, it is reserved at
meal-times for the father and mother while the children and
servants eat at the big table. In Ireland the kitchen table is a
flimsy construction, and its place is against the side wall, under
a window. Not infrequently it is hinged to the wall as a 'falling
leaf table' which drops when not in use, thus enlarging the
open space in front of the fire.

Bishop Pococke describes the Tirawley (Mayo) table as 'a
long sort of stool about 20 inches high and broad and two yards
long',[2] clearly designed to be stowed away along a wall. Small
tables which have been found in the bogs are little more than
small boards, their four short legs being cut from the solid.
They are provided with holes by which they could be transported or hung up when not in use (Fig. 26). It follows that
table-chairs were unnecessary: long, low, narrow stools or three
legged 'creepies' would serve, and the children would have
squatted eastern-fashion on the floor.

The table, therefore, in the words of a Swedish student of
Irish ethnology, 'never attracted the social activities of the
house, and there are no ceremonies connected with the places
at the table, as in countries where the table is the predominating

[1] T. O'Crohan, *The Islandman* (1934), 40.
[2] *Pococke's Tour, 1752* (1891), 87.

social and family centre'.[1] The table has never supplanted the
fireplace as the focus of social living, a function it has served
since the dawn of humanity. As so often happens, folklore
endorses this finding: there is an Irish saying that it is unlucky
to shake hands across a table. The table or 'board', which in
the English language gave its name to a committee, has not
replaced the fireside as the place where the Irish countryman
talks—and talks business. When food is left out for the fairies
or for visitors from the other world it is placed in front of the
fire, and at Hallowe'en seats for the returning dead were arranged
around the fire.

Fig. 26. Table, cut from the solid, from a Co. Armagh bog. It measures 20 in.
by 12 in.

Similarly the fireside, not the table, attracted whatever means
of illumination was available. The hob-lamp took the place of the
table-lamp. Even when paraffin came in the oil lamp was still
hung in the chimney. The older native oils, derived from fish
and burnt in open lamps, were very unsavoury, and it was ex-
pedient to allow the fumes to escape with the chimney smoke.
The iron crusie or open oil-lamp, its shape almost unchanged
since classical times, was to be seen nearly everywhere around
the coast until late in the last century (Fig. 27) but the paraffin
lamp quickly swept it out of existence. Medieval crusies from
Spain, Italy and north-western Europe are very similar to
recent Irish examples, and it was from the Rhineland, it is said,
that the crusie was taken to Pennsylvania, where it first suc-
cumbed to the new mineral oil. Stone moulds of uncertain age
known from Scotland and Ireland show how the iron pans were
hammered into shape. Inland, the place of the crusie was taken
by resinous splinters of bog fir kept by the fire till tinder dry,

[1] Å. Campbell in *Folk-Liv* (1937), 234.

89

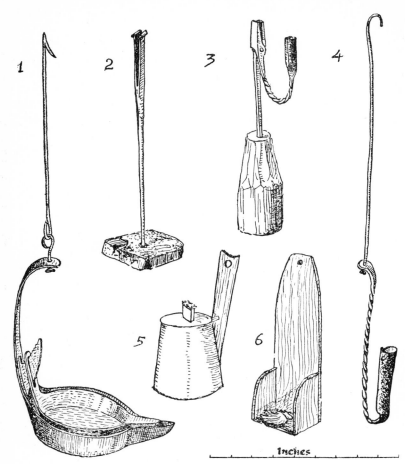

FIG. 27. Light-holders. (1) Crusie, Co. Antrim (scale × 2). (2) Fir-split holder, Co. Antrim. (3) Rush and candle-holder, Co. Antrim. (4) Weavers' candle-holder, Co. Armagh. (5) Hob lamp, Co. Cavan. (6) Scollop shell lamp, Aran Islands.

and by rush-lights held in iron pincers mounted on wooden or wrought-iron stands (Fig. 27). Candles of resin, tallow and beeswax were also made at home by dipping prepared strips of cloth repeatedly in an iron grisset and rolling out the candles on a board. Such candles played an important part in various church festivals and at wakes, and though they are now bought they are made by hand in a few towns by chandlers who carry on a medieval tradition. One Dublin firm, established in 1488, manufactures large church candles of beeswax by methods which can have changed little with the centuries. In the home the candles were supported in wrought-iron holders or stuck into a turf by the fireside. Tall standard holders, often with adjustable fittings, were designed to give light to the weaver at the loom, and they are most typically found in Ulster (Fig. 28). The fine embroidery which occupied the women in the linen districts must have imposed a great strain on the eyes: there are stories of a single candle serving as a central source of light for a ring of seamstresses, each of whom held her work against a bottle full of water which acted as a magnifier.

In Ireland, as throughout Atlantic Europe, the dresser ranks as the most important and elaborate piece of furniture in the kitchen, and its position is prescribed by custom. It stands either against the side wall or against the partition between kitchen and bedroom. Since this partition is of no great anti-quity we can be sure that the original place of the dresser was against the side-wall and that it has developed from, and taken the place of, shelves built into or attached to the side-wall. In part of Ulster it is referred to as 'the shelf'. I have already mentioned the tiers of stone shelves set in the wall which are preserved in the deserted houses of the Slievemore cluster on Achill Island. It is believed that the fashion of open crockery shelves was diffused from the court sideboards of the later Middle Ages in France and England, and it may be surmised that the wooden dresser was readily accepted in Celtic lands to replace wall shelves, from Elizabethan times on. The adoption of delph and tea-drinking in the eighteenth century no doubt accelerated the spread of the dresser, which had become, by that time, an essential part of Irish kitchen furniture (Plate 1). The corner-cupboard, evolving in much the same way from corner-shelves, is another article of furniture with a north-west European distribution. Similarly the coffer or store-chest spread through western Europe from the later Middle Ages onwards, replacing skin, straw, hollowed wood, or basket-work containers.

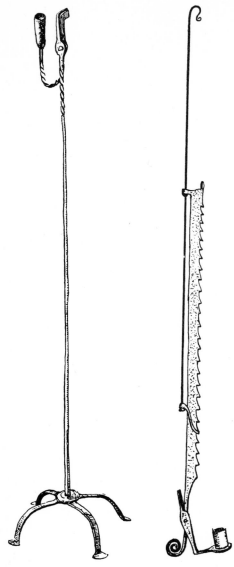

FIG. 28. Weavers' light-holders, Co. Armagh. Height, 3 ft.

Low stools and benches seem to have been the traditional form of seating, and no doubt the floor served for the children. Travellers noted that this was the best way to avoid the smoke:

> By sitting low, on rushes spread,
> The smoke still hover'd overhead;
> And did more good than real harm,
> Because it kept the long house warm.[1]

Fireside seats, more or less fixed, were often of stone, a solid block of wood or a large lump of turf. In the 'round about' hearths which were common in parts of Co. Antrim, and which people who remember them have described to me, the seat behind the fire, a log of wood, was known as the dais, a dialect word for a bench or seat which appears to be of north English origin. Solid seats of coiled straw or rushes were also common (Fig. 29) but the favourite fireside stool was the three-legged creepie, resembling a milking stool and like it finding a firm hold no matter how uneven the floor. There is little evidence of chairs of any antiquity. A three-legged type found in parts of the west, with a triangular seat and a narrow one-piece back has probably evolved from the creepie but looks Germanic. The nearest approach to a distinctive Irish style is the straw or rush-seated chair, which finds its best-known homes in Co. Down and Co. Limerick. High-backed armchairs made entirely of coiled straw rope after the manner of a beehive used to be found in the west, and since they can be paralleled in many parts of western Europe from the Orkneys to Spain it is probable that their manufacture is a peasant craft of some antiquity (Fig. 29). Cradles, too, were made of straw as well as of wood and basketwork, and they were sometimes suspended from the roof. I have heard of a cradle being improvised by laying a horse-collar on the floor. The phrase 'rocked in a pot' applied to an illegitimate child is said to derive from the use of a large fireside cooking pot as cradle and hiding place: round-shouldered infants were therefore suspect.

Down to recent times it was the custom to keep most of the dairying equipment in the kitchen, and in the traditional peasant house the upright churn still occupies a place against the wall,

[1] W(illiam) M(offatt), *The Western Isle* (1724), Canto 2.

FIG. 29. (1) Co. Antrim chair. (2) Co. Down straw-seated chair. (3) Creepie.
(4) Armchair of coiled straw-rope, Co. Cork. (5) Straw seat, Co. Clare.

usually opposite the fire. The absence, in a country predominantly pastoral and consuming large quantities of milk products, of a building or room set aside as a dairy is at first sight strange. Milk cattle, however, were closely identified with the woman of the house, and as we have seen they commonly shared the kitchen with the family. Owing to the scarcity of winter feeding-stuffs, moreover, the supply of milk must have been, down to a couple of centuries ago, largely confined to the summer months and butter-making was therefore undertaken at the booley houses. It must have been difficult to store the considerable amounts of milk products required for winter food, especially when one remembers that most of the peasant houses were made of wattles, sods or mud, and there is some evidence, as we shall see in Chapter IX, that they were kept underground under the old Celtic economy, in even temperatures and safe from the depredations of animals.

However this may be, the kitchen is the traditional place for keeping the churn, and for churning. The stave-built upright plunge churn, prototype of the metal milk-churn which at first faithfully copied its shape, belongs to a family of wooden vessels which has been diffused across the Old World from Ireland to Tibet and now survives most abundantly towards the limits of its range (Fig. 30). Made by local coopers, Irish churns display a considerable variety in shape and size, the shapes differing regionally, the sizes depending on the number of cows kept on the farm, for they were 'made to measure'. The small barrel-shaped churn of the south-west, with a narrow vertical mouth, would appear to be the older style. The mouth, designed to hold a lid through a hole in which the churn staff passes, is usually a separate unit attached to the body by a join—the crib—skilfully contrived and concealed under one of the encircling hoops. Some old churns have hoops of split rods, hazel or sally, but it was reckoned lucky to have one of the hoops of rowan. The staves are invariably of oak: the circular base is made in three pieces, dowelled together and having the joins sealed with rushes. Small churns which have been dug out of the bogs are generally found to have been cut from the solid, and they often have projecting lugs perforated for ease of transport. Those with holed lids were certainly churns, but others

95

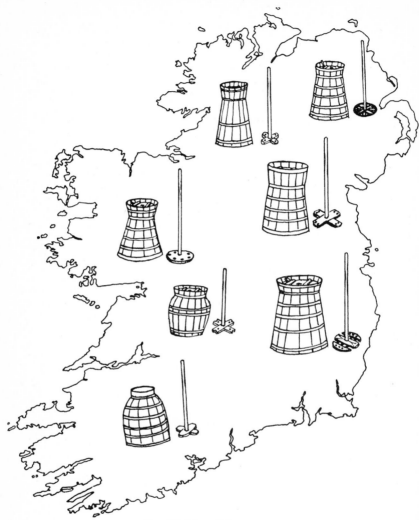

FIG. 30. Map of churn types.

were probably kegs for carrying milk: they have a rim of hoops
which would allow a cloth or skin cover to be securely tied on.

A most interesting stave-built churn dating from the ninth
century was discovered by Gerhard Bersu during the excavation

of a rath (farmstead) at Lissue, Co. Antrim, in 1946.[1] Its barrel-shaped body has the unusual refinement of an oval mouth, designed for pouring, with an iron rim-mount over which a cloth could be tied. A central iron band has two rings attached, evidently for suspension. A century ago, that is a thousand years after the Lissue churn was in use, we know that butter was made not far away on the shores of Lough Neagh by swinging the churn to and fro, suspended from the roof timbers. The Lissue churn could also have been used to carry milk from the summer pastures to the homestead. There are stories in the Mourne Mountains of milk transported in this way which would turn to butter by the automatic churning of the rough journey home from the hills. Evidently the lidless churn is the older type, and I have seen large specimens in Donegal. It was presumably from a churn of this kind, slung from a pony's back, that the Donegal child was observed 'peeping and screeching' as the pastoral cavalcade moved up to the summer booleys in the days before the Great Famine.[2]

The simplest form of churn dash, found along the west coast, terminates in a wooden cross. A similar Norwegian dasher has the ends of the cross joined with a sally ring, and a rope of cowhair is said to have been used for the purpose in Scotland. It was considered lucky to have the cross-pieces made of two different woods; indeed everything about the churn had to be made 'right'. In the whole business of handling milk luck was more important than labour, and butter-making in particular was a task fraught with unseen dangers. Often the butter would mysteriously refuse to break, and many were the precautions taken and the remedies sought. It seems that the old Irish method was to churn from the whole milk, and it was customary until recently to pour the skim milk into the churn along with the risen cream. It should be remembered, too, that the butterfat content was low, and that since many peasant farmers had no more than one cow at a time in milk, its quality would be more variable than the milk of a large herd. The unaccountable variations in the success of churning were widely attributed to the intervention of witches or fairies.

[1]G. Bersu, *U.J.A.*, X (1947), 30–58.
[2]Lord George Hill, *Gweedore*, 24.

Bad luck could not always be avoided, but at least it was desirable to make the toil less wearisome, and to this end a number of ingenious fittings were applied to the churn staff. Most of the examples I have seen, in the north-east, depend on the recoil of a strong spring to lift the staff, and they may well have been evolved from a spring pole, such as is used for the pole lathe, attached to the roof timbers.[1] Other devices enabled the staff to be moved in both directions by an arrangement of levers hinged to a couple-baulk. These engines, which have almost entirely gone out of use, were known as glaiks (Fig. 31).

Fig. 31. Glaiks for churning, Co. Down, with milk 'keeler' and piggin, Co. Donegal.

Here we may mention other things which were hung from the roof timbers: in the more prosperous homes sides of bacon and portions of the autumn-killed ox, the mart; in poorer houses the salted ling or other 'kitchen'. And there was a strange custom of keeping in the roof, to bring luck to the livestock, part of a carcase, such as an animal's leg. This undoubtedly had its origin in the days when living-room and byre were under

[1]For another device, fitted to the churn, see my *Mourne Country*, Fig. 84.

one roof. A relic of this practice may perhaps be seen in the sheep's bones that one occasionally finds tucked away in the keeping-holes of old-fashioned houses. Above the door the Bridget's Cross gives protection from fire and other dangers.

Besides the churn the old-time farm will have a wide range of other wooden dairying utensils, some stave-built, others carved or turned from the solid. They will include milking-piggins (Fig. 31), cream-skimmers, ladles, butter-scoops, and -prints, butter tubs and buttermilk butts. A shallow stave-built 'keeler' or a large turned bowl is kept for setting milk (Fig. 31). The solid and often shapely carved cups and methers (literally mead bowls) are already archaeological specimens (Fig. 65), and many of the other wooden containers are going the same way, including the little stave noggins described in an earlier chapter.

VIII

FARMYARDS AND FENCES

THE paved area in front of the traditional Irish farmhouse is known as 'the street', a word here used in its original sense of a pavement. The old style street is usually cobbled, and occasionally, especially along the coast where the materials lay to hand, neat arrangements of waterworn pebbles made a pretty pattern at the door. This is a technique of prehistoric origin which is found along the Atlantic coasts and in the Mediterranean region. The area around the hearth also may be pebbled, but I have not seen in Ireland the entire kitchen floor so treated, as in parts of Wales. There may be a stone bench against the front of the house near the door, and here, or in specially constructed wall coves across the cobbled street, pots and buckets are put out to dry (Fig. 32).

Immediately in front of the house is the traditional location of the dungheap. 'The dunghill before each door' was commented on by nearly every nineteenth-century traveller. The apologists, it is true, remind us that tenants would not move the dunghill for fear of having their rents raised because of 'improvements'. But its proximity to the dwelling house need occasion no surprise when we recall that down to a century or two ago, in remote parts, the dung was allowed to accumulate at the end of the living-room. We recall that in 1837 a school teacher wrote that some houses in Donegal had 'within their walls from ten to fifteen tons weight of dung, and only cleaned out once a year'.[1] Nowadays, however, from hygienic motives, the manure is removed to a less conspicuous part of the farmyard, though if possible still in sight of the door, for the farmer likes

[1]Lord George Hill, *Gweedore*, 17.

to keep an eye on his wealth. The muck-heap is the source of good crops and good luck, a potent symbol of well-being: 'where there is muck there is luck'. It was the custom, recorded for instance in the Glens of Antrim, to stick a sprig of rowan tree upright in the midden on May Eve to protect the farm from mischievous fairies. The muck symbolizes the fertility of the farm.

FIG. 32. Keeping-hole for pots, Co. Down.

In many parts of the country, especially in the northern counties and in Co. Wexford, the entrance to the farmyard is dignified by a pair of massive stone gate piers, generally built-up from field-stones in the form of a conical topped cylinder and kept whitewashed. There are many modern variants in concrete, and the old style piers are steadily disappearing and are often hastened to their end by carelessly driven tractors or lorries. They seem far too massive for the gates they carry, resembling twin bastions defending the entrance to a fortified enclosure (Figs. 5, 33). In some areas, probably under the influence of improving landlords or land agents, field entrances are also dignified by built-up stone piers, and it is possible to explain the fashion as part of the agrarian revolution which resulted in enclosure. In the virtual absence of well-grown oak trees they provided an Irish alternative to the oak gate-post of the English farm, sturdy enough to carry the iron gate which for the same reason took the place of the five-barred oaken gate.

101

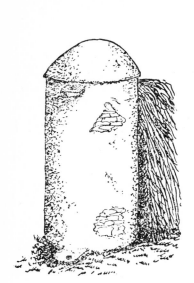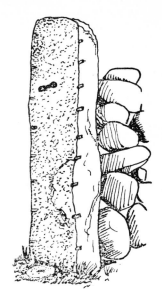

Fig. 33. Gateposts, Co. Down. *Left:* built-up pier with stone hinge and **spud-**stone. *Right:* granite slab with iron hinge and spud-stone.

The shortage of suitable timber also led to the disappearance of the native wattled house and of the introduced timber-framed house, and the fact that such houses were more combustible (and that wooden gates, as one observer remarked, would have been stolen for firewood) was of less importance. The prototype of the stone piers of the farmyard may perhaps be seen in the great entrance pillars of the fortified 'bawns' erected by the seventeenth-century planters. Yet the style is quaintly archaic, and they have often been compared to miniature round towers. Very stout examples do indeed resemble the stone beehive 'clochauns' which we describe later, except that they are solid. In their construction the method of marking out the circumference and maintaining a vertical line by means of a string attached to a central post which is later removed is primitive enough. Moreover the method of hanging the gate is archaic. It is the harr-hanging which is found also in Scotland, the Lake District, Cornwall and Brittany and has survived in these stony refuge corners of Europe. The gate swings like a fire-crane, not on hinges or rings-and-hooks, but directly on its heel, on a projecting iron spud which swivels in a stone socket. These stone sockets or spud-stones are frequently seen arou.d old farm sites, and very similar stones in Mesopotamia go back into the fifth millennium B.C. In the days before the iron gate was introduced wooden gates were hung in the same way, and we know from Scotland that they were sometimes tipped with stone.[1] A projecting stone perforated to hold the top of the gate-post (Fig. 33) has now been replaced, as a rule, by an iron eye.

In Co. Armagh I have heard the farm gate-piers referred to as the man and wife of the house, and one of the pair may have a flat top whereon, it is said, the fairies like to dance. The old people used to place the two first plates of champ—the Hallowe'en festival dish of mashed potatoes—on the top of the pier.[2] While all this may be nothing more than an exuberant play of fancy we cannot overlook the megalithic practice of selecting alternating pointed and flat-topped monoliths for some of their ritual erections, symbolizing, it is thought, male and female. The twin portal stones of many megalithic chamber graves come to mind, and pairs of such stones now standing in isolation, as at Lisdivin in Co. Tyrone,[3] may well have been a symbolic entrance to some vanished ceremonial enclosure. The tradition of large entrance piers dies hard. Not infrequently today the first thought of an improving farmer is to erect imposing concrete pillars at the entrance to his property. They are as a rule garishly painted and pebble-dashed, a poor substitute for their simple whitewashed forerunners.

In the early nineteenth century field gates were almost unknown except near towns, and we read of the rustic forerunner of the iniquitous barbed wire—a hay-rope strung with thorns.[4] In boggy areas one commonly sees the gnarled root stumps of bog trees doing service as a gate, much as the Canadian pioneer will make a temporary fence with grubbed-up stumps. The huge

[1] A. Mitchell, *The Past in the Present* (1880), 127.
[2] Michael Murphy, *At Slieve Gullion's Foot* (1940), 64.
[3] O. Davies, *U.J.A.*, 2 (1939), 169.
[4] G. V. Sampson, *Memoir*, 288.

defensive horns of the long-extinct Irish elk, dug from the bogs,
have been utilized for this purpose! That the gate-piers are more
significant than the gate is evident when one sees a bundle of
thorns or a collection of decaying farm implements doing service as a stop-gap between a pair of magnificent pillars. Where
stones of suitable dimensions are available, in granite or limestone country, for example, single uprights take the place of
the built-up piers (Fig. 33). In the Aran Islands the field-walls,
a single stone in width, have no permanent openings, but
phantom gates—a portion of wall which is knocked down and
rebuilt as required—are defined by upright slabs (Fig. 34).

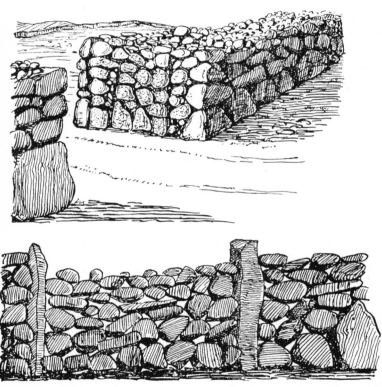

FIG. 34. *Above:* a 9-ft. wide wall in the Mourne Mountains. 'Monumental
relics of secular toil, such walls may record by their successive accretions periods
of agricultural activity through the ages.' *Below:* stone gateway, Aran Islands.

This was formerly the custom also in Connemara and Co. Clare, and it finds an explanation not so much in the scarcity of wood or iron for gates as in the desirability of giving the wind no way into the fields. Such stone walls, seemingly artless constructions of rough boulders, are characteristic of the thin-soiled hillsides throughout Ireland. Most of them are of no great age, for permanent enclosure on this scale is comparatively recent, yet dry-stone walls were built by the men of the megaliths, and there was a lingering tradition of wall-building among the stony hills, which blossomed with intricate garlands of dry-stone walls when enclosure came. What distinguishes these boulder walls is their flimsy lace-like appearance when seen against the sky. Herein lies their strength, for they are full of holes and offer less resistance to the wind than a solid wall. They are most characteristic of hillsides where stony moraines and drift-boulders occur: other types of stone call for different treatment, and taking into account those fences which are partly or entirely made of sods or earth there is an endless variety in the tens of thousands of miles of ditches which mark out this now much-enclosed land.

To speak of a ditch without defining the Irish meaning of the word is to mislead the English reader. It is used in the sense of dyke, a raised bank, and it is not difficult to see why, since the positive and negative earth-ditch usually accompany each other, the word should change meaning. The older meaning of 'ditch' in the north of England was a bank. Similarly in Normandy the word 'fosse' is applied to a raised bank dividing the fields. An Ulster M.P. is said to have caused much amusement at Westminster in a debate on fox-hunting when describing how Irish horses jumped a ditch by changing feet on top! In the north of Ireland as in Scotland the open drain alongside the ditch is known as the sheugh.

We know from archaeological evidence that many existing types of ditch are of prehistoric antiquity. The dry-stone walls of the circular enclosures known as cashels and the earthen ditches of the countless raths of the Dark Ages were, by and large, little more than farmyard fences. Scores of existing farmsteads occupy the old sites and even when, as is more usual, the farms are on sites of fairly recent choice the ditch surrounding the farmyard tends to be a substantial construction. Where the farm is a survivor of a clachan, the small fields near the house, little more than gardens in size, are surrounded by massive winding walls attractive to the eye and always worth examining. Over rough ground they pick their way erratically, incorporating great boulders which could not be moved and which, centuries ago perhaps, became the nuclei of smaller boulders cleared from the fields. Knotted tangles of walls ten or twelve feet thick have resulted, monumental relics of secular toil. Such walls may record by their successive accretions periods of agricultural activity through the ages (Fig. 34). When more stones are removed from the fields they are added as an outer skin, and one can easily recognize the latest additions by the bleached unlichened nakedness of the stones. Archaeological material may be accidentally incorporated in the core of the wall. The wall-builders, too, apparently had a habit of thrusting into the crevices curiosities picked up when working in the fields or bits of abandoned tools, and I have occasionally found prehistoric polished stone axes which their finders had pushed into a wall. The core of the wall is likely to contain similar oddments and bits of pottery, so that the excavation of old walls can be quite profitable to the archaeologist. In Denmark it has been possible to date ancient field-walls to various periods stretching back into prehistory, mainly by means of the stray objects they contain.

In Ireland the clearest evidence for the antiquity of some field boundaries comes from the remains found buried under the bogs. Examples in Co. Londonderry have been described by Dr. Oliver Davies as consisting of irregularly piled stone slabs with standing stones set at intervals.[1] Some of these ancient walls, which country people in Ulster call Danish fences, seem to have enclosed large areas and appear from their contour-alignment to have been head-dykes, enclosing land once arable, but now overgrown with peat, and demarcating it from the rough outfield. I have seen examples both in Ulster and in Munster which are of massive dry-stone work tied to great standing stones set at fairly regular intervals. Often it is only the standing stones, deep-bedded by the builders, that remain to puzzle the archaeologist. A characteristic of these fences is that

[1]O. Davies, *U.J.A.*, 2 (1939), 61–65.

many of the stones are set vertically or diagonally.[1] Others of the same character, or equally massive earthen banks, may be observed to radiate from some of the raths or 'Danish forts' which we now know to have been farmsteads of the Dark Ages and, since they seem to have been single farms held in severalty, the enclosures which they presuppose are likely to be co-eval with the raths. Indeed Professor O'Riordain has claimed that the existing earthen field fences around the group of raths at Cush in Co. Limerick closely follow those of the late Bronze Age which were 'essentially similar' . . . 'the present-day field system is the direct descendant of the ancient one'.[2]

Much smaller and more irregular are the walls one sees associated with areas of megalithic settlement, though this may be because of their great age. Indeed one example recently discovered during the excavation of a megalithic tomb in Co. Down, which was older than the construction of the cairn and partly preserved by it, was built in coursed dry-stone work.[3] We have as yet little information to draw on but it seems likely that these oldest walls were mainly the result of the casual piling-up of stones cleared from little patches of cultivated ground. Some of the great walls associated with clachans and referred to above may well be built on the foundations of such lines of stones pitched around and between bedded boulders which could not be moved. Yet the size of some of the stones built into these ancient walls is astonishing. I have watched a loose-limbed farmer, who seemed to inherit the physical characters as well as the skills of the megalith builders, handle with superb ease great boulders which one would think it beyond human power to move. A stout timber or iron bar and a sturdy slipe (Chapter XIII) are the tools used. Alternatively boulders may be buried *in situ* if there is sufficient depth of soil, but until recently there was a reluctance, for superstitious reasons, to break up large stones. I have not come across the old miners' practice of cracking stones with fire,[4] and except near towns or quarries the splitting of field stones by means of wedges, 'plug

[1]O. Davies, loc. cit., 62

[2]S. P. O'Riordain, *P.R.I.A.*, 45 (1940), 83–181.

[3]A. E. P. Collins and D. M. Waterman, *Millin Bay, a late Neolithic Cairn in Co. Down*, H.M.S.O. (1955), 8.

[4]But A. Young (*Tour*, 2, 115) describes the process near Killarney in 1778.

and feathers', or explosives is a comparatively recent development. These methods took a heavy toll of the megalithic
monuments of granite-quarrying districts such as the Mourne
Mountains in the nineteenth century, though superstitious tales
are still told of the misfortunes which befell the stone-workers.

Another type of stone ditch popular in the limestone plain of
east Galway is curiously similar to the Scots Galloway dyke
and may well have been introduced by improving landlords or
their agents. The lower portion of the ditch is a dry wall of
small stones about two feet high carefully levelled on top, and
on this rests a wall of boulders of lace-work type two or three
feet high. The heavy superstructure not only secures the lower
part with its weight but, perhaps because of its slight overhang
and tottering appearance, is said to deter cattle and sheep from
approaching the wall (Fig. 35). The low walls of loosely piled

Fig. 35. East Galway ditch of Galloway type, and cross-section.

stones on Rathlin Island are said to act as a deterrent on the
principle of the modern electric fence: I was told that animals
give them a wide berth once having learnt that they collapse
almost at a touch. At the other extreme are the ten-foot walls
which run for miles around many demesnes, isolating them
physically from the surrounding country so that only at the
entrances or the now numerous gaps does one get a glimpse of
the decayed grandeur inside. A good many of them are 'famine
walls' built to relieve distress during famine years, in return for
a meagre allowance of food and a wage of perhaps a few pence
per day.

Throughout the lowland farming country the commonest ditch is an earthen bank faced on one side with stones and planted with quicks slipped in near the base among the stones (Fig. 36). This was the 'approved mode' of enclosing the land

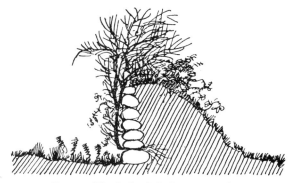

FIG. 36. The hedged ditch, cross-section.

advocated by the reformers from the late eighteenth century onwards, but it was noted that 'the planting of hedgerows was repugnant to the practice of the country' and in many districts the hedges were neglected and the livestock still had to be tethered in the fields.[1] The tradition of temporary fences died hard. 'A year's ditch passeth for a very strong fence', wrote Sir John Davies to the Earl of Salisbury in 1606. These sod fences were deliberately thrown down after harvest, and the decayed sods enriched the soil. The *Advertisements for Ireland* published in 1623 state: 'Their fields lie open and unclosed. Where wood is plentiful they hedge in all their corn with stakes and bushes and pull them down in the winter and burn them.'[2] When fixed field-divisions were adopted, the hedgeless earthen bank was preferred in many parts of the country, usually growing a luxuriant crop of brambles and gorse (whins). These were a useful source of firewood and provided both shelter and food for the livestock, the 'pounded whins' being fed to horses. The knocking stones, flat slabs or stone basins where the whins

[1]*Report on the Estates of the Drapers' Company in Ireland*, 1829.
[2]*Advertisements for Ireland* (1623), Ed. G. O'Brien (1923), 33.

were 'melled' with a wooden maul, are sometimes to be seen
in the farmyard, and there were a few water-driven 'whin-mills'.
Their use is almost forgotten as is the custom of growing a
field of whins to provide fodder. This was done in Co. Cavan
and it is a recognized method of land utilization in the poorer
parts of Brittany. A gorse hedge near the homestead is still
popular as a place for drying clothes on washing day. 'Firing
being scarce', wrote Gabriel Beranger of the barony of Bargy
and Forth, 'they plant all their ditches with furze, which serves
them for firing, and is reckoned equal in value with the produce
of the land.'[1] Small farmers in Co. Down preferred wide earthen
ditches because, as Binns was told: 'we have both sides of the
ditch for feeding the cattle, and whins to bruise for the horses'.[2]
The economy of the grass-grown ditch becomes clearer when we
realize that on boulder-strewn hillsides where wide stone
ditches separate the tiny fields a high proportion of the land is
sterilized. Such wide earth banks often serve as footpaths where
the land is wet, and in Co. Limerick I have seen cart tracks on
top of them. This habit may go back to the wide balks between
some of the openfield patches, which were used as access ways
where the boggy fields were too soft to take a cart. Such double
ditches, when faced with stones on both sides, are undoubtedly
an old type of fence, for they are characteristic of many raths or
Dark Age farmsteads. These 'dry fences' are common in Co.
Kerry and also in north Antrim, and they occur in Brittany, and
in parts of Anglesey and north Pembrokeshire. In stony country
the filling of a double ditch may be of loose stones gathered from
the fields, and here again we have ancient examples in the enclosing walls of small cashels which are the equivalent in thin-
soiled areas of the raths of the lowlands.

What nearly all these many types of field fences have in common is their untidy appearance. Dry stone walls tend to be
cyclopean, lacking the precision of those of north England or
the Cotswold country. Rough glacial boulders are a poor substitute for oolite, and one recalls the comment of Sir John
Russell that Irish architecture suffered because of the virtual
absence of Jurassic rocks in the geological series. Rarely does

[1]Lady Wilde, 'Memoir of Gabriel Beranger', *J.R.S.A.I.* (1876), 132.
[2]J. Binns, *Miseries and Beauties*, 1, 60.

one see a well-kept or neatly trimmed field-hedge and never a staked and pleached hedgerow to compare with those of the English lowlands. The whole art of hedging is poorly developed, and the craft of laying a hedge almost unknown. The thorns are allowed to grow freely—as though they were the true fairy thorns which must never be damaged—and cut back ruthlessly at long intervals, when the many gaps are stuffed with dead thorns. The truth is that it is the bank rather than the hedge which makes the fence, and the thorns do little more than provide some shelter for livestock. But while the earthen banks grow tall hedges they will not support good hedgerow timber. The few starved ashes, sycamores or stunted beeches compare very unfavourably with the great oaks and elms of the English Midlands. Arthur Young brought his English common sense and prejudices to bear on the subject: 'To permit a hedge to grow too long without cutting not only ruins it for a fence but spoils the trees that are planted with it . . . I never saw a single capital tree growing on these banks.' And consequently, 'the greatest part of the kingdom presents a naked bleak dreary view for want of wood.'[1] Elsewhere he writes, of Mitchelstown in Co. Cork, 'An oak, an ash, or an elm is almost as great a rarity as an olive, an orange or a mulberry.'[2]

The planting of hedges and hedgerow timber had been advocated by improvers since the sixteenth century. The Ordinances for the Government of Ireland (1534) lay down that 'every husbandman having a plough within the English Pale shall set by the year twelve ashes in the ditches and closes of his farm'. The ditch-bank was evidently already a feature of the farms in the Pale, and it is interesting that there, as generally through the east and north of the country, the ash—providing the most useful timber for general farm use—is the favourite hedgerow tree. But it is in the closes (the farmyards) that one sees most trees today, chief among them the sycamore whose dense foliage gives protection from the winds and from the prying eyes of neighbours. Next to the sycamore in popularity, and similarly providing a thick cover, come the beech and the conifers, and it is noteworthy that none of these species is

[1]Arthur Young, *Tour*, 2, part 2, 66.
[2]ibid, 2, 272.

111

native to the country. Around the coasts the sycamore is almost the only tree that persists, for it will stand up to the salt-laden gales everywhere save on the most exposed parts of the west coast. R. U. Sayce has recorded the belief, from Montgomery-shire, that 'sycamore trees keep the fairies away and stop them spoiling the milk',[1] but this bit of lore cannot be of any great antiquity since the tree did not reach Britain from its home in the mountain belt of southern Europe until the sixteenth century. It presumably arose from the association of the tree with the farmyard. In Ireland the sycamore probably came in with the early seventeenth century planters, though the beech may be a medieval or even older introduction. Both trees had many economic uses, especially for dry-coopering, that is the manufacture of provision casks and butter firkins, and the sycamore is an excellent wood for turnery. Later, as the linen industry became mechanized, the beetling mills demanded sycamore for the great beam of the engine and beech for the vertical beetles.

The lay-out of farm buildings seems to have been, in the native single-farms, as haphazard and formless as was that of the houses themselves in an old clachan. As separate farms with outbuildings ('offices') became fashionable improvements after the middle of the eighteenth century, the latter were built for convenience of access and they were put close to the farmhouse, either attached to one end or lying parallel to provide a wind-break. Only in the planted areas does one find old examples of planned 'courtyard farms' where the house and offices enclose a square or rectangular yard. I fancy the stone or wooden 'hovel-stands' with their picturesque mushroom-like staddle-stones are also confined to planted districts. In the west a favourite method of making stacks is to build them about a central pole. (See p. 164.)

The wayside stile is another absentee in the native Irish countryside, as is the footpath which is its companion. Short-cuts are rarely worth while in a land of tiny fields, and if there is a right of way there is sure to be a tolerable road. In fact there are so many farm lanes and access ways to mountain, seashore or bog that an economist might regard the amount of land so taken out of cultivation as excessive. It has been

[1] R. U. Sayce, *Montgomeryshire Collections*, 45 (1938).

calculated that in some thickly settled and much-enclosed town-lands the land wasted in ditches may amount to a quarter of the whole area.[1] The peasant proprietor, however, would regard the loss of land as the price he pays for his independence, remembering 'the fights, trespasses, confusion, disputes and assaults' which were 'the natural and unavoidable consequences' of the openfield rundale system.[2]

[1] *Devon Commission*, 1, 422.
[2] Lord George Hill, *Gweedore*, 22.

IX

KILNS AND CLOCHAUNS

WHILE the timber building has almost entirely disappeared from the Irish scene, there survives an archaic
tradition of building in dry stone which is best illustrated in the
humble structures erected for special purposes in or adjacent
to the farmyard. Since stonework has a much better chance of
survival than timber it is possible, even without excavation, to
trace the descent of some of these small buildings through the
ages. They include corbelled animal houses (clochauns), corn-
drying kilns, sweat-houses and turf-shelters. We shall consider
also small outhouses of sods or wattles, including soot-houses
and animal shelters. Some of these, reduced in scale and status,
are the successors of buildings once erected for higher purposes.

The clochauns of south-western Ireland, corbelled stone structures, nowadays used mainly for keeping pigs or poultry, are indis-
tinguishable from the monastic huts such as are found on the
precipitous island of Skellig Michael off the coast of Co. Kerry.
Similar stone huts accompany monastic settlements in other
parts of Ireland—and also in the Hebrides and in islands off the
coast of Brittany—and they have been preserved, thanks to their
sanctity or their isolation, as examples of a mode of building
which was common when Christianity reached the west. Some
clochauns in the Dingle peninsula, Co. Kerry, have been erected
within living memory, but we also know that this type of
construction is far older than Christianity in Ireland, that it
was already two millennia old when Christian converts adopted
it for their dwellings and their oratories. It is probable that
some of the megalith-builders lived in clochauns and that their
magnificent corbelled tombs have alone survived because they

were buried under great cairns such as those at New Grange on the River Boyne. Clusters of ruined clochauns surrounded by old field walls litter the hillslopes of the Dingle peninsula near Fahan; but we can only guess at the age of these 'beehive farms'. Some of the large oval clochauns would give standing room to as many as sixty people. Many of the existing farms in the district have at least one round clochaun, used for keeping pigs or poultry or for storing milk or turf (Fig. 37).

In the Aran Islands both oval and circular stone-roofed buildings are to be seen, though most of them are ruined. O'Flaherty in the seventeenth century described them as being 'so ancient that nobody knows how long ago any of them was made'.[1] The oval houses measure up to 21 ft. by 12 ft. internally; they are rectangular inside and some have two opposite doors (Pl. 3). Smaller round huts are also known.[2] In north-eastern Ireland, too, in north Louth and south-east Down, both round and square clochauns have been constructed down to recent times for housing pigs and poultry: a few are still in use.[3] The corbelled pigsty is known also in Wales,[4] and has been recorded in Caithness and the Orkney Islands.[5] Very similar corbelled buildings attached to old farms on Dartmoor are said to have been used as ash houses, for holding the embers taken from the fire at night.[6] One example, now used as a chicken house, is described as a winnowing hut.

Other parts of western and southern Europe can show both ancient and recent examples of corbelled constructions, though most of them, in so far as such a timeless style can be dated, were probably erected within the last two or three centuries, and some of them are known to have been built within living memory. They are found, either in ruins or serving as shelters or as animal- and tool-houses, in south France, especially in and around the Central Plateau, in Spain, Portugal and Majorca, in the heel of Italy, in the western Balkans and in Crete, where the mountain dairies appear to be very similar to the stone

---

[1] R. O'Flaherty, *H'Iar Connaught* (1684), 68.
[2] Å. Campbell, *Folk-Liv*, 1938, 173–96; G. H. Kinahan, *P.R.I.A.*, 10, 25.
[3] R. H. Buchanan, *U.J.A.*, 19 (1956), 92–112.
[4] I. C. Peate, *The Welsh House* (1944), 42.
[5] A. Mitchell, *The Past in the Present*, 71.
[6] *Trans. Plymouth Institute*, XVIII (1944), 34.

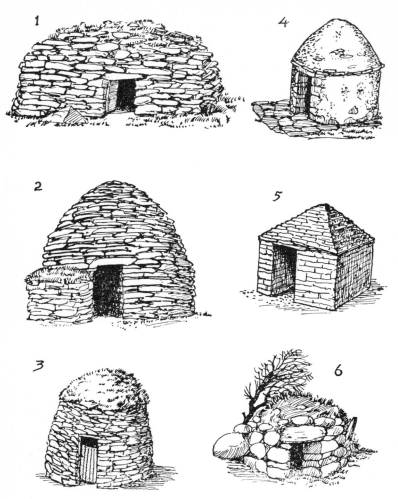

Fig. 37. Clochauns. (1) Oval house, Aran Island. (2) Hut, Skellig Michael. (3) Poultry house, Dingle. (4, 5) Pigsties, Co. Down. (6) Sweat-house, Co. Leitrim.

booley huts and shielings of Ireland and the Hebrides. The corbelled buildings of Vaucluse, in the mountains behind Avignon, are both round and rectangular, the latter bearing a striking resemblance to Irish oratories of the type of Gallarus,

116

Co. Kerry, which is believed to date from the sixth or seventh century. Whether or not the origin of this style of building in western Europe should be placed, as I am inclined to believe, in the megalithic period, there can be no doubt that it represents, in various parts of the Mediterranean-Atlantic route, the survival of an ancient method of building. It has had a long life in exposed hilly districts where suitable materials lay to hand, especially where the interests of simple shepherds and cattlemen were dominant. Villages of houses with domed or conical stone or mud-brick roofs are a feature of south-east Italy and Syria, and of the dry belt stretching eastwards to India.

Some of the Co. Kerry farmyard clochauns are still used for storing milk; their thick walls are admirable for maintaining even temperatures. Their association with the pig may also be an archaic feature, for the pig was perhaps the first domesticated animal to be brought to Ireland, and although much altered in breed, it still thrives best in warm, draught-proof surroundings recalling the sultry jungles of its original south-east Asiatic home. The well-worn phrase about 'the gentleman that pays the rent' not only summarizes the role of the pig in recent historic times but carries a humorous hint of the veneration in which the pig was once held in southern and western Europe. Here archaeologists have postulated an early Neolithic matriarchal 'swine-culture', vestiges of which would explain the fact that the pig was the only cult animal of the oldest of the Greek mysteries, the Eleusinian.[1] Later pork became the favourite food of both the Roman and Celtic worlds. In parts of Ireland the pig is driven into the house for luck on May morning, and the pigsty figures in a strange ritual for certain cures, e.g., a sufferer from mumps should be led with an ass-halter three times round the sty! Further, there is surely a supernatural quality in an animal which is reputed to be able to see the wind! In many parts of the British Isles, especially in Scotland, it is unlucky to speak of a pig when fishing at sea. Superstitions about the pig are numerous in Scotland, and in the Highlands there was formerly a tabu against keeping pigs and eating pork. This was apparently true also of those parts of the north of Ireland which have had close connections with the Western Isles.

[1] C. O. Sauer, *Agricultural Origins and Dispersals*, 37.

In discussing the association of pigs and clochauns, which may well have reached Ireland together, reference must be made to a curious variety of underground 'outhouse', the stone-built souterrain, which is frequently found attached to ancient farmsteads of the Dark Ages. Many thousands have been recorded from all parts of the country, and they have their counterparts in Scotland, Cornwall and western France. Stripped of their cover of earth, the chambers which are incorporated in many souterrains would resemble free-standing clochauns. The long galleries which are perhaps the most characteristic element in souterrains could have originated as passages into the buried chambers. Some of the chambers may have served as pigsties, but it is a more plausible theory that these structures, long regarded as refuge places, were primarily storage places, designed to maintain an even temperature for keeping food and especially milk products. The custom of building souterrains, which must have called for considerable labour and skill, seems to have stopped, after a long life, before the early Middle Ages. We do not know what cultural factors were responsible for this change of custom, or what forms of storage took the place of the 'coves', but the change marks one aspect of the decline of the old Gaelic world of rath and tuath which had passed its zenith by the tenth century. The practice of building underground storage places, however, did not entirely die out. K. Danaher has recorded stone-lined structures in Donegal, associated with still remembered booley-sites, which are said to have been used for storing butter.[1] One wonders whether the custom of burying butter in the bogs (Chapter XIV) was generally adopted when souterrains were no longer built.

The souterrains, whatever their original purpose, have occasionally been pressed into service as hiding places for outlaws, for illegal possessions or small livestock. It is known that the Irish, in the worst days of landlordism, were in the habit of hiding their stock to avoid confiscation when they were in arrears of rent. Some examples, which had not been opened within living memory, were found, when entered, to reek strongly of animals. And I know one souterrain in Co. Antrim which is littered with the remains of home-made bombs dating

[1] K. Danaher, *J.R.S.A.I.*, 75 (1945), 204–12.

from 'the troubles' of the early nineteen-twenties. Souterrains have also been used for other illegal activities which were enjoyed irrespective of political party, such as the making of illicit whiskey—poteen—an activity which is not yet entirely suppressed and which called for secrecy. I have more than once been shown specially-made underground hiding-holes where the poteen-makers went to earth when the gaugers were scented.

In the category of temporary shelters we place the wretched 'fever-huts' erected to isolate victims of infectious diseases in the famine years. We cannot wonder that no detailed descriptions are to be found, but the account of a structure of 'turf built up in the form of a cone, with an entrance scarcely large enough for a dog to crawl through'[1] hints that some of these huts presented features of interest to the ethnographer. Temporary windbreaks erected by turf-cutters are also of considerable interest. One which I saw in Co. Fermanagh (Fig. 38)

FIG. 38. Bog shelters, Co. Fermanagh. Left, for turf-cutters; right, partly dug out of the bog, for calves.

was built of birch rods bent over and neatly thatched with branches and rushes. The construction of animal shelters in great variety, too, built of sods or wattles, doubtless perpetuates skills once devoted to human habitations. I illustrate in Fig. 39 an outhouse with a solid hipped roof, known as a flat roof.

Unusual, because so far as I know confined to Achill Island, are little soot-houses erected for the special purpose of manufacturing supplies of soot and ashes as fertilizers. It is probable that we have to deal with a custom which has died out elsewhere and has maintained itself here in insular isolation. It will

[1]*The Saxon in Ireland* (1851), 143.

be recalled that Achill was the last Irish home of booleying, and there may be some connection between the two practices, the soot-houses being the diminutive descendants of the winter dwellings whose roofs, on this theory, were stripped in spring in the days when the whole family migrated to the summer pastures. At any rate the soot-house season runs from October to May, that is the winter half-year. In the Hebrides it was customary to strip the soot-laden thatch of the black-houses annually for use as manure, and the roof was left without a smoke-hole to encourage the deposit of soot. The smoke 'oozes out over the whole roof, giving the house, when seen from a distance, the general appearance of a dung-heap in warm wet weather. The object of the roof is . . . to accumulate soot.'[1]

Fig. 39. Soot house, Achill Island; animal shelter with walls of whins and 'flat roof', Co. Cavan.

The soot-huts are rectangular gabled structures, measuring some ten by five feet externally and about eight feet high. They are built either out in the fields, where peat and sods are at hand, or near the farms, in which case they often serve in summer as hen-houses. The low side-walls are of dry-stone construction though when built in the fields they are more usually of sods: the entrance, in the gable, is only some two-and-a-half to three feet high. The roof structure is of the simplest, consisting of a ridge pole against which bits of driftwood serving as rafters rest without ties of any kind, the whole being kept in place by a great thickness of sods laid horizontally, the lowest layer resting on the thick wall-tops. At the end of harvest the huts

[1]A. Mitchell, *The Past in the Present* (1880), 53.

are repaired and re-roofed with sods, and turf fires lit inside are kept smouldering with wet sods until the spring, when the huts are half-full of ashes and the soot-laden roof-sods are ready to collapse. The roof is then broken up and the soot and ashes spread on the ridges as potato manure (Fig. 39).

Although I know of no parallel in other parts of Ireland it seems likely that the custom of removing the roof-covering of the winter-house was once fairly general, at any rate in houses of the old Achill type, which in many details closely resembled the Hebridean black-house. I should be inclined to correlate the custom with the roped style of thatching, which betrays little of the care of other styles and in the old form where the ropes were weighted by hanging stones had a distinctly ephemeral appearance. Where sods were used for walls as well as roofs the whole house would have become a convenient source of fertilizers for the infield. This may be the explanation of the remark made by Dr. Madden that in the south of Ireland 'cottar houses of dirt, sticks and straw were generally removed once a year'.[1] There are indications met with in excavations of houses in Dark Age raths that reconstructions were more frequent than would be justified by ordinary wear and tear. In Sutherland, down to the early nineteenth century, sod-houses were abandoned periodically and pulled down to be utilized as manure, a new hut being erected near by. In this instance the cause was said to be that the accumulation of filth had rendered the place uninhabitable,[2] but this underestimates the tolerance of the Gael. The soot-houses, at any rate, seem to perpetuate old custom, and one thinks back to the earliest days of agriculture when crops were sown in the highly productive soils of newly burnt woodland. Faith in the use of fire persisted longer than the woods. Burning the land, we shall see in Chapter XI, was a very general practice down to the famine years when rough pasture was being reclaimed for potato-growing.

We come now to a group of stone structures built to serve as kilns for drying or burning. The drying-kilns were principally needed for drying corn before it was ground, though flax-drying kilns were also required in the days when the fibre was extracted

[1]Dr. Madden, *Reflections and Resolutions* (1738).
[2]Quoted in F. T. Smith, *The Land of Britain*, Part 3, Sutherland.

by hand. The corn-drying kiln is a culture-trait clearly adapted to the climatic conditions of the Atlantic coasts of Europe. In extreme cases, as in the Faroe Islands—where even barley does not ripen fully—the ears are kiln-dried before thrashing, but the purpose of the Irish kilns was to harden the thrashed grain before grinding. They can be traced back archaeologically to the last centuries B.C. and on present evidence their introduction may be linked chronologically with grain-storage pits and with the rotary quern. Thus the custom of parching the grain in the straw would be a survival of an older culture layer associated with the saddle-quern and the mortar and possibly with harvesting by pulling the corn by the roots.

One early type of kiln was made of wattles plastered with clay, and was perhaps used like an oven, being heated before the corn was put in it to dry, but those which have come down into recent times were stone-lined pits into which a long flue was led. The fuel used was peat. It is stated that down to famine times every townland in some parts of the country had its kiln, though in other parts they went out of use long ago when landlords, following Anglo-Norman custom, insisted that all corn should be ground at the mill. In Co. Cavan for example, 'every estate has its cornmill and the tenantry is bound under severe penalty to grind their corn thereat and pay toll'.[1] These watermills should be distinguished from the native clackmills, built over little streams and driven by small horizontal wheels. They were characteristically held in joint ownership, as were the kilns. The Mayo kiln is described as resembling a large tobacco pipe, the circular stone-lined bowl being dug into a sloping bank and the horizontal stem or flue emerging lower down the slope. A bee-hive cap of timber and thatch was the only part visible. In it a straw-covered wattled hatch gave access to the kiln floor, a wooden frame half-way down the bowl of the pipe, on which thrashed sheaves were spread, heads to centre. The grain, laid on this, took about twenty-four hours to dry. The taste of the oatmeal made from grain so dried was said to be delicious.[2] A man who had seen a similar kiln working in Co. Antrim told me that the corn was laid on a linen sheet

[1] C. Coote, *Cavan* (1802), 251.
[2] H. T. Knox, *P.R.I.A.*, 26 (1906-7), 265.

resting on a well-prepared bed of drawn straw spread on a hurdle, and he recalled the phrase 'soft as kiln bedding' to illustrate the care devoted to the operation. The Gaelic language has quite an extensive vocabulary describing every detail of the floor and the bedding of a corn-kiln. Because of the risk of fire, the Laws stipulated that the kiln must not be placed within so many paces of the dwelling house.

Lint-kilns, for drying flax after it had been taken from the retting dams, were in general use in Ulster in the days of hand-scutching, and a few half-ruined specimens are still in existence. As with corn-kilns—and lime-kilns—they were of two kinds, which may be termed pot-kilns and pipe-kilns. The former are described in Co. Armagh as 'small sod buildings, left open at the top . . . built by the sides of fences near the cabins: they are four or five feet in diameter, and have a hurdle of sticks placed across them at a convenient height (about four feet) on which a small quantity of flax is spread to dry over a turf fire'.[1] The stone-built kilns, known in Co. Tyrone as 'farrows' were similar in construction to the 'tobacco pipe' corn-kilns. The flax, well shaken and loose, was placed on end on a wattled platform set across the bowl of the pipe. When dried it was beaten on a melling-stone with a heavy wooden mell until every stalk was flattened and it then passed to the hand-scutcher.

As the corn-drying kiln has been superseded by the kiln attached to the country grist-mill, so the small lime-kiln has given way, over most of the country, to the large quarry-kiln. At the same time coal has replaced turf as a fuel. The little circular pot-kiln of sods or stones filled with alternate layers of turf and limestone may be met with in the west, but in general the home-burning of lime did not long survive the Great Famine. Down to that time, wherever limestone could be obtained, almost every farm or farm cluster had a lime-kiln. It was the importation of guano and later of artificial manure that put an end to a most advantageous practice. The application of lime to acid soils is a comparatively recent practice, but one likes to think that the little pot-kiln was in use long ago to burn lime or sea-shells for the whitewash with which the mud houses were lightened and brightened. Kelp-kilns, similarly (see Chapter

[1] I. Binns, *Miseries and Beauties* (1837), I, 178.

XVI), had their great days in the eighteenth and nineteenth centuries, but small-scale wrack-burning is far older than this. In the later eighteenth century, when framed windows and brick chimneys became fashionable in the more prosperous lowland farms, the bricks were locally burnt in circular kilns plastered with clay.

Another class of outbuilding, allied to the clochaun in construction, is the stone sweat-house, the Irish version of the Turkish bath, which the Germans, indeed, call the Irish bath. There is a theory that the idea reached Ireland with Christian missionaries who were accustomed to Roman practices, but heat-treatment as a cure is so widespread throughout the world (cf. the sweat-houses of Finland and pre-Columbian California) that one thinks of remoter origins. What is certain is that they were visited for cures within living memory in several parts of Ireland. In west Cavan twenty-five sweat-houses have been listed in one district, and many more are known to have been destroyed. A French traveller of the late eighteenth century observed that 'wherever there are four or five cabins near each other there is sure to be a sweating-house'.[1] And old people in Cavan confirm that every four or five families once shared a sweat-house, in which sweating cures were taken in summer and autumn (Fig. 37, 6).

The sweat-house is a dry-stone corbelled structure, measuring internally from four to seven feet in diameter and rather less in height. A low lintelled doorway is the only means of access though some specimens have a roughly constructed chimney flue to allow the smoke to escape. This was closed with sods during the treatment, as was the door. The fire of turf—straw and bracken seem also to have been used—had been kept burning inside for a day or two previously. The floor, normally an earthen floor though some examples were cobbled or paved, was then swept clean and strewn with green rushes. On these, or on grass sods or low stools which they took in with them, from two to as many as six or seven persons would sit, naked and sweating profusely. After half an hour or so they would emerge and cool themselves either in a near-by stream or with a bucket

[1]De Latocnaye, *A Frenchman's Walk through Ireland* (1796–97). Ed. J. Stevenson (1917), 193.

of water. I was told on Rathlin Island that eligible girls would take a sweating bath to clear their complexions before the annual visit to the Lammas Fair at Ballycastle on the mainland. They were in demand also during kelp-burning operations—a notoriously filthy occupation. Not all sweat-houses were built of stone. Wood-Martin quotes accounts of some which were dug into an earth bank and 'finished with sods', while others were excavated in turf banks.[1] He also records that water was sometimes poured on stones inside the sweat-house, 'thus converting it into a vapour- as well as a sweat-bath'.[2]

More intimately linked with the house is the turf-shelter, the Irish equivalent of the English coal-shed. In the drier eastern part of the country a built shelter is not necessary, and the peats, skilfully built into a huge turf-stack protected from the driving rains by a wall or gable, perhaps improve by exposure to the winds, but in the wetter west unless the turf is under cover it must be dried in small quantities in the loft or by the fire before burning. In parts of Kerry the turf is stored in large clochauns : elsewhere narrow oblong or oval stone enclosures are erected, their walls loosely built to allow the wind to blow through. The peat-store or cleit of St. Kilda was similar—an oblong corbelled stone building with open joints.

The well is another essential item of equipment of farm or clachan, and it is often provided with a corbelled stone cover. Since springs are abundant, except in bare limestone country, the wells are not deep and few are fitted with windlasses. In their absence quite elaborate ramps with stone steps are sometimes needed to obtain access to the water, and the whole structure being roofed, some examples (for instance in the south-east of Co. Down) are considerable architectural feats (Fig. 40). In the limestone districts the woman of the house may have to walk as much as half a mile to carry drinking water from a dip-well. It is now carried in buckets but was formerly transported in stave-built piggins balanced on the head. The peasant makes a virtue of necessity by asserting that almost every spring well yields 'the finest water in all Ireland, and never runs dry'. Wells are regarded as chancy things, not to be

[1]Wood-Martin, *Elder Faiths*, II (1902), 166.
[2]ibid., 165.

lightly meddled with, and if the water is not as good as usual you will be told, in the phrase used for an ailing human being, that the well is 'not *at* itself at all'.

FIG. 40. Well-covers, Co. Cavan and Co. Down.

Finally we come to a miscellaneous assortment of outbuildings and shelters built to house various animals and birds. Elaborate pigeon houses (ducats) designed to house hundreds of birds seem to be confined to the east and south coasts and to areas planted by English or Scots. They are no doubt manorial in origin but some existing examples were built in the early nineteenth century, though they are no longer in use. In these areas the smaller farms may have little pigeon houses made for a dozen birds, and the humblest stable is likely to have a pigeon hole or two in the gable. The birds formerly nested in hanging nests of plaited straw.

Cavities in the thick walls about many old farms were built as dog-kennels or duck-houses, and simple shelter holes ('boles' in Ulster) were intended to house assorted three-legged iron pots (Fig. 32). An interesting variant is the bee-bole, a shelter for the bee-skep, a few examples of which have been observed in eastern Ireland.[1]

[1] R. M. Duruz and E. E. Crane, *English Bee Boles* (1953). (National Beekeeping Museum Pamphlet No. 1.)

X

PLOUGH AND SPADE

STRONG arms have been the Irish labourer's passport to labouring jobs overseas, and it may be recalled that the word 'navvy' derives from the canal-diggers or navigators, many of them Irish, who opened the waterways of industrial England. Later it was Irish labourers who built the first railroad tracks of North America. Those arms were toughened by spade-work in field and bog, for the Irish spade is much more than a gardening tool: it was, and still is in backward areas and in the boglands, an implement for field cultivation and for cutting turf. The small field pattern of all except the most fertile regions is in part a reflection of this historic fact. An acre or two and often less in area, the tiny hillside fields are a measure of spade work just as the wide prairie wheatlands mirror the multiple plough or the mounded garden plots of an African village are the mark of women's work with mattock and digging-stick. Even in the deep-soiled lowlands where the plough is now universal the observant eye, still more the viewer from the air, will pick out the narrow ridges made by the spade faintly showing, as in a palimpsest, through the more regular pattern of wide plough ridges. In hilly country, especially in the west, the spade is still in common use in the fields, and the traveller moving about Ireland in spring, when the potatoes are being planted, will notice an astonishing variety of spades in use. Even in districts where the plough is universal the spade may still be pressed into service to deal with stony patches or awkward corners, and I have seen it supplementing the plough in another way by being tied on to a lea plough to convert it into a double-sided drill plough.

127

The Irish spade is not a digging implement: it is essentially a ridge-maker or hand-plough, adapted to the business of undercutting and turning the sod. Its narrow bent blade is ill fitted to the lifting of soil, and for this purpose the long-handled shovel is used, an efficient implement for lifting loose earth and placing it with precision where required, for example to fill holes on the ridges. The Irish spade is more specialized and more primitive than the 'common or garden' English spade (Fig. 41).

The evidence of the Irish Law Texts and the discovery of plough coulters on sites of pre-Norman date show that heavy

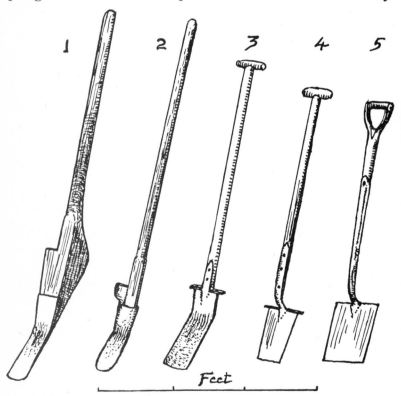

FIG. 41. Spades. The five examples form an approximate evolutionary series. (1) Loy, Co. Leitrim. (2) One-eared spade, Kerry. (3) Two-eared bent ridging spade, Fermanagh. (4) Treaded garden spade, Wexford. (5) English spade.

ploughs were known in parts of Celtic Ireland, but the light plough or *ard* almost certainly prevailed, and it is unlikely that ploughs of any kind were employed outside the 'few favoured acres' of the infield. A light plough, at any rate, would be unfit to break the tough sod of the outfield, which was allowed to rest for long periods. Even today the answer I have been given when I have asked ridgemakers in old outfield why they were using spades has been: "Tis too tough for the plough!' Ploughing 'by the tail', similarly, becomes intelligible only if one envisages it as restricted to infield cultivation. The iron plough with curved mould board did not reach the outlying corners of the country until late in the nineteenth century, and down to the time of the famine iron ploughs were used only in progressive areas where there were improving landlords. The prototype of these ploughs was the Scottish two-horse swing plough invented by James Small about the year 1765. By the end of the century it had reached Ireland (and also Norway) and it was a powerful instrument in breaking down the archaic system of openfield husbandry. The Irish were amazed when they first saw a ploughman with a Scots plough both driving the horses and holding the stilts.[1]

Under the traditional system ploughing was 'merely marking the land with furrows'[2]: a spade or mattock was commonly needed to turn back the earth, and to force the share into the ground it was often necessary to have a man walking alongside the plough, pressing down on the beam with a stout stick. No bits or reins were used, and the plough itself required two men or a man and a boy, 'one to hold and one to drive', that is one holding the plough stilts and the other leading the horses by walking backwards before them. Evidently the man at the handles needed to give all his attention to the plough. It was, as a Cavan man described it to me, a process of 'jerking up and down'. Many of these practices were probably taken over from the days of ox-teams. Ploughing with oxen is believed to have died out in late medieval times, though it was reintroduced by some landowners in the late eighteenth century. The small farmer did not use oxen for the plough because unlike horses

[1] R. Thompson, *Meath* (1802), 111.
[2] I. Weld, *Roscommon* (1832), 656.

they could not be put to other purposes such as going to the fair.

The wooden plough has now been almost entirely replaced by the iron plough, but in many districts a wooden plough, often converted from a lea plough, is preferred for opening drills (Fig. 42). The potato growers of the kingdom of Mourne in Co. Down, for example, find that it suits their stony soils and is less likely to be damaged by boulders. The rough wooden mould-boards carry the earth with them and distribute it more evenly than the iron drill-plough, which tends, moreover, to 'put a skin' on the soil and to pile up pointed ridges which would require to have their tops flattened later.

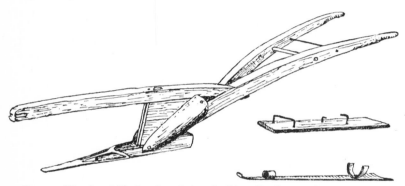

FIG. 42. Wooden drill plough and plough slides, Co. Down: the lower slide is of iron.

The improved wooden plough did not reach remote hill regions until roads were built after the middle of the eighteenth century. Even in the nineteenth century it is described as a newcomer in Co. Donegal, where spade labour had previously been supplemented only by 'a crooked stick armed with a bit of iron, with a second stick grafted to it to give two handles'.[1] This archaic implement must have resembled the wooden 'ard' (araire) of Mediterranean lands. It was so light that when the improved wooden plough with mould-board was introduced into Donegal the ponies were not equal to the task of pulling it. In west Cork the new wooden ploughs were not to be

[1]John Hamilton, *Sixty Years Experience as an Irish Landlord*, 47.

seen on the small farms until after the Great Famine: 'the things called ploughs would only scratch the surface, a log of wood sharpened and shod with iron'.[1] This 'poorer sort of plough' was made of alder in Co. Londonderry.[2] Observers attributed the Irish addiction to cross-ploughing to the fact that the ribs of unploughed land could only be broken by this means. Small squarish cultivation plots and fields are a natural consequence of cross-ploughing.

It seems that even these light ploughs, quite incapable of penetrating lea ground, were pulled by three or four horses abreast, 'so weak and small are the horses'.[3] Thus 'coaring' (coaration) was necessary, though one suspects that tradition rather than need lay behind the large teams. In the seventeenth century four horses abreast pulled the plough by the tails in Co. Clare, 'which was the custom all over Ireland. The tackle and traces being made of gadds or withies of twigs twisted, would be broken to pieces otherwise . . . But the horses being sensible stop until the ploughman lifts the plough over the rock.'[4] At the same time we find complaints from the midland counties that the native plough was 'heavy and unmanageable, distressing to men and horses.[5] Here we probably have to deal with the descendant of the heavy Anglo-Norman plough.

Unfortunately we have no details of the Irish *ard*. One would like to know, for instance, whether it turned the furrow or rather threw the earth—for it merely scratched the soil—to the left or to the right. It has been found that in certain parts of western Europe left-sided ploughs are traditional whereas, of course, the common plough is almost universally right-sided. Mr. Robert Aitken has traced the left-sided plough in a clearly defined area of south France and north-east Spain.[6] The explanation may be that in these areas cultivation was originally done with a foot plough, for which the right foot was used, so that the soil, as with the Scottish caschrom, was turned to the left, and that the plough when adopted became a traction-

[1]W. Bence Jones, *A Life's Work in Ireland* (1880), 20.
[2]G. V. Sampson, *Memoir* (1814), 290.
[3]W. Shaw Mason, 2 (1816), s.v. Sligo.
[4]*Dineley's Tour in Ireland* (1661), Ed. J. Graves, (1870), 162.
[5]W. Shaw Mason, 2 (1816), s.v. King's Co. and Queen's Co.
[6]R. Aitken, *Man*, 1953, 286.

version of the foot-plough. This is an almost unexplored field of rural history. Mr. Aitken is of the opinion, however, that the left-sided plough goes with the use of the right hand as holding hand.

At any rate it is interesting to find that in Ireland the majority of diggers use the right foot, and although in theory the wooden foot-rest of the native one-eared spade can be fitted either to left or right of the narrow blade it is, in the west, almost invariably on the right side. Presumably only habitually left-handed people use the left foot. In eastern Ireland, on the other hand, and particularly in the Protestant districts of the north-east, the left foot is normally the digging-foot, though judging from the proportions of right to left (about one to three in the north-east), the old Irish stocks continue to dig with the right foot. Hence there is a basis of fact in the phrase 'digging with the wrong foot'. (To say that someone digs with the other foot is in Ireland an oblique way of referring to his religious faith.) The old Irish spade, we have seen, is a highly specialized tool. It may have been preceded by some kind of hoe or planting stick such as are represented today by the graffan or the steeveen which we describe in the following chapter.

We have no direct evidence of Bronze Age ploughs in Ireland, though marks of furrows have been observed underneath burial barrows of that period in Jutland and Holland and it has been claimed that the *ard* had reached the west Baltic region before the end of the Neolithic phase. However this may be the sod-cutting spade, which could be supplemented by the wooden shovel, is not likely to have been introduced much before the beginning of the Christian era, since it required an efficient knowledge of iron-working. By facilitating the building of ridges it would have improved crop yields during a climatic period, the sub-Atlantic, which was even wetter than at present. A mould-board plough capable of forming ridges did not reach Ireland on present evidence until about the seventh century, and as we have seen it had not been adopted in parts of the west until the nineteenth century. Thus the narrow spade, coming into use at about the same time as oats, would have been a factor in stabilizing settlement by permitting ridge cultivation on the outfield grazing ground round about. This is speculative, but it is at least clear that with the introduction of the potato in the seventeenth century it was the spade that facilitated the breaking-in of rough pasture by means of 'lazy-beds', and so made possible the great expansion of cultivation and population in the century before the Great Famine. To this day the one-eared spade, in endless variety, has kept its medieval simplicity and diversity, though it is fast disappearing in favour of the two-eared spade. It may still be seen in the west and south, and a heavy variety is at home in the upper Shannon basin, in the counties of Leitrim, Sligo, west Cavan, Longford, and Roscommon. This is the loy (Fig. 41) a veritable foot-plough with a massive heavy handle expanding on one side into a foot-ledge and below into a stout heel which acts as a pivot when the undercut sod is being turned over in ridge-making. 'This machine they prefer to ploughs', wrote McParlan.[1] Seasoned old men will tell you that they couldn't make ridges unless they had a loy, and they add, scornful of the rising generation, that 'the young people going nowadays couldn't carry a loy'. There was much opposition to the light two-eared spades when they made their appearance in the early nineteenth century. They were objected to above all because, the diggers not wearing boots—the native shoe was at best a flimsy raw-hide cover—the iron would cut their feet. To this day the Irish two-eared spade is distinguished from the English spade by having iron foot-plates (Fig. 41).

The metal spade probably began its life as a mere cutting edge of iron attached to the mouth of a narrow wooden spade. It is still little more than an attachment to a wooden shaft, consisting of an open iron socket which folds around the end of the shaft and passes at an angle into a strong narrow blade. I regard the loy as the most primitive type because the pivot or 'lift' is largely in the heel of the wooden shaft or 'tree', whereas in the rather lighter Munster spade—variants of which are also found in Kilkenny and Galway—the whole pivot is provided by the bent blade. The Longford-Cavan loy, which is adapted to heavy glacial or peaty soils, is a very clumsy digging tool, though well adapted for sod-turning. In experienced hands the loy 'would go in of itself' thanks to its weight and the expanded

[1] J. McParlan, *Leitrim* (1802), 25.

mouth which opened a way and prevented the blade from wedging.

It was reckoned that twelve men armed with loys could turn an acre a day.[1] This compares not unfavourably with the estimated rate of 'ploughing' with a caschrom, and is nearly twice the speed of spade digging. In the Munster spade the foot-rest is a separate piece of wood which is wedged into the open socket to one side of the shaft, normally the right. The shape of this wedge, and the dimensions and curve of the iron blade, vary from one district to another. When new the spade mouth has two points resembling a fish-tail, or the blade may taper to the mouth to facilitate digging in light gravelly soils. The old Galway spade has its footpiece cut out of a single piece of wood to which a separate handle is attached. This is considered to lessen the shock when the spade is thrust into the ground, and the device is frequently found on old-fashioned turf spades. A curious forked spade formerly common in Mayo also has this feature. This is the 'gowl-gob', a two-eared wooden spade with twin narrow iron-shod blades, and it was reckoned to be very suitable for making ridges in loose sandy or boggy soils (Fig. 43). This may be the last survival of a prehistoric spade, for 'a two-pointed pronged spade' is said to be an ancient Mediterranean tool,[2] and a 'bidente' is used in parts of Spain.

The two-eared iron spade which is replacing the loy in its last lairs has gradually ousted the one-eared spade in most parts of the country during the course of the nineteenth century. But in doing so it has copied even the minor variations of the spades it replaced, so that the spade remains an index of regionalism, a tool of sociological research as well as an instrument of labour (Fig. 44). Until water-driven tilt-hammers were introduced for the manufacture of spades—perhaps half a dozen of them are still in operation—they were made by local blacksmiths for local customers. A good spade-maker occasionally won a reputation which might be compared to that of a medieval sword-forger. The smith needed two helpers to hammer out the metal plates, and the work was very heavy.

---

[1]Coote, *Cavan* (1802), 31.
[2]*The Cambridge Economic History* (Eds. J. H. Clapham and E. Power), I (1941), 94.

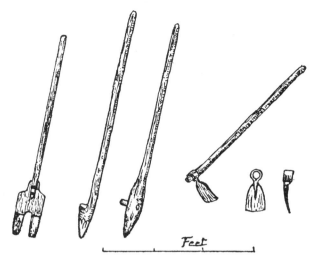

FIG. 43. 'Gowl-gob', Co. Mayo; steeveens, Longford and Cavan; and graffan, Kerry.

The precise requirements of each group of townlands forming a neighbourhood-unit resulted from the balance of many physical, human and economic factors—such as conditions of soil and slope, methods of digging, types of crop, length of arm and leg—cemented by usage and sanctioned by tradition. The 'spade gauge book' of a County Tyrone factory, which has lately closed, lists some 230 different patterns, not counting the special turf spades, and it served only Ulster and the west. I quote the dimensions for the length and breadth, at shoulder and mouth, of the spades of a few districts in Ulster to illustrate the variety and precision of the gauges: Armagh, 18 in. $\times$ $5\frac{13}{16} \times 6\frac{11}{16}$; Omagh, $17\frac{1}{2} \times 5\frac{1}{2} \times 6\frac{1}{4}$; Dungannon, $17\frac{1}{2} \times 5\frac{7}{8} \times 5\frac{7}{8}$; Portrush, $16 \times 6\frac{3}{4} \times 6\frac{1}{2}$; Kilkeel, $15 \times 6\frac{1}{4} \times 4\frac{1}{4}$; Monaghan, $20 \times 4\frac{7}{8} \times 6$. It will be noticed that the spades vary not only in size but also in shape, some having 'broad points', that is expanding at the mouth, some 'narrow points', that is tapering, and others being parallel sided. The blades range in weight from 3 to 6 lb., in length from 13 to 22 in., in width at the shoulder from $3\frac{1}{2}$ to 8 in. and at the mouth from 3 to 8 in. In addition great attention is paid to the longitudinal

135

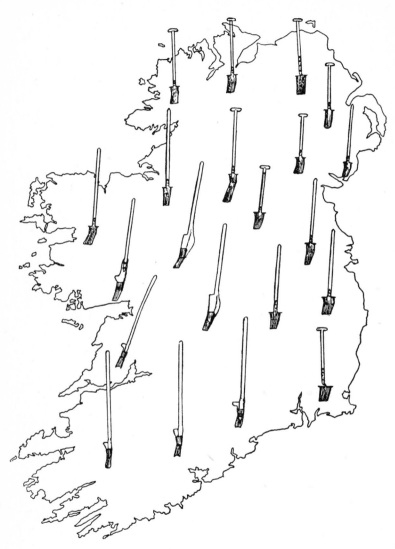

FIG. 44. Map of spade types.

136

bend or 'lift' of the blade and to the lateral bend or 'dish'. The lift may be well distributed or it may be concentrated at one point: it may be curved or cranked.

The shape of the blade being thus precisely standardized for each area, various sizes are made to suit individual users and also the seasons of the year. Thus four or five spades of different sizes, ranging say from 13 to 17 in. in length, will be seen on sale in the market towns. In addition some longer spades may be offered for old-fashioned folk, for the blade of the spade is now made shorter than it used to be. These shorter spades, required for digging potatoes, retain the often awkward shape of the long spring spade—designed for ridge-making—which is going out of favour with drill cultivation.

The Irish spade differs from the English not only in its narrow bent blade but also in its thickened sides, its foot-plates, its straight handle and the short straight straps or tails to which the handle is attached. Whereas the English spade derives its digging power from the curvature above the blade, in the Irish spade the curvature is all in the blade. Moreover the Irish prefer a long shaft (4 ft.) without hand-grip, though in Ulster the shaft is short (3 ft.) and headed, i.e. fitted with a cross-piece at the end. The headed shaft, however, is replacing the long headless shaft which is better adapted to the process of sod turning than to digging. With the headed shaft the control of the spade is mainly in the hand that grips the head, which thus tends to be the right hand: consequently this type of spade goes with left-footed digging (Fig. 41).

These differences are largely explained by differences of function, for the primary purpose of the Irish two-eared spade, like the loy which it has replaced, is to turn the sod. It is a hand plough rather than a digging tool, and it owes its remarkable development to the expansion of potato cultivation in the eighteenth and nineteenth centuries. To the new crop, as we shall see, the old method of burying the seed in prepared beds was quickly adapted, for ridge cultivation was ideally suited to a root-planting culture, and in fact potatoes are grown in ridges on the Andean plateaux. Thus the adoption of the potato helped to perpetuate tools and methods of cultivation which might otherwise have died out. Nowadays, however, drill-cultivation has replaced lazy-beds over most of the country.

Some ridge-making tools have almost entirely disappeared, for example the mattock and the breast-plough, which were once characteristic respectively of the south-west and the north-east of the country and which may still be seen occasionally in Cos. Kerry and Antrim. The mattock ('graffan') is a tool of ancient lineage which finds its parallels in Wales, in Spain and Mediterranean lands, and throughout the tropics (Fig. 43). In Kerry and west Cork it has had many uses—for breaking sods and

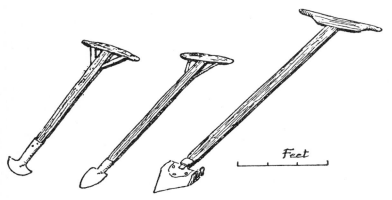

FIG. 45. Flachters or breast-ploughs, north-east Ireland. (1) North Antrim. (2) Co. Tyrone. (3) Mid-Antrim.

clods on the ridges, for loosening the earth of the furrows before shovelling, and also for cutting sods for ridge-making, for 'paring and burning' and for roof-covering. Arthur Young describes the process of graffaning a field by rolling the sod with the foot as it was cut: it was reckoned very heavy work.[1] The breast-plough or flachter (Fig. 45) served the same purpose in Cos. Antrim and Londonderry and earned the same reputation. This instrument is now largely restricted to paring bogland in preparation for turf-cutting. During the second world war I broke in a neglected mountain garden by making lazy-beds with a flachter and I heartily agree with the verdict of an Antrim labourer: 'half a day with it was enough for any ordinary

[1] A. Young, *Tour*, 2, 10.

mortal, but there was ones made a profession of it and could keep on most of a day.' The normal flachter is wingless after the Scots pattern: the winged blade of English type, curiously restricted to mid-Antrim (Fig. 45), is probably a landlord's introduction.

XI

LAZY-BEDS

IN the Western Isle, as throughout Highland Britain, climate and custom have conspired to limit the farmer's work in the fields to little more than half the year, from March to October. It is geared to a régime of spring-sown crops, supplemented since the agrarian revolution by intensive hay-farming. Wheat-growing is now encouraged under the Republican drive towards economic self-sufficiency, but it is a risky crop except in the drier eastern lowlands, and though it was the chief cereal in early prehistoric times there is some evidence to suggest that it was then a spring-sown crop. Barley has been grown in small amounts since early times and was especially popular in remote places during the great days of poteen-making, but it is now insignificant as a crop in comparison with oats and potatoes. Before the coming of the potato the oats (corn) crop was all-important, and the routine of its cultivation set the pattern of the farming year and was closely integrated with pastoral needs. In bad seasons even the oats may not ripen properly, and their safe harvesting is at best a gamble in the oceanic climate of the west where autumn is the wettest season of the year. Thus great toil was endured and every care taken in the preparations for sowing, rites of propitiation were performed during the growing season, and every chance of harvesting the crop was quickly seized. It was in the nature of a rescue operation, and indeed the Irish farmer always speaks of 'saving' his harvest. The normal worries of a cereal farmer are here accentuated, and the harvest period is so vital that autumn in rural Ireland is always referred to as 'harvest'.

Spells of fine weather in spring and harvest were times of

intense effort, when the toilers were spurred on by rivalries in their efforts to avoid the bad luck which tradition wisely bestowed on the laggards. The seasonal festivals which marked the end of these periods of strain—at the beginning of May and November—were not merely celebrations of work completed and a new season begun, but also the occasion for the release of emotional stresses. The Irishman's capacity for bouts of strenuous work, and his more notorious addiction to spells of complete idleness, are surely related to the experience accumulated through countless springs, harvests, and winters. Winter was a dead season for man as for the world around him. It was no time for fairs, fighting or raiding, for selling or even stealing animals which were not worth the trouble of stealing: the problem was to maintain life in them.

Long tradition explains the neglect of winter ploughing which is still characteristic of the greater part of Ireland. The infield stubble was required to augment the very poor and limited outfield grazing available for the wintering stock. There are some townlands, in the west, where to this day all the fields become common grazing during the winter, and only the strongly-enclosed 'gardens' are safe places to grow cabbages, for instance, or a little rye for the thatch. Moreover even with improved ploughs the grass tends to grow in the furrows of ploughed land during a mild winter. And when it is recalled that much of the old infield land was on sloping ground, if only for the sake of the natural drainage thus provided, it can be conceded that there was wisdom in not breaking the earth in winter and opening the way to soil erosion. Moreover the loss of fertility by the leaching of exposed soils can be serious.

Preparing the land for seed had thus to await the spring, and pressure of time as well as the uncertainties of weather strengthened the tradition of co-operative labour in the form of pooled plough-teams in the infield and gangs of ridgemakers in the outfield. The plough-team, normally of four horses or oxen supplied by as many neighbours, had to be supplemented by spade and mell, for the furrows were badly turned, and after the seed-bed had been prepared and the corn sown the seed was covered with shovelled soil. In order to facilitate drainage, in the days before field drains, the land was ploughed in ridges or 'lands' some ten or twelve feet wide, separated by trenches which provided the soil for burying the corn. Lazy-beds, that is spade-ridges for potatoes, made even heavier demands on many hands (Fig. 46). A writer in the 1830s describing the scene in the fields as neighbours worked together in teams, remarks that 'these congregations give vivacity to the labour . . . and occasionally an animated shout is set up by the whole body'.[1] The pooling of labour resources, 'sharing' or 'morrow-ing'—there are several terms for this co-operative system—is still by no means uncommon even if there is nowadays less need for it. It not only cements social relationships but provides the stimulus of competitive effort. In the north of Ireland Protestant and Roman Catholic neighbours frequently share their labour in this way.

FIG. 46. Ploughed ridges, Co. Cavan, and spade ridges (lazy-beds), Co. Mayo.

By tradition the vital spring-time preparations are hedged around with tabus and omens. The ploughman should turn his horses with the sun, from left to right, to invoke its blessing on the work, and when yoking or unyoking his team his horses' heads should be facing south. Friday—which is regarded as a lucky day to begin all operations not needing iron—is the best day to begin sowing, and Good Friday is best of all. The sower going forth should begin his labours with the solemn words 'In the name of God', and he should give the horses a handful of corn from the seed-bag and throw a handful of earth over each horse's rump. Ashes from the turf fire were sometimes mixed with the seed for luck and there are traditions of the ashes of the midsummer bonfires being kept for this purpose.

In some parts of the country, chiefly in the south and east, the sower carried a straw seed-basket, and this is presumably

[1] Isaac Weld, *Roscommon* (1832), 660.

an English introduction since 'sowing baskets' are listed in the medieval pipe-rolls of the Pale. In parts of the west, for example Mayo, a skin tray was used for sowing. But the usual Irish method is to sow from a linen sheet, kept specially for the purpose, which is tied round the sower. The seed is thrown with a one-handed cast, and it is not everyone's privilege to be allowed to undertake this important task. It calls for skill and concentrated care, for 'a missed bit' is a bad omen, foretelling death. The seed should all be safely 'buried' by the beginning of May, and in Co. Armagh the first cuckoo's call was taken as a sign. To be found sowing corn after this was a mark of deep disgrace: the laggard was labelled 'a cuckoo farmer'.

With modern ploughs and improved drainage it is not often, save in the tiny fields of the west, that one comes across cereal crops sown in ridges, but the lazy-bed method is very generally employed for potatoes and other crops where the spade is used, though the great bulk of the potato crop is sown in drills. The potato ridge presumably derives its name, lazy-bed, from the fact that the sod under the ridge is not dug: the bed is built up on top of the grass with sods and soil dug from the trenches between the ridges. Not only does this method make full use of the humus and decaying grass but it prevents the sets from becoming waterlogged and rotting, for the whole bed is raised above the water-table. And the unbroken sod checks the downwash of plant nutrients. The trenches or furrows between the ridges provide open drains, and the lazy-beds are always carefully aligned with the slope of the land. Moreover, when the trenches are dug a second time for earthing the potatoes, they often go deep enough to penetrate the hard layer of iron pan which tends to form under heavily leached soils by the washing down of iron salts. This the old-fashioned plough could not do. Breaking the impermeable pan not only improves the drainage but provides minerals which are returned to the topsoil when the potatoes are earthed. The ridges in which potatoes are grown in their Andean homeland appear to be similar to the Irish lazy-beds, and tuber crops throughout the tropics are planted in ridges or mounds, but the ridge-technique is certainly older than the potato in Ireland. Clearly an efficient shovel is a requirement in the construction of ridges of any width, and it is here that the long-handled shovel comes into its own. In Britain such a shovel, which remains characteristic of south-west England, is of at least Roman antiquity. Specimens from the Roman period are, however, made entirely of wood, and several similar shovels of unknown age have been found in the Irish bogs (Fig. 47). In the west, down to famine times, the common shovel was made of a single piece of wood, usually willow, shod with a narrow strip of iron along the edge.[1]

Fig. 47. Long-handled shovels used for finishing the ridges. The wooden one was found at Glenoe, Co. Antrim.

In some districts potato ridges are made with the plough, either with an ordinary lea-plough or else with a special paring-plough, fitted with a wide sock, which reproduces the special feature of the lazy-bed, that is, it does not break the grass of the bed but inverts a wide sod on to it from either side. In both instances the trench is then broken up by a plough with the mould board removed to provide earth for shovelling on to the ridges. The much wider corn ridges were normally made with the plough, except in those retarded mountainy districts where the plough seems never to have been adopted. Wheat was grown on narrower ridges, some five to seven feet wide. In Co. Londonderry it was customary to plough a 'rid-hint', that is, to take a second furrow out of the subsoil of the trench to facilitate drainage.[2] We can readily picture the arable land as eighteenth century observers saw it, with 'the strips piled high and the furrows scraped bare'. Lazy-beds vary in width according to local conditions and conventions and may be as little as

[1]W. R. Wilde, *Catalogue* (1857), 207.
[2]G. V. Sampson, *Memoir* (1814), 282.

PLATE I

Traditional farm kitchen, Co. Down. Note baking-board on table (*left*) and meal ark to left of dresser, with beetle hanging above.

(*By kind permission of Ulster Museum, Belfast*).

PLATE 2

Butter-making in a Co. Antrim farm kitchen.

PLATE 3

Beehive house (clochaun), Irishmurray, Co. Sligo.

PLATE 4

"Lashing" rye, Aran Islands. Note the woven belt (criss) supporting the hand-woven tweed trousers.

PLATE 5

1. Flax in stook in drumlin country, Co. Down. Flax-dam on right.

2. Spreading flax from the dam, Co. Down.

PLATE 6

1. Shearing oats with the toothed sickle, Co. Antrim.

2. Thrashing oats with flails, Co. Antrim.

PLATE 7

Winnowing oats with a skin wight, Co. Donegal.

PLATE 8

1. Slide-car with peat-kish, Glens of Antrim.

2. Wheel-car, Glens of Antrim.

PLATE 9

1. Cutting turf (underfooting) in a Co. Fermanagh bog.

2. Building a peat stack, Co. Antrim.

PLATE 10

1. Spreading mud turf with long-handled shovel, Co. Meath

2. "Running" the spread turf.

PLATE 11

Kelp gatherers near Fair Head, Co. Antrim.

Kelp-burning, Co. Antrim.

PLATE 12

1. Curraghs, the Aran Islands.

2. Dragging home the hay in the west of Ireland.

PLATE 13

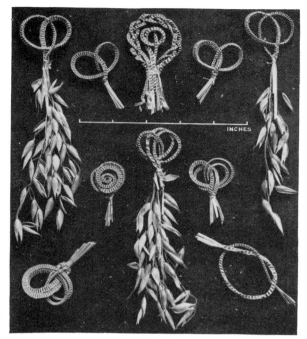

1. Harvest knots, Co. Armagh.

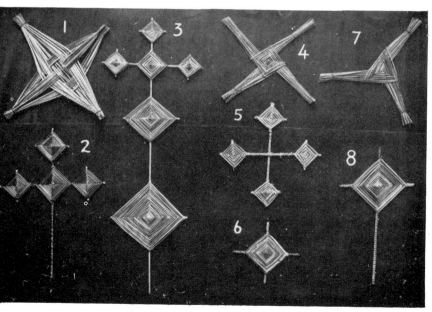

2. Bridget's Crosses, Co. Armagh.

PLATE 14

Salruck graveyard, Co. Galway, with tobacco pipes left on graves.

PLATE 15

1. Holestone "altar", Inishkeel, Co. Donegal.

2. *Above.* Pilgrim's prayer-tally, Gouganebarra, Co. Cork.
Below. Rags on bramble at a wart-well.

PLATE 16

Holy well at Doon, Co. Donegal. Crutches and bushes (*behind*) swathed in rags.

two feet or as much as eight feet wide, the furrows between them being from one to three feet in width. These dimensions and the different methods of building the ridges are intimately related to the depth and quality of the soil and to the types of spade used in each locality. Both the breadth and length of the ridges are commonly measured by the spade, and the term score-ground, applied in Co. Kerry to potato land let in conacre, that is from year to year, refers to twenty spade-lengths. When the crop is lifted the ridges are roughly levelled, and the following year they are split, that is the new furrow is dug in the middle of the old ridge.

It is not easy to describe the process of ridge-making with the spade and impossible to portray all the varieties of technique employed. It is back-breaking work, yet it is performed with an easy rhythm and a seemingly effortless and almost mechanical efficiency. In its simplest form the grassy strip which is to become the furrow is notched centrally down its length and the sods on each side are each undercut by two spade-thrusts and levered over on to the beds, where they lie flat, grass to grass, like closed hinges (Fig. 48). Normally the manure has already

FIG. 48. Lazy-beds.

been spread on the beds, and if the potato sets have also been planted all that is needed to complete the ridge is to break the earth of the furrow and shovel it on to the ridge. More commonly, however, the beds are fully prepared before the sets are planted, and it is the task of the women and children to follow the ridgemakers and thrust the potatoes into the sandwich of sods and manure. This is the method appropriate to the wetter west, for it means that the ridges can be prepared beforehand as opportunity offers. What is known as the Munster mode of planting 'with the back of the spade' is to thrust the narrow spade through the inverted top sod and drop the set behind the blade as it is levered forward. On the average three rows of potatoes go to each bed, but there are also one- two- and four-set ridges.

A special wooden dibber known as the steeveen, kibbin (little spade) or gugger is employed for planting in Cavan, Leitrim and Longford and may perhaps be correlated with the heavy loy as another archaic tool which has kept its hold in that area. The steeveen with its conical head (Fig. 43) will break through the toughest sod and open a way for the young sprouts. Typically 'guggering' is woman's work, the children following, dropping in the sets and closing the hole with a fork or a mell. I like to think that the steeveen is descended from that universal tool of the women of humble cultivating societies, the digging or planting stick, remote ancestor of the spade. It is a plausible theory that the crops of wheat and barley sown by the first Irish cultivators were planted in this way in the ashes of burnt woodland on the mountainsides. Larger dibbers or 'stamps' with several teeth for planting corn were used until quite recently in some counties, for example Armagh (Fig. 49).

FIG. 49. Dibbers and (*centre*) sowing fiddle, Co. Armagh.

They are probably the descendents of specimens introduced by English 'planters' of the early seventeenth century. It is the dibberhole which is referred to in the rhyme which has outlived the action it once accompanied:

146

Four seeds in a hole,
One for the rook
One for the crow
One to rot
And one to grow.

The sowing fiddle which scatters seed broadcast and which
may frequently be seen in use in some districts, for example
Co. Down, is another introduction from England which has
survived here longer than in its presumed home (Fig. 49).
The fiddler makes a striking figure, seen from a distance, as he
strides steadily up and down the field with his silent instrument;
he must beware of changing his pace whether going uphill or
downhill or the crop will grow in uneven strips.

In many parts of the world burning of the vegetation is a
necessary preliminary to shifting cultivation, and the use of
fire in the preparation of the outfield for ridge cultivation therefore raises some interesting questions. We know that the burning
of sods pared from rough pasture, sometimes called 'den-
shiring' from its reputed Devonshire home, was widely practised
in Ireland down to the time of the famine. In the early nineteenth century nine-tenths of the potatoes grown in Co. Clare
were planted on burnt land,[1] and a special skinning plough was
used to pare off the sod. Elsewhere the graffan and flachter
were put to a like purpose. From a description of Donegal in
1880 it seems that the drying and warming of the soil were
regarded as more important than the fertilizing ashes: 'There
is on the fresh bogs a process of heating resorted to in the
Spring, i.e., the end of April and the first half of May: the piles
of earth are never allowed to burn out into a fire but combustion
is kept stopped up within the mass . . . the heated earth, not
ashes, is scattered and the first crop put in.'[2] Where the land
was of fairly good quality only the furrow sods were burnt.
They were stood on edge to dry and then burnt in piles on the
ridges, after which the ashes were spread and the potato sets
planted in them, to be covered with earth dug from the trenches
in the usual way.[3] The process of paring and burning seems to

[1]H. Dutton, *Clare* (1808), 36.
[2]*Report of the Royal Commission on the Land Law (Ireland) Act, 1881* (1887),
Appendix B, 137.
[3]R. Thompson, *Meath*, 272.

have been greatly accelerated in the eighteenth century, thanks no doubt to the stimulus of contemporary English practice, but it may well be that the custom perpetuates the prehistoric method of clearing the land for cultivation. The fact that burning the land was prohibited by various Acts of Parliament in Ireland would point to its being another abominable native custom, like ploughing by the tail. We have referred to the graffan as a skinning tool of ancient lineage, and may add that in Devon and Cornwall the implement used 'in the infancy of the art of paring'[1] was a mattock or adze which also served as a clod-breaker. The 'hack' of the Pennine country comes to mind here. The flachter, the Highland equivalent of the breast-plough which became the standard English paring instrument, may well be, in fact, the ancestor of the breast-plough, and I suggest that it came into use for skinning the outfield before burning and planting. We know that outfield cultivation of burnt-over forest lasted in France, in the Vosges country, into the eighteenth century, and the custom probably survived long enough in Ireland to be replaced by 'paring and burning'. This view is certainly in line with the other evidences of cultural continuity from prehistoric times. The customs of throwing the ashes of May Day and Midsummer bonfires into the fields and the mixing of peat ash from the hearth with the seed corn may be magical residues of the ancient practice of firing the land before sowing.

We shall describe in a later chapter the various methods of carrying manure to the fields: here we may refer to another simple implement which serves in the preparation of the ridges. This is the clod-breaking wooden mallet or mell, resembling a croquet mallet (Fig. 1). The subject of our drawing might have been taken straight from the Luttrell Psalter of the fourteenth century, but it is a mell which I saw in use in Co. Armagh a few years ago. Hurling sticks served the same purpose in some southern counties,[2] and one wonders whether the Gaelic game of hurling evolved in this way by playfully knocking a rounded stone among the rigs. Patrick Geddes amusingly, if erroneously, traced the origin of the game of golf back to the

[1] *Loudan's Encyclopaedia of Agriculture* (1831).
[2] W. Tighe, *Kilkenny* (1802), 182.

idle Scots shepherd who with his crook knocked a white sea pebble into a rabbit hole among the dunes. And one recalls the theory that the game of cricket, with its 22-yard pitch, had its beginnings in the English openfields among ploughboys (players) and landlords' sons (gentlemen) who threw clods at the ploughman's marking sticks across the chain-wide acre strips completed at the end of a day's work. At any rate cricket has not strayed far from the English openfields and village greens, and in Ireland it clings to the larger towns and to the English-settled areas along the east coast.

Among other implements for preparing the soil the roller is probably of no great antiquity, though examples of wood or stone are of considerable interest. Alternatively, flat boulders or specially-built clod-slipes are driven over the ploughed ground, the driver being carried along on the platform thus provided and adding to its weight. I have seen the former in Co. Wexford and the latter in Co. Down. In the west the breaking of clods on the ridges is done by hand with a heavy rake (Fig. 1), and the 'harrows' which were formerly pulled by the horse's tail was a similar implement, a block of wood armed with a few wooden teeth. Even the larger harrows were a source of amusement to visiting farmers like Arthur Young, 'more fit to raise laughter than soil', as one observer put it.

The weeding and protection of the young corn were serious matters in the days when a patch of oats provided a family with its only cereal food. The tethering and herding of livestock were universal habits, and hand-weeding was another task for the young folk. O'Flaherty writes of Connacht: 'They go and lie prostrate or sit upon the corn, to weed it with their bare hands, leaving nothing behind but pure corn'.[1] Swedes are almost invariably weeded and thinned by hand. Thistles growing in corn or flax are pulled with special pincers or 'clips' made either of iron or more usually of wood, of a type which is illustrated in the Luttrell Psalter. The very similar French weeders known as Havre pincers were also used for catching eels. Docks were removed with a heavy forked spud (Fig. 50). There were other less arduous ways of inducing a bounteous crop. The custom of placing a sickle in the corn-field at the

[1]R. O'Flaherty, *H'Iar Connaught* (1684), 59.

149

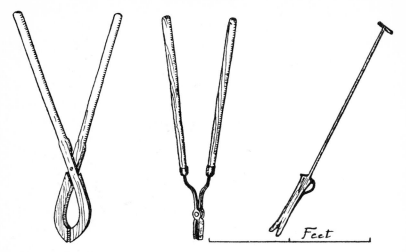

F ɪ ɢ. 50. Weeding 'clips', Antrim and Armagh, and iron dock-lifter, Antrim.

Midsummer festival was an easy way of showing the spirits of the corn what was expected of them. You might also hope to transfer ill-luck to someone else's crop by burying a dead animal, a piece of meat, or even an egg on his land. It would be worth while listening for the call of the cuckoo on the first day of July, for to hear it was a sign of a good harvest. Prognostications were so many and so easily procured that they apparently provided a fatalistic society with a ready means of avoiding steady work. In some parts of the country, docks, thistles and couch grass were apparently regarded as a good sign, because they kept the crop warm.[1]

[1] W. Bence Jones, *A Life's Work in Ireland*, 87.

XII

HARVEST

THANKS to the necessity of 'winning' (seasoning) hay and corn in the fields before the crops are carried home, harvest time drags on from late summer to the edge of winter, and the word 'harvest' as we have seen is a synonym for autumn. In this pastoral Irish country the hay harvest is nowadays of vital importance in farm economy, yet I cannot find any evidence that hay played a significant part in the traditional Gaelic system of farming. It is the sickle, not the scythe, which figures in folk-lore and in place-names, and the scythe seems to be a relative newcomer in most parts of the country. It requires a stone-free sward which would be hard to seek on hill farms. The business of hay-making was, I believe, of little importance until the economic changes of the agrarian revolution and the introduction of rotation grass. In the North the date of the first hay-cutting is fixed by a celebrated but relatively new festival, the Orangeman's day on the 12th of July. After hay comes flax, which is pulled from late July to mid-August, followed by wheat and barley in the areas where they are grown, by the corn harvest in September and the potato-lifting in October. In bad years hay may still be uncut in late August, the mountain corn is green even at the end of September, and late-cut corn sometimes stays stacked in the fields up to Christmas—indeed there are records of the grain being reaped after Christmas[1]—but traditionally all harvest work was completed by All-Hallows.

In Scandinavia it has been claimed that hay-making began in pre-historic times as a result of the climatic deterioration which took place during the last millennium B.C. In Ireland with its

[1]For example in 1817. J. Donaldson, *Upper Fews*, 25.

milder winters there seems to have been no such response. Although there has been hay-making on the rich meadows of Co. Meath, for example, since medieval times, when the English openfield system was introduced, I have found no literary or archaeological evidence for it anywhere in early Ireland. Indeed Giraldus Cambrensis expressed surprise in the twelfth century that the Irish neither made hay nor built stalls for cattle, and despite his untrustworthiness I believe his witness may be accepted in this instance. Hay-making would have begun on the river bottoms (callows, holms) which, being liable to floods, were not available for winter grazing: this meadow hay is today much less important than 'upland' hay, the significant term used for rotation grass. The hay-making season is nowadays a time of toil for all members of the family, but I suspect that the period from midsummer to late July was under the old order a slack season, the time for raiding and fighting, and catching the English bending in the hayfields. For the Irish it was the 'blue month', when food was scarce (July is also called 'the hungry month') and the meal bins empty. In Ulster at any rate, for reasons which may be older than King William III, July is the holiday month and the time for faction fights. Sir John Myres used to say that in the Mediterranean world, where there is little grass to make hay, the month of May was the slackest time of the summer, the favourite time for fighting instead of hay-making. In Ireland as in classical Greece the winter climate made it difficult and unsportsmanlike to go to war at that season.

To judge from present practice on the tiny farms of the west of Ireland, grass was cut as required from field-banks and odd corners, a creelful at a time to give to the cow as a 'bribe' at milking time, and it was woman's work. The hook used for this purpose, the grass or scythe hook, is smooth-edged, unlike the saw-toothed corn sickle, and what hay was made in former times was probably cut for the most part with the hook. The livestock would be fed in winter mainly on oatstraw, and grazed on the infield stubble, supplemented by the outfield grasses which had been allowed to mature while the bulk of the stock was at the summer booley-grounds. We may be sure that what little hay was saved was treated much as it is on mountainy farms today. The scythed grass is shaken out by hand and spread thinly over the field. When partly dry it is gathered into windrows and lapped or coiled, that is folded against the leg over the forearm into small 'lap-cocks' resembling a lady's muff, the hole permitting the wind to pass through and the smooth rounded top allowing the rain to run off. Like all practised hand-work it is a job carried through with apparently mechanical indifference, but the old hands will take care to ensure that the laps are properly made and laid down so that they are aligned with the prevailing wind. Even on rich lowland farms the hay will be 'lapped' if it is first season's grass grown, as in Ulster, for the seed, which is a valuable export. Alternatively seed grass is tied in sheaves and 'gaited' like flax or stooked like a cereal crop (Fig. 51).

FIG. 51. Laps of hay, gaits of flax and stook of wheat, with 'hudders'.

When dry the laps are shaken open and built into small cocks or lumps which are later enlarged into hand cocks. Or if the hay is in good condition it is made, chiefly in the drier parts of the country, into larger ricks or tramp cocks which are trodden down firmly and secured with a hay-rope (Fig. 52, 10). The process of hay-making is thus, like the winning of turf (Chapter XIV), one of gradually increasing the size of the pile as the material is dried by sun and wind. The cocked hay is left standing for some weeks in the fields to season, so that it seems to the English visitor, as Arthur Young remarked, that the Irish are generally two months 'making or marring their hay'.[1] The explanation given is the necessity of avoiding overheating, but English critics say that it is the farmers who dislike getting overheated! A more charitable view is that by the

[1] A. Young, *Tour*, 2, 246.

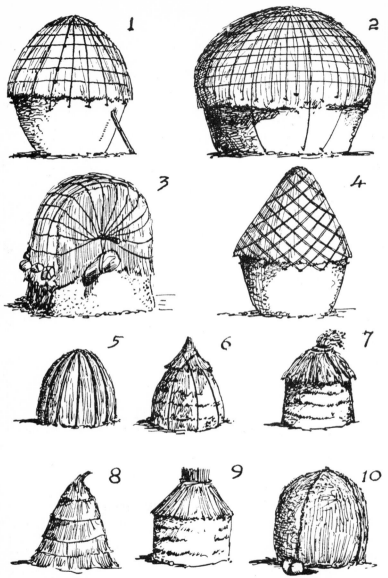

Fig. 52. Stacks and huts roped in many patterns. (1) Cavan (flax). (2) Cork (hay). (3) Mayo (hay). (4) Antrim (oats). (5) Donegal (hay). (6) Donegal (oats). (7) Down (oats). (8) Down (seed hay). (9) Cavan (oats). (10) Down (tramp-cock of hay).

time large-scale hay-making developed it had to fit into a fixed rota of farm work which kept men busy in late July and August at flax-pulling and turf-carrying, so that the cocked hay had to wait. Today the baling machine is speeding up the process, but the bales, whether from the need of seasoning or from force of habit, are left piled in angular cocks scattered over the hayfield.

Carried at last to the haggard on rick-shifters or slipes—formerly on slide-cars or the backs of men and ponies—the hay is built into small circular stacks (pikes). As a protection against wind and rain they are thatched with rushes forthwith and roped (Fig. 52). Since the stacks are thatched before they have had time to settle, the pegged or scolloped thatch found in England is not used. Not only do ropes hold the thatch more securely but it is a simple matter to tighten them as the stack sinks. In the simplest form of roping, hanging stones are attached to the rope ends so that the adjustment is automatic. But where the roof of the stack is not rounded but conical a straw-rope is wrapped round in a spiral which can later be tightened by vertical ropes pegged into the lower part of the stack. One sees this spiral roping also in parts of western Britain. Several other patterns of roping are found, some making a complete network; and the shape of the stack also shows many regional variations (Fig. 52). The size and shape depend not only on local custom but to some extent on the weather and the condition of the hay. Small rounded stacks are most usual, for they are wind-resistant. They are characteristic too of much of Highland Britain from Caithness to Cornwall.

The scythe has not entirely given way to the mowing machine on small farms in whose tiny fields it would anyhow be difficult to turn a machine. The Irish scythesmen, though not so well known as the spalpeens or reapers, had their brief day in the English harvest-fields, and those who remember working 'across the water' in the nineteenth century tell of great feats of piece-work. I was told of one heroic figure who could scythe seven acres in the day, 'and four lifters wouldn't lift after him'. Henry Stephens, in 1855, reckoned that the English labourer would scythe four acres of oats or barley in a ten-hour working day.[1]

[1]Quoted in E. C. Curwen, *Plough and Pasture* (1946), 98.

The Irish prefer the long-handled scythe. The sned, about five-and-a-half feet long, has the lower handgrip offset, and a pointed iron spike is sometimes driven into the end of the sned to anchor it safely when honing (Fig. 53). A test of a well-

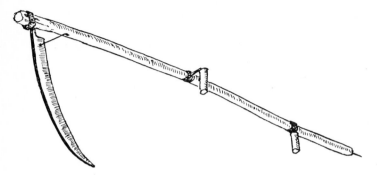

Fɪɢ. 53. Long-handled scythe, Donegal.

sharpened scythe is that it should 'cut wool moving downstream', and there was a special charm used in sharpening. The sanded scytheboard (strickle) has now given way to the artificial stone, though hones of natural stone, including the fossilized wood of Lough Neagh, are used locally. A smith-made scythe-blade is highly prized and long after its legitimate life has ended lengths of it will be utilized for choppers and turnip knives. For full efficiency one must be measured for the fitting and hanging of a scythe. The lower handle should be at arm's length from the bottom of the sned, the upper one distant from the top by the length from elbow to finger-tips. The two handles should also be a cubit apart. The angle of the blade is determined by swinging the left leg and adjusting the blade until its point comes within a nicely determined distance of it when the sned is held upright against the right leg. The scythe cradle, for gathering the swathe as it is cut, is rarely met with in Ulster, save for makeshift devices such as a bit of sacking fitted against the 'grass-nail' which joins sned and blade in the angle where they meet. In the south and south-east of the country, where the scythe is an old introduction, quite elaborate cradles both of wood and of finely-wrought iron are to be seen.

When the scythe was transferred from the mowing of hay to the cutting of corn during the second half of last century there was much opposition from the reapers, sometimes for the good reason that little fields full of great boulders or the stumps of bog-fir gave no space to swing a scythe, and a single blow on the fast-moving point may ruin the blade. But one suspects that conservatism was rooted in magic. It is said that the rice-growers of Malaya refuse to use a scythe because its slashing motion would frighten away the spirits of the rice. Some such notion may have strengthened the Irishman's condemnation of the scythe. And I find another curious parallel with the Far East. The Malayan reaper hums like an insect while he is cutting the rice, perhaps to soothe the spirits of the living crop. In Ireland there is an old belief that an insect kept in a little box fastened to the handle of hook or scythe will bring luck and give the blade greater cutting power. Both scythe and sickle are personal possessions and their luck is personal: they are loaned with reluctance. When a sickle is borrowed it should not be passed directly from hand to hand but thrown on the ground and then picked up. This belief, which applies to all pointed objects, may be explained by the danger of handling a sharp tool, for bad luck is often related to bad practice.

But before coming to corn harvest the handling of flax should be described. Unpleasant handling it is, even if not quite so onerous (and odorous) as working with hemp or jute. When grown for fibre flax is harvested after the pale blue flowers have fallen but before the seed ripens, and because it is the stalk that is being harvested it is not cut but pulled up by the roots. 'Lint' is a crop of the small family farm, for many hands are required, teams or 'boons' of anything from half a dozen to thirty people gathering from neighbouring farms and working together in a festival spirit which reaches its climax in the evening dance. The tough flax is hard on the hands and the stooping is back-breaking. But the beets (sheaves) are carefully put together, for they have to be spread after retting and the stalks should lie evenly. The three handfuls which compose the beet are laid down at slightly different angles so that they will separate easily. A standard beet is reckoned to be 22 inches in diameter. The bands (ties) are prepared beforehand and consist of two lengths of green rushes knotted at the flowering end. When tied, the end of the band is thrust under towards the head of the beet, that is 'with the grain' of the flax. The beets are carried as soon as possible to be steeped (drowned or dubbed) in the flax dam or 'lint hole' where soft peaty water has been standing for some days to warm up. If they cannot be steeped forthwith the beets are built into stooks, for they are damaged if left lying on the ground. The beets are placed upright in the dam, with a slight inclination to facilitate their later removal, and when well packed may be covered, if the water is deep enough, with a horizontal layer or 'sheeting row' on which large boulders are placed to keep the flax under water. The process of retting (rotting) takes from seven to twelve days and is soon advertised by a foul and penetrating odour as the core or 'bone' of the stalk decays. Then the slimy, stinking beets are taken out of the dam and 'grassed', that is spread on grass, usually a new-mown hayfield. This is a skilled but dirty (Pl. 5, 2) job. To ensure that the stalks do not stick together the beets are shaken loose over the left forearm so that the flax lies evenly in ordered rows. After a couple of days it is once more tied into beets, but if the weather is bad it is first 'gaited' for a day or so to complete the drying (Fig. 51). This provides one of the more picturesque scenes of flax harvest, for the gaits look like the skirts of invisible dancers or the tents of a fairy host. The drying stalks of each beet are gathered and spread around the leg to make a hollow broad-based cone which will stand upright. It seems probable that gaiting was at one time a method of drying cereal crops as well as flax in these difficult Highland regions. The 'gaitner' was a recognized member of the harvest gang in Northumberland in the early nineteenth century. 'He follows close on the reapers and, the corn being laid in the band near the tops of the corn, he . . . brings the sheaf up to the left knee, gives the band a peculiar twist and sets the sheaf upright, giving it a half turn so that the skirts fly out to look like the cover of a beehive'.[1] Gaited corn was said to 'win' well and it was carried to the stack without stooking.

Ideally the flax after gaiting is ready for breaking and scutching, and in the old days when the farmer was also a

[1] *Loudan's Encyclopaedia of Agriculture* (1831).

weaver it would be hung in the rafters to be used as required. Nowadays the scutching-mills cannot store all the flax they handle, so that the farmer stacks it in the fields until the mill can take it. It is built into large oblong stooks variously known as barts, sleighs, hovels or rays, containing as many as a hundred beets or more. The barts are two-storied. On top of the first storey, which consists of three rows of beets on each side, a row of sheaves is placed along each eave like wall-plates, and others are laid transversely between them. On these, in turn, a central row is placed lengthwise to act as a support for the upper storey, and against this row two or three layers of sheaves are laid like rafters on each side. The hipped roof is then thatched with grass or rushes roped on (Fig. 54). The bart[1] is thus kept

Fig. 54. Flax dam, stooks and bart.

dry while its open structure allows the wind to blow through, drying the beets and also lessening the risk of its being blown down. The farmer-weaver, needing the fibre, might have to dry the flax in a kiln after it had lain spread for a few days (Chapter IX). The whole sequence of breaking (melling) the flax, scutching, cloving, hackling, spinning, weaving, and bleaching was then carried out by hand. The water-driven scutching mill was introduced in the eighteenth century though hand-scutching continued in some districts into the present century. All processes are now mechanized apart from a little high-quality hand-loom weaving in Ulster, and very little flax is home-grown even in the traditional linen districts.

[1]'Bearts' of oats are referred to in medieval documents. See W. R. Wilde in *Census of Ireland 1851*, Part 5, Vol. 1, 98.

Corn harvest did not begin until a certain set day which differed in various parts of the country, and the appointed day was a time of much excitement. The following description of the Reaping Blessing in the Scottish Highlands would probably apply to Ulster, though I have not found a record of it in Ireland. 'The day the reaping began was one of commotion and ceremonial. The whole family repaired to the field dressed in their best . . . the father of the family took his sickle and, facing the sun, cut a handful of corn. Putting it three times sunwise round his head, the Reaping Blessing was sung'.[1] We know that in Ireland it was the custom for the first sheaves cut to be scutched or lashed, that is the grain was beaten out without using the flail. The winnowed grain was parched over the fire, ground in a quern and boiled in time to make a breakfast for the reapers.[2] This ceremonial breakfast undoubtedly preserves archaic practices.

Reaping with hook or sickle is by no means uncommon on little hill farms where fields are small and uneven, but the days of the great 'gatherings' are no more, when down to late in the last century as many as seventy men might have been seen at work. Most of the lore of these reaping boons has passed away unrecorded, and we get only glimpses of the terrible strain imposed on the toilers and the compensating gaieties. The pressure was most severe when to the rivalry between workers was added the drive of a pace-setter, for it was a mark of disgrace not to keep pace. In Ulster the leader of the boon was 'stubble hook', so called because his ridge was the first of the 'set', next the stubble. (A set was the number of ridges equal to the number of reapers in the boon). The driver, called 'corn-land', took the rig or land next to the standing corn, and between the two the other reapers on their ridges would strive to keep a straight line. 'A bad shearer', runs the Ulster saying, 'always gets a big rig and a blunt hook'. But a spirited reaper, I have been told, 'would die upon the rig before he would suffer "corn-land" to pass him'. Between each set a rest was taken at the 'land-end' and it was an interlude of 'crack and courting'. If we may judge from a Scottish custom, any visiting

[1] A. Carmichael, *Carmina Gadelica*, I (1928).
[2] *Béaloideas*, 10, 293.

stranger was accosted and held down on the ground, a woman would lie on top of him and another woman would tumble them over.[1] Such horse-play was more than a consequence of the high spirits of harvest, the 'rural saturnalia' described by Richard Jefferies in *The Toilers of the Field*. Displays of the rites and symbols of fertility were closely bound up with the bounty of harvest.

There were many variations in the methods of reaping, or shearing—to use the old term—depending on the type of hook, which might be smooth or notched, on the width of the ridges, the condition of the crop and so on. The toothed sickle is probably the older implement, going back to the time when iron was a new metal and could not be given a sharp steel edge. Whereas the smooth or scythe hook is wielded with a slashing cut which may spill the grain, especially of rye, if the crop is ripe and the edge not kept very keen, the sickle is pulled towards the shearer, who holds each bunch as it is cut, pressing it back into the standing corn. As a rule three handfuls or 'loghters' go to each sheaf, the bands of which are prepared beforehand and laid out for the reaper to place the loghters on them straight from the hook (Pl. 6, 1).

The term shearing implies that the crop was cut close to the ground as wool is clipped from a sheep, and indeed urban officials have been known to confuse the operations. Pride was taken in a stubble-field that looked as if it had been shaved. 'Low and clean' was the injunction, 'cut it down to the living earth!' 'Down with the head and up with the tail' were my instructions when I lent a hand at harvest in the Glens of Antrim. Mercifully one worked uphill: where the land was level the reaper would go down on one knee, wearing a knee-pad. If the ridges were wide there might be two shearers and one binder to each ridge, the shearers working from the furrows on each side, the depth of which minimized the amount of stooping required. A 'crack hooksman' could reap and tie fifty twelve-sheaf stooks a day, or say an Irish acre ($= 1\frac{2}{3}$ English acres). It is necessary to have worked with a gang of reapers to appreciate the relentless pace of the work and at the same time the care with which every operation is carried out. There must be no

[1] M. Banks, *British Calendar Customs*, Scotland, I (1937).

heads of corn at the wrong end, or they would be missed in thrashing with the flail, and for the same reason the ears of the straw band-knot should lie towards the top of the sheaf. The sheaves should be laid with their butts to the wind, for these need most drying. The bands should be tied with nice judgement, tight but not over-tight: one should not be able to put the toe of one's boot under the band when one stands on the butt of the sheaf.

As in all farming operations conducted in traditional ways, music and magic to ease the labour were part of the scene. There were shearing songs to match the rhythm of the sickle, and its efficiency was improved by keeping a fly or other insect imprisoned in the handle; perhaps its incessant activity was meant to speed up the work. Another strange belief was that luck followed the reaper who carried a child on his back. The world of magic and fairy was close by at harvest time: it was believed that the top grain (pickle) of every stalk of corn was empty because it had been taken by the fairies and was their due. The sheaf had its share of lore, too, related possibly to its semblance of human shape. A curse could be worked by sticking pins into the joints of the straw, and the sheaf might be properly waked and buried so that as it withered the object of the curse would decline. Stooks with their 'hudders' (Fig. 51) (hooding sheaves) also take on human forms, and I have known various terms for these large stooks applied as nicknames to broad-based country women. 'The last sheaf' also is known as the cailleach or hag.

Beliefs and customs connected with the last sheaf are legion and find their counterparts in many parts of the world. 'Winning the churn' was an incentive to the reaper, for good luck attended those who had their rigs sheared quickly if only because they avoided the ill-luck of being last. Stories are told of rigs being left unclaimed and uncut because their owners feared to incur 'the famine of the farm', of having the hag to feed until next harvest. The basis of this belief was that the last sheaf was sometimes hidden overnight in the corn of lazy farmers, who would watch at nights and reap by moonlight to avoid what was an omen of misfortune or death.

The last handful of standing corn, selected for the purpose,

162

was twisted into a three-stranded plait. Standing back at a mark, the reapers threw their spinning hooks at it in turn until it was severed and 'stretched'. At this a triumphant shout was raised. The cailleach was sometimes 'waked' before it was lifted: the 'corpse' was hung round the neck of the triumphant slayer, who was guest at the subsequent 'churn' (the harvest feast and dance) and who was fated to be the reaper who would be first married. It was, perhaps, more usual for the cailleach to be put around the neck of the master or mistress of the house. From the threat of being hanged by it they would purchase their freedom by providing the churn supper, for which special food was prepared. There are many variant practices but it is clear that they all turn on the same themes, the spirit of the corn and the luck of a speedy harvest. In some districts the cailleach was known as the hare, and the cry which kept the toiling shearers to their task was; 'We'll put the hare out of it today!'

It was customary to hang the churn in the kitchen, either over the door, on the dresser, or about the chimney hearth, and to keep it until the following harvest, when it was given to the cows. Or it might be fed to the horses on the first day of ploughing. In some houses the last sheaf was preserved year after year, and I have seen specimens half a century old. One of these was dressed with coloured papers, hinting that there was formerly more ceremony connected with the last sheaf than has survived. These dressed cailleachs figure in the harvest festival decoration in some churches in Co. Armagh, where also miniature corn ricks surmounted by a harvest knot are displayed, the Church thus having won over and preserved the pagan symbols of harvest (See Tailpiece).

Harvest knots or bows are decorative twists of straw which were worn by the harvesters, and are still quite commonly carried by young men at harvest time in some districts (Plate 13, 1). Girls would wear them in their hair, boys in their coats, and in former times they were exchanged by the sexes as a sign of mutual attachment. They are made in a fine plait of two straws tied into loops or interlaced, those worn by the girls having the ears of the corn left on. The best examples are made from wheat, and some exceptionally fine specimens are made from grasses and flax. The many practical uses of straw will be described in a later chapter and its employment in fashioning various kinds of dolls, ceremonial dresses and masks, for example on St. Briget's Day. Certain protective charms were also made of oat-straw, for example the Bratóg Brighde (St. Briget's rag or mantle) worn by the fishermen of Tory Island as a protection against storms. Here the explanation may lie in the power of wind over bits of loose straw which by association gives the straw the secret of controlling the wind. This is the basis of the phrase used in Co. Cavan to describe something which circulates quickly: 'going round like the straws'. It was the custom to ward off storms by running with a handful of straws from one farm to another.

With corn, as with hay and turf, the harvesting proceeds by building up stooks and ricks of increasing size according to the nature of the crop and the weather conditions. Little stooks (footings) of four or six sheaves are the first stage in the construction of the twelve-sheaf stooks (ten standing and two inverted hooding sheaves) which, however, are generally confined to wheat (Fig. 51). It is the general practice to build the little stooks of corn, after one or two weeks' seasoning, into hand-stacks which are of a convenient size to make a load for the rick-shifter, or for the tractor-lifter which is replacing it. The shapes of these miniature stacks, varying from one district to another, are often extremely picturesque, and their serried rows marching up the hillsides give the autumn fields a populated appearance. Their many names (hut, shig, bart, adag, and so on) would indicate that they are no novelty, and these little field stacks are as characteristic of Wales and Scotland as they are of Ireland (Fig. 52). A picturesque variety of hay-stack, commonly seen in Connacht, is the sheep-cock, built around a tall pole which prevents the cock from collapsing when eaten away at the base.

XIII

CARS AND CARTS

PEASANT communities concerned primarily with livestock which can be moved on the hoof have little need for elaborate means of transport. Long-tried devices adapted to the difficulties of the terrain continue to be used even in this age of tractors, and Ireland can show a remarkable variety of archaic farm vehicles of simple types. The heavy lumbering wagon would be out of place and out of scale in this environment. It is included in medieval inventories of manors and monasteries but it never took hold of the country, and although some landlords re-introduced English farm wagons in the eighteenth century, they were soon 'laid aside'.[1] The common Irish car was better adapted to the needs and skills of the people as well as to the condition of the roads.

The Irish low-back car, which is not yet extinct, is a light vehicle fitted with block wheels rigidly attached to a rotating axle (Fig. 55). Arthur Young commented that the loads they carried were 'such as an Englishman would be ashamed to take in a wheelbarrow'.[2] Yet he praised them because they required only one horse and did little damage to the roads. Prior to the eighteenth century there were very few roads except for those connecting the towns, and it seems that even the humble low-back cars were rare outside the urban spheres. For farm-work the wheel-less slide-car was used almost everywhere, supplemented by sledges, panniers, back-creels, and burden-ropes. It was progressive landlords who initiated, in the interests of the new agriculture, the construction of roads on their estates; and

[1]A. Young, Tour, 2, 22.
[2]ibid., 2, 59.

when the making and repair of 'cross roads' became a public charge it was done on the basis of baronies, and the Grand Juries—composed largely of landlords—became responsible, under the presentment system, for local road-making and repairing. Thus from about 1760 onwards a fairly close network of roads began to be established in the richer parts of the country—especially about the big demesnes—and the way was open for the more capacious spoke-wheeled cart which held its own until in our own day it is being replaced by the lorry and the tractor-trailer.

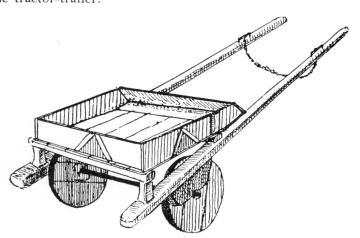

Fig. 55. Wheel-car, Co. Antrim.

In the face of abundant evidence as to the backwardness of rural transport and the rarity of wheeled vehicles and made roads until quite recent times, it is startling to read of the prominence of chariotry and of the rapid movement of armies in the Irish legendary histories. In fact, up to date, the archaeological evidence which would clearly establish the use of chariots in early Celtic Ireland is scanty. There can be little doubt, however, that horse-drawn spoke-wheeled vehicles were a significant element in Celtic culture, and it is known that the Romans took into their language nearly a dozen Celtic names for horse-drawn vehicles.[1] Such fragments of harness as have been re-

[1] E. M. Jope, *U.J.A.*, 13 (1950), 57–60.

covered from early Celtic sites in Ireland suggest that the horse was held in high regard and was perhaps reserved for pageants, combats and ceremonies. The detailed evidence in the legendary histories of ancient Ireland for the existence of roads, however, is clear. The fact that the Celtic roads are rarely traceable today is understandable in view of the physical conditions of the country, especially the prevalence of obliterating bogs. Moreover the road system must have decayed with the decline of Celtic culture. In any case it is evident that the use of the chariot was confined to the highest castes, and that its humble relation the block-wheeled car was fated to outlast it. The finely-spoked wheeled vehicles of the Celtic invaders were as much out of place in Ireland as the great wagons which later overlords introduced from England. The block-wheeled car, if not previously known in Ireland, may have been the native response to the impressive magic of the Celtic wheel, or it may have reached this country with Celtic camp-followers. We shall see that it could have been developed from the slide-car which almost certainly preceded it in Europe. The term 'wheel-car' as used in Ireland refers to the block-wheeled car and is clearly meant to distinguish it from the wheel-less slide-car. The spoke-wheeled cart is a newcomer in most parts. Nevertheless there is evidence that a light spoke wheeled cart continued to be used in early Christian times: an example drawn chariot-wise by two horses is figured on the eighth century Ahenny Cross in Co. Tipperary. It seems that such light carts were used for personal transport, for example St. Sampson took one with him, according to an eleventh-century account of his travels, to carry his books across Cornwall on his way from Ireland to Brittany.[1] And the spoke-wheeled cart must have been known in the planted areas since the Middle Ages, so that it is very probable that in parts of the country the cart has had a continuous life since early Celtic times.

But we should first examine certain archaic methods of transport which depend on the carrying power of beasts and men, or rather women, for in simple societies the bearers of children are also the burden-bearers. The romance of rural

[1] O. G. S. Crawford, 'Western Seaways' in *Custom is King* (1936), 196.

Ireland has so often been symbolized by a bare-footed colleen bashfully hiding behind a creel-carrying donkey that it comes as a shock to discover that the animal is a relative novelty in the Irish scene. There is no evidence of the use of the ass as a beast of burden in Ireland until the beginning of the nineteenth century. Professor Mahaffy, who wrote learnedly 'On the Introduction of the Ass as a Beast of Burden into Ireland',[1] pointed out that the little donkey was conquering Hibernia when the Great Duke was subduing Iberia. In fact asses came in to replace the Irish horses which were being drawn on in large numbers to maintain the British cavalry in the peninsular wars. Although they were apparently introduced, like so many other novelties, by way of Scotland, they proved unsuited to the comparative rigours of the climate of the northern coasts of Ireland, and it was in the west of the country that they fitted best into the physical and social environment. It is strange to reflect that a culture-trait so well adapted to a region which has ancient physical and human relations with Iberia should have been so long in reaching Lusitanian Ireland and should have got there by the back door, through Ulster.

Down to recent times, then, the horse—a pony, not a heavy cart horse—was the universal draught animal and beast of burden save where poverty or environmental difficulties imposed carrying duties on men, women and children. There were places such as soft bogs or slippery seashores where even pack-horses could not find a footing, and there went the women and children with their back-creels to carry the peats and sea-wrack. In spring, when the men were fully occupied with ridge-making, the transport of manure seems to have been the special task of the women, though in time the ass came to relieve them of this duty. The manure creels or pots (pardogs) of a fashion which has been recorded all along the Atlantic coastlands from Spain to Scotland, have a hinged or slip bottom which allows the load to be dropped where required (Fig. 56). Nowadays the creels are hung in pairs on the donkey's wooden straddle (pack saddle), and in the west it is no uncommon sight to see convoys of asses so laden picking their way from the dung-hill to the fields. I have also seen hay being transported by hanging

[1]*P.R.I.A.*, 33 (1916–17), 530–8.

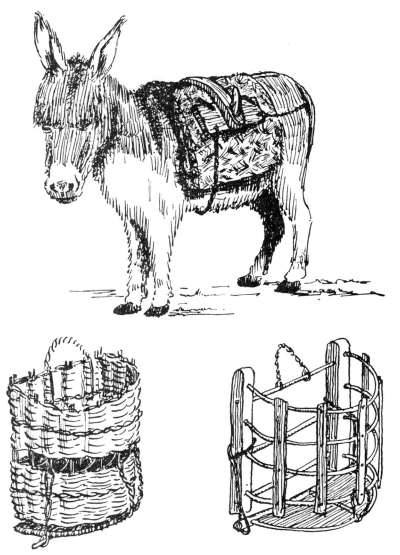

FIG. 56. Ass with straw pads and straddle, Co. Fermanagh. Creels with slip-bottoms for manure, Co. Galway and wrack, Co. Down.

tied bundles on to the straddle-pins, and both sheaves and firewood are occasionally carried on light V-shaped wooden frames. A similar carrying frame is known from Spain. There are several varieties of straddle, and a pattern found on Clare Island, in which one side engages in a hole bored through the other side, finds a parallel in the Shetland Islands and among the Lapps of north Norway: it could be of Norwegian origin. For long hauls the pack animal was undoubtedly the chief means of transport until the coming of the spoke-wheeled cart. For short distances the burden rope (Chapter XV) or the carrying creel was more convenient and it is still not uncommon to see the back-creel, the carrying basket or the hand barrow used for transporting turf or wrack over rough, soft or slippery ground (Fig. 57).

In some parts of the country, especially along the east coast, a form of sled fitted with a box body is kept for the transport

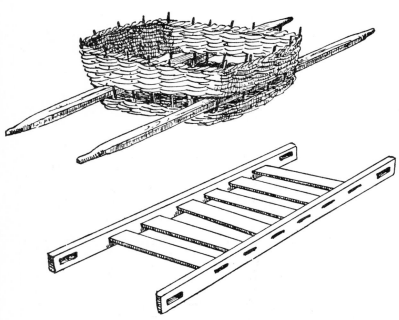

FIG. 57. Turf-basket, Co. Armagh and hand barrow, for carrying nets, Co. Antrim.

of manure, though it is also used for carrying earth on steep slopes where the soil is washed away and is tediously replaced. In this form of sled the runners are deep and set close together so that the load can be tipped out over the side (Fig. 58, 4). The sled or slipe is a transport-agent of remarkable versatility, ideally suited to small-scale operations involving heavy loads, and it persists because for some purposes no more convenient method of transport can be devised. In the apple-orchards of Co. Armagh, for example, a large, low box-slipe, involving little lifting of the apples, conveys the gathered crop to the store with a minimum of jolting, and it is frequently drawn by a tractor. Similarly the flat slipe finds its uses in hauling large stones in quarry and field, side by side with, and supplementing, elaborate modern machines. To the great advantage of its low body is added its suitability on slopes which are too steep or soils which are too sodden to take wheeled vehicles.

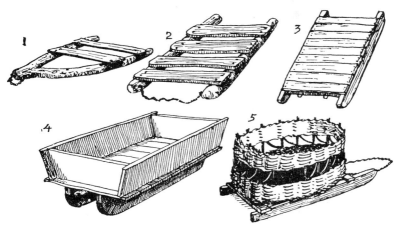

Fig. 58. Slipes. (1) Forked slipe, Co. Antrim. (2, 3) Stone slipes, Co. Down. (4) Manure slipe, Co. Down. (5) Turf slipe, Co. Antrim.

The simplest form of slipe consists of nothing more than a forked branch or young tree with a drag-chain secured to the point of the V (Fig. 58, 1). This forked sledge is not shod and it finds its principal use in moving large boulders from the fields. Some examples I have examined are made of holly which,

171

in addition to its strength, is reputed to have special sliding qualities. A forked slipe can be dragged over rough, trackless, boulder-strewn hillsides, where it will make and widen its own path as it goes. In such circumstances, given a favourable gradient, it can be man-hauled, and the persistent use of similar sledges for transporting large stones in other regions of megalithic culture such as the Dordogne—and indeed in Assam for surviving megalithic cults—hints that it comes down to us from very early times. The present distribution area of the forked sledge in Europe, from Scandinavia round to the western Mediterranean, can be correlated with many archaic culture-elements.[1] Its preparation calls for no tool more sophisticated than an axe—even a stone axe would suffice—and as I have watched huge stones being sliped from the fields I have easily imagined myself transported to a clearing in a long vanished Neolithic forest.

The standard flat slipe is a rectangular platform supported on two low parallel runners which may be shod with iron. It will be found on many farms and serves numerous purposes—for hauling stones, potatoes or turf, or for transporting the plough or the harrows from field to field (Fig. 58, 2, 3). There is, however, a simple, light slipe, made either of wood or of iron, which is kept specially for moving the wheel-less plough (Fig. 42). The wooden form finds exact parallels in Sweden and the east Baltic lands.

In the Antrim Glens, where topographic conditions and isolation have preserved an unusually full series of archaic vehicles, I have seen a light forked slipe loaded with sacks of peat being man-hauled, the forked end being lifted off the ground by a rope bearing on the puller's shoulder. This is in effect a slide-car, and although the Irish slide-car is always pulled by a pony, it may be noticed that the Swedish slide-car, used mainly for carrying hay, is often man-hauled. No doubt the forked form is the more primitive and there is some evidence to suggest that it was from a forked slide-car that the first European carts and wagons were evolved by the addition of

[1] E. E. Evans, 'Some Archaic Forms of Agricultural Transport in Ulster' in *Aspects of Archaeology* (Ed. W. F. Grimes), (1951), 108–23; J. M. Mogey and G. B. Thompson, *Man*, 51 (1951), 3–5.

wheels and a draught-pole. The body of the traditional ox-cart of Spain and many parts of India is suggestively triangular in shape.

The horse-drawn, wheel-less slide-car consists in its simplest form of two parallel poles, serving both as shafts and runners, fastened together by cross-pieces which form a carrying platform (Fig. 59). It was widely used down to the eighteenth century, but is now confined in distribution almost entirely to Ulster and in function mainly to the transport of turf from mountain bogs down steep tracks to the valley farms. For this purpose a large creel or kish is secured to the carrying platform, and it will take loads of potatoes or manure as required, but as a vehicle for general farm use the slide-car is now virtually extinct. That it has lingered so long in the mountainous corners of Ulster is perhaps due to the fact that the creel-carrying ass did not supplant it as it did in the milder south and west of Ireland (Pl. 8, 1).

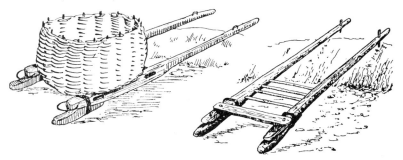

FIG. 59. Slide-cars, Cos. Tyrone and Antrim.

This primitive vehicle, which can be constructed entirely of wood—in treeless districts even bog-timber was utilized[1]—is of high antiquity and of great ethnographic interest. It has been contended that the one-horse wheel-car evolved from a slide-car to which a log roller had been fitted, and in view of the fact that the wheel-car has a revolving axle such an evolutionary sequence seems probable. Gösta Berg thinks that this evolution took place in the heart of Asia,[2] but there is the possibility that

[1]H. Dutton, *Clare* (1808), 65.
[2]Gösta Berg, *Sledges and Wheeled Vehicles* (1935), 140.

the block wheel was independently invented in north-western Europe, or at least adapted from the log roller as a native response to the novelty of the spoked wheel.

A feature of the Ulster slide-cars which distinguishes them both from Scots and Welsh examples and from most other slide-cars is the provision of separate wooden runners or 'shoes' which are pegged to the ends of the shafts and can be replaced when worn out. They have the effect of reducing somewhat the slope of the platform and its load. Formerly a special slide-car was kept for carrying corn, the sheaves being supported by a hooped frame of osiers which finds parallels in Sweden and Finland. Another archaic feature was the harness, which was constructed, until quite recent times, entirely of wood, straw and withies (Fig. 69).

Slide-cars, 'strange survivals from the twilight of history',[1] are found not only in Highland Britain and the Baltic lands but in many parts of east central Europe, in Siberia, China, Siam and the Indian Deccan. Such a distribution points to a dispersal in high antiquity, probably from western Asia. There is no direct archaeological evidence of ancient slide-cars but it has been plausibly argued that the well-known 'cart tracks' of Malta were made by slide-cars some 3,000 years ago.[2] This humble vehicle is well suited to simple societies, whose transport needs are few, and to country, especially hilly country, without made roads, where the wheel would be out of place.

In Ireland the wheel-car clings to the same districts as the slide-car and serves much the same purpose, but it may occasionally be used for longer journeys by road, for example to take an animal to the fair. (Slide-cars are very injurious to roads and were driven off them by ordinances against their use on the highways). On steep slopes the wheels, being secured to a rotating axle, act as a brake on each other. Measuring only some two feet in diameter, they are composed of three segments of wood dowelled together as in the oldest known Mesopotamian wheels, and shod with an iron hoop. They revolve under the car inside the shafts, so that the body must be raised to give clearance. It is supported by vertical struts morticed into the

[1] A. C. Haddon, *The Study of Man* (1898), 161.
[2] H. S. Gracie, *Antiquity* (1954), 91–98.

174

rear ends of the shafts, which are, however, left projecting so as to take the weight of the tilted car when it is not in use. It is these projecting shafts or 'trams' which give the wheel-car the appearance of a slide-car on wheels and seem to confirm the suggested evolution (Fig. 55).

In eighteenth-century Ireland possession of a wheel-car was a mark of social distinction, and entire districts were without wheeled vehicles of any kind. Down to the middle of the nineteenth century it was considered 'respectable' to go to 'meetings' in a wheel-car in the Presbyterian parts of north Antrim. In the course of the nineteenth century, as the larger spoke-wheeled cart was adopted by prosperous farmers, the little wheel-car sought refuge in the poor mountainous districts where we find it clinging precariously today. As late as the 1914–18 war one was in use on a farm on Black Mountain, within the city boundary of Belfast (Pl. 8, 2).

The wheel-car has its place in history because it was the ancestor of the nineteenth century jaunting-car which Lloyd Praeger rightly lists as one of the essentially native Irish products.[1] The platform of the wheel-car, to which a box body or a wicker-work creel was secured when goods were being carried, became a seat, covered with a straw mat, when the vehicle was used for social occasions. The passengers sat on each side, back to back, their feet dangling near the ground or resting on a hay-rope slung fore and aft, which could accommodate any length of leg. By the end of the eighteenth century this 'side-car', fitted with wooden foot-rests, had become a standard hiring vehicle, and it needed only the substitution of spoked for solid wheels, the addition of springs and consequent alterations of height to give the Irish jaunting-car which Bianconi adopted in 1815 and later developed into the four-wheeled long-car.[2] There can be no doubt that 'the Bians', traversing the highways and byways of the whole country, made a contribution to the social and economic life of Ireland which was, in its day, as important as that of the railway in the latter part of the century or the motor bus in the twentieth century.

The spoked wheel, which throughout the eighteenth century

[1] R. Ll. Praeger, *The Way that I Went* (1937), Ch. I.
[2] I. J Herring, *U.J.A.*, 3 (1940), 115–22; *U.J.A.*, 7 (1944), 42–46.

was reserved for coaches and the carriages of the rich, was popu-
larized by its adoption for farm carts (Scots carts) under the
improving zeal of landlords towards the end of the century.
In Ulster, which has always looked to Scotland for its inspiration, the Scots cart was first used for transporting linen, and
one thinks of it spreading along the improved roads and being
copied and adapted to local needs and traditions. Around
Lough Erne, for instance, one reads of large one-horse carts,
adopted by carriers in the early nineteenth century, which had
'trams' or rearshafts four feet long,[1] and these projections,
surely a reminiscence of the long slide-car runners, are still
characteristic of the 'flat' carts of the west and south-west (Fig.
60).

The Scots cart with its four-foot wheels was able to take twice
the load of the native wheel-car, and as industry increased and
roads were improved through the nineteenth century it drove
the block-wheeled cars off the roads. But for rough work in the
fields and bogs various types of slipe were preferred: the cart
was little used for harvesting and its possession was to some
extent a sign of prestige. (Unlike the native car, the woodwork
of the cart was and is brightly painted, usually in red and blue.)
The slipe and slide-car were better adapted to moist ground,
to undrained fields and the uneven surface of ridge and furrow.
As roads and farm practice were improved it was a new version
of Scots cart (Fig. 60) which ultimately drove out the slide-
car and the wheel-car in Ulster. It seems that the older varieties
of Irish carts were derived from the Leith cart of the eastern
lowlands of Scotland.[2] The body consisted of little more than a
slatted platform without fixed sides and ends. This 'flat cart',
as distinct from the 'box cart', is the usual pattern of farm cart
in the west of Ireland and, fitted with springs, is the common
hawker's cart. As a farm cart it suits the small farmer because
it can be used for a variety of purposes by fitting different kinds
of sides, for example tall slatted 'crates' for carrying turf.

Towards the middle of the nineteenth century there was
evolved, in Lanarkshire and the neighbouring counties, the box
cart with upright panelled sides perhaps derived from the

[1] L. Atthill, *Recollections of an Irish Doctor* (1911), 44.
[2] R. L. Edgeworth, *An Essay on the Construction of Roads and Carriages* (1813).

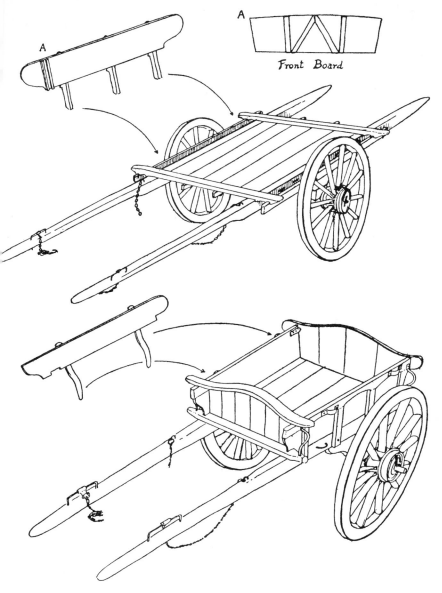

Front Board

FIG. 60. The Scots cart in Ireland. *Above:* the flat cart with projecting trams, Killarney, Co. Kerry. *Below:* the improved box cart, Cushendall, Co. Antrim (after G. B. Thompson).

177

wagon, a sturdy vehicle which was manufactured by large Scottish firms and exported far and wide and also copied locally. Its distribution can be readily traced because it carried an unusual design on the front board—the 'spectacles'—consisting of a pattern of linked circles out cut of an outer layer of horizontal boarding which is applied to the main vertical boarding of the front-board. The design is further emphasized by being painted a contrasting colour, red or blue. The spectacle design became a kind of trade-mark of the Lanarkshire style of cart. It may have evolved simply by the gradual enlargement of two curving strengthening boards at top and bottom, until they met to form a design which became standardized (Fig. 61). C. F. Tebbutt is inclined to seek an origin in the magic *oculi* such as occur in prehistoric pottery and to this day on Mediterranean boats, but it is difficult to see the connecting links.[1] If one looks for a more practical origin it could be argued that when freshly painted front-boards were first fitted to carts they were marked and damaged by the rump and tail of the horse. At any rate I have occasionally noticed a spectacle-like pattern rubbed by the horse on to the paint of Scots carts not fitted with the recessed front-board. On this theory the board was strengthened by means of panelling while at the same time the shaped recess gave the horse's rear a little more space and saved the paint.

In Ireland the Scots cart with 'fiddle' (spectacle) decoration has an interesting distribution corresponding closely with the area of historic Scottish influence, from east Down across Antrim to Londonderry and north Donegal. It has replaced the flat-cart over much of Ulster, but the latter survives in south Fermanagh, in an area where thatched houses with hipped roofs are also found, representing an older culture-layer. In Scotland it is found throughout the Highlands and Islands, in the central lowlands and the south-west. In eastern England the Scots cart has replaced older forms over a wide area extending from Lincolnshire to North Bedfordshire and from Essex to South-east Nottinghamshire. Mr. Tebbutt believes that it was first introduced to the fenlands by improving farmers who, in the second half of last century, looked to the Scottish lowlands as a model of farming methods. In all these areas the original

[1] C. F. Tebbutt, *Man*, 55 (1955), 113–17.

spectacle design was retained but in time instead of being panelled it was merely painted on the front-board. In Ulster carts of this kind, lacking the tilting device of the Scots proto-type, have been made until recent years by many local wheel-wrights, and it is interesting to notice how the original panelled design, which is present on old specimens, has been replaced by painted motifs which break up into many varieties, some of which are shown in Fig. 61. Mr. Tebbutt illustrates similar sequences of derived decoration on English carts.

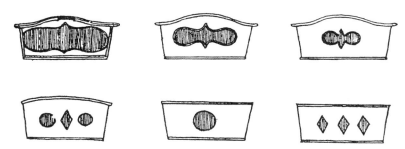

Fig. 61. The 'fiddle' design on the Scots cart in north-eastern Ireland. The front-boards illustrated are all from Co. Antrim and suggest both the derivation and the deterioration of the design. The upper examples are panelled and painted, the lower simply painted. The recess in the 'cape' of the first example is for the horse's tail.

The Scots cart with its box body, ideal for holding sacks of corn or potatoes, is not suited for carrying home crops, and both in Scotland and Ireland it is supplemented by a specialized harvest carrier known as the rick-shifter. This is a large plat-form with low wheels, fitted with a windlass by which the cock of hay or hut of corn is dragged into position on the platform. It is often dispensed with in moving hay cocks to the haggard, for they can easily be pulled or 'traced' along the ground simply by harnessing a horse to a chain placed around the base of the cock, a method which was used in the eighteenth century (Pl. 12). Six bullocks 'yoked as for ploughing' were employed for this purpose in Co. Meath.[1] The rick-shifter appears to have evolved

[1]W. Thompson, *Meath* (1802), 217. See also J. M. Mogey and G. B. Thompson, loc. cit.

from the platform carts of the East Scottish or Leith type. Edgeworth remarks in 1813 that carts of this kind were common in the Low Countries and many parts of France. What more likely than that this model should have reached Scotland by way of the port of Leith? The district bordering the Firth of Forth was an area of rapid agricultural improvement after 1750, and it was to it that Irish landlords turned for new ideas at the end of the century. The rick-shifter was probably evolved at some period from the same source, for Edgeworth tells us that the platform carts of the Low Countries were fitted with windlasses attached to the shafts. But it is risky to speculate on these matters: for example, a simple horse-drawn hay-rake, now rarely seen, used to be considered characteristically Irish and was popularly known as a 'tumbling paddy'. This rotating sweep is stated to have been introduced from America in 1850.[1]

[1]*Agricultural Implements and Machinery* (Science Museum), 1930.

XIV

TURF AND SLANE

IT should perhaps be explained that this chapter has nothing to do with horses, for the word *turf* in Ireland keeps its old meaning—as in German *torf* and French *tourbe*—and is the equivalent of the English word *peat*. Only in the extreme north-east of the country, in districts settled by Scots planters, does one hear turves cut from the bog referred to as peats. The cutting-spade, a highly specialized tool, is known as a turf-spade or sleán, a Gaelic word which may be anglicized as slane.

Moving about the Irish countryside one is never long out of sight or scent of turf. The scent arises not from the bogs themselves, which for all their accumulated decay are free of the odours of putrifaction, but from the surprisingly sweet smell of burning turf which announces their proximity. For the returning exile nothing so surely tugs at the trigger of memory: the faintest whiff of turf smoke hanging in the damp air is enough to recall the whole scene, the glowing fire on the hearth, the half-light of the kitchen, the great turf stack at the gable and all the toil that went to its making. And in the background is the bog itself, save at the cutting season a quiet empty place, holding a stillness which deepens when the curlew's cry fades away or the startled pipit drops back into the heather. Green and gold in spring, it beckons with waving bog-cotton in summer and glows with reds and russets as of a great peat fire in autumn. These are scents and scenes not readily forgotten.

The use of turf as fuel is nowadays an index of isolation and economic self-sufficiency. Mechanical excavation of fuel for power plants is being successfully applied by Bord na Mona (the Irish Turf Board) but for domestic fuel nothing can replace the costly hand-cutting, -wheeling, and -turning. The calorific value of peat is less than half that of coal, and its bulk makes transport costs high. Small coal-boats put in at harbours all round the coast, and in the larger towns, whose adjacent supplies were early exhausted, coal has been the chief fuel since the days when Dean Swift vainly advised the Irish to burn everything English except their coal. During the second world war, however, even Dublin had to depend on turf brought from the west and stacked in immense piles in Phoenix Park. Some peat is still burnt in the towns, especially in the interior of the country, but it is in the small farms that the bulk of the annual turf harvest is consumed. So necessary was a supply of peat in former times that proximity to a turf bog was a factor in land values. As to the antiquity of its use as fuel in Ireland we have little evidence, though Pliny describes its preparation in ancient Germany. Petty tells us in the second half of the seventeenth century that 'their fuel is turf in most places',[1] although Professor O'Brien, writing of the same century states that 'until the woods began to sink to very small proportions, turf was not at all employed for heating.'[2] The difficulty is that such a lowly pursuit as peat-cutting is not likely to be mentioned in the Irish law texts, and if we rely on documentary evidence alone we might suppose that all sorts of ancient practices were introduced by the English who first described them. To judge from the bright red ashes one frequently sees in the excavated hearths of Dark Age habitations peat was used as firing before history begins in upland areas and along the wind-swept coasts. But we may accept the view that over most of the country turf-cutting on its historic scale developed, probably under the stimulus of improved techniques brought in by English settlers, after the major forest clearances of the sixteenth and seventeenth centuries. There is evidence from some parts of the country, for the eighteenth century, that the cutting of peat for winter use was one of the occupations of transhumant herders who took their livestock to the bog pastures in summer.[3] But it is unreasonable to suppose that the great labour involved

[1]Sir W. Petty, *The Political Anatomy of Ireland* (1691), 82.
[2]G. O'Brien, *The Economic History of Ireland in the Seventeenth Century*, 44.
[3]W. Harris, *The Ancient and Present State of the County of Down*, 125.

would have been undertaken so long as supplies of timber were available, though Petty observed that 'the cutting and carriage of turf was easier than that of wood.'[1] We may think of turf as supplementing and then coming to replace wood fuel, though in fact some wood is still very desirable to supplement the slow-burning turf, especially the quick-burning gorse and bog-fir which are the most readily available sources in treeless areas.

It is calculated that at least one fifth of the country is coated with bog, but a small proportion of this could be classed as reclaimed bog. It occurs not only in all the mountain areas but also, and more conspicuously, in the ill-drained hollows of the lowlands where glacial deposits had blocked the natural flow of waters or human occupation had brought about environmental changes. It is estimated that in recent years over 5 million tons of dried domestic fuel have been cut annually, representing a weight as cut of some 40 million tons. At this rate the supply is reckoned to last for 500 years, but this makes no allowance for the increasing exploitation of peat for the thermal generation of electricity and for the extraction of by-products. There is, however, a slow accretion of peat in many areas, though this consists mostly of sphagnum peat and the good-quality fen and forest peats of the deeper bogs are not being replaced. In fact these deeper layers tend to remain untapped either because the water cannot be drained away, or because layers of tree-stumps defy the attacks of both spade and mechanical digger.

The main causative factor in bog-formation is waterlogged soil, which checks the decomposition of vegetable remains. It therefore depends to a considerable extent on climate and on the balance between precipitation and evaporation. It is generally held that past phases of bog-growth can be correlated with periods of climatic deterioration, and horizons which are believed to mark the changed conditions can be traced in most of the deep bogs. In Scandinavia the most important of such 'recurrence horizons' has been dated by pollen-analysts and archaeologists to about 400 B.C.: the stormy sub-Atlantic climate whose beginning is thus chronicled is believed to have improved somewhat early in the Christian era, but to have suffered two further periods of worsening about A.D. 400 and

[1]Sir W. Petty, op. cit., 82.

A.D. 1300. Attempts to extend this chronological scheme to cover Ireland have not been successful, and the current view is that some at least of the recurrence horizons should be attributed to ecologic changes brought about by human action which led to the redistribution of water and the blocking of drainage. Admittedly the basal Boreal peats of lowland bogs, and the Atlantic peats which succeeded them, must have been formed without any appreciable human interference, for in those periods traces of man are either absent or few and limited in distribution, but from sub-Boreal times onwards, after 2500 B.C., we have to reckon with human societies equipped with tools and domestic animals capable of working far-reaching changes in environmental conditions. The blanket bogs which cover the mountain slopes and in the west spread indiscriminately over hundreds of square miles of upland and lowland alike are admittedly associated with areas of heavy precipitation and high humidity, but the significant fact is that some of them can be shown to have been initiated in sub-Boreal times following extensive clearance of the woodlands which previously grew there. Walking over the upland bogs, I have stepped on to the roofing slab of a great stone monument which once stood seven feet clear of the ground: it had been completely engulfed in peat formed since its erection. Study of the bottom layer of this bog showed that it contained pollen grains of cereal type and of weeds of cultivation such as ribwort plantain.[1] Leaching of soils exposed by shallow cultivation and the formation of iron-pan seem to have followed human occupation of the sandy moraines and residual soils to which early man was attracted by their dryness and by the lightness of their forest cover. The extensive areas affected, despite the presumably small population, may be explained if we suppose that cultivation was temporary and that settlements were moved every few years.

These blanket bogs are rarely more than six or eight feet thick and many stretches have been reduced by turf cutting and erosion to a mere skin with occasional residual hags betraying their former depth. The so-called raised bogs of the lowlands, in contrast, are not easily cut-out: they are often very deep,

[1] G. F. Mitchell, *P.R.I.A.*, 53B (1951), 159.

averaging some twenty feet, and they have had a far longer life. In their natural condition their surface is slightly convex, and they may come to stand, perversely, above the level of the surrounding countryside, though they began life in ill-drained hollows where reeds grew to make fen-peat. These lower layers tend to be alkaline in nature and when the upper layers are cut away the bogs may be turned into productive cropland if adequate drainage can be provided. Small areas of this type occur to the south of Lough Neagh, but Ireland has nothing to compare with the English fenlands. Yet the Irish bogs take their place in the agricultural economy as summer grazing grounds, formerly for mixed stock and for cattle in particular, latterly mainly for sheep. In the past, too, considerable use was made of buried timber dug from the bogs,[1] of oak for roofing beams and of pine for kindling and resinous 'splits' to give light. The long 'trying iron' with which buried timber was located is shown in Fig. 66, together with the massive 'fir hatchet' and 'fir rooter'.

To the ecologist the bogs provide a unique field of research into the history of the occupation of the country by plants, animals and man. In the waterlogged depths of the peats everything is preserved, even the tiniest seeds and insects. Centuries of successive summers are chronicled in countless pollens of trees and grasses which the botanist can identify and thereby reconstruct the changes of vegetation from prehistoric times down to the recent past. When man appeared on the scene not only did he leave his pathways and possessions in the bogs, but, as we have seen, he was an agent in their growth. His tools of stone and copper, bronze and iron, evolving in that order, are found lying at levels which can be correlated with the vegetation-history by analysing the pollens that cling to them. Thanks to the labours of Knud Jessen and Frank Mitchell we now have an approximate chronological sequence of landscapes and human cultures in Ireland going back several thousand years.

The pollen grains from the lowest layers of the upland bogs include those of shrubs such as hazel, birch, rowan and thorn, as well as, occasionally, those of cereals and the weeds of cultivation. Evidently the clearings soon became threatened with forest and field weeds, and these companions of the earliest

[1] E. E. Evans, *Irish Heritage*, 142; A. T. Lucas, *Béaloideas*, 23, 71–134.

farmers, both the flowers of the fields and the shrubs of the forest edge, took on a special significance which they have retained in the peasant mind to the present day. There is powerful magic in the flowers of May, in the hazel twig, the fairy birch, the rowan branch and above all in the flowering hawthorn. This most beautiful of trees first became common in the Neolithic period. In a later chapter we shall consider some of the enduring spiritual aspects of man's association with this environment of his own making. At about this time, too, when the Neolithic economy was both absorbing the older population and being supplemented by metal tools, pollen studies reveal a marked decline of the elm tree which has been explained by the use of its bark and branches as cattle fodder. The oak forests, however, persisted in strength, and were presumably treasured for their supply of pig-fattening mast. Alder also was abundant, occupying soils which were too damp to be cultivated.

The onset of the sub-Atlantic climatic deterioration in the last millennium B.C. seems to have accelerated the peat-forming processes. Both oak and elm decline, but the birch tree spreads widely. In County Antrim, for instance, extensive oak forests growing up to heights of 1,000 feet were overwhelmed in the spreading bogs. The pine had become rare by the end of prehistoric times, though it may have lingered into the historic period on sandy eskers and on the dried surfaces of some of the raised bogs. Despite climatic change and human interference, considerable oak and alder forests survived here and there into the seventeenth century, but these last remnants of the Irish forests were almost all destroyed by the military and economic demands of that troubled century. Among the many consequences was the almost universal exploitation of the peat bogs for fuel. In addition great quantities of turf were consumed by the linen bleachers from the late eighteenth century, and kilns for burning lime and bricks and for drying agricultural produce made considerable demands on the bogs. A minor traditional use which may be mentioned in passing was for the preparation of charcoal for smith's work. The peat was charred in pits.

For all its toil turf-cutting provides a welcome break from the routine of farmwork, a time when friends and neighbours come together away from the familiar surroundings of fields and houses. There is a marked loosening of inhibitions at this time. The occasion is something of a festival, of picnic meals and keen appetites, so that tea is said to taste better at turf-cutting than at any other time. After the March winds and the lengthening days of spring have dried the bog surface there is a stirring in the homesteads, the well-worn tools are pulled out of their hiding-places and the smith is kept busy repairing spades and barrows. Bright new tools litter the town pavements on fair day, and the countryman chooses his new slane with an exhibition of caution that seems superfluous until one remembers that an ounce of weight or an inch of length can make the difference between smooth ease and back-break. April, everywhere the driest month of the year, is the best month for cutting: an early start gives the turves a better chance of drying, but the planting of crops keeps the men busy till the end of the month, so that May is the likeliest time to see them in the bogs. There is an old belief that to facilitate drying, peat should be cut when the moon is waning (Pl. 9, 1).

A whiff of turf smoke drifting from a hidden fire where the tea is brewed is the first sign that the bog is peopled. If it is a deep bog you will look in vain for signs of activity, but once you have been seen dozens of heads pop up from deep cuttings and the diggers welcome a break for a smoke and a 'crack'. Turbary rights are extremely complicated, but with the decreasing demand for turf there is little dissension even when banks are communally owned. Nowadays each family generally has its own bank or cutting-face, but it is customary for two or three families to pool their labour and work at each bank in turn. The owner of the bank by tradition provides food for the helpers. On the average a week's cutting provides sufficient fuel for each family, but the time taken and the amount required depend on the nature of the bog and on the quality of the turf. Ideally the season's cut should contain a proportion of brown top turf, that is light sphagnum peat for summer firing, and a proportion of black bottom peat for winter use: this is moist humified peat which dries hard as a brick and burns almost like coal. The amount required is measured by the load, that is the load of a small one-horse cart. I was told in Donegal that a good team of four men, cutting, lifting, wheeling and spreading, could account for twenty-five loads in a day, but, my informant added, 'they would need to be strong in the back and weak in the head'; as at corn harvest competitive cutting and 'striving' brought intense excitement and severe strain.

'Opening up' a bank involves first of all the removal of the top layer of tough fibrous peat—'flow' or 'fum'—to a depth of a foot or so. It grows heather, tough grasses or mosses and makes poor firing, though there are districts, especially on the islands, which have exhausted their turf and burn nothing but the even more fibrous sods or 'rough-heads' skinned off the rocks. The common spade is usually employed for opening a face, supplemented often by a sharp nicking tool, a hay-knife or a portion of an old scythe-blade hafted for the purpose. In parts of north Ulster the thin top-layer of the mountain bogs is removed with a small variant of the breast-plough known as a flachter or flaying-spade, one of the tools which this region shares with western Scotland (Fig. 45). The term breast-plough is a euphemism, for it is really a groin-plough, pushed forward by thrusts of the thighs and groin.

The bog parings are generally spread on the cut-over bog below the bank, where they give a dry footing for the barrow-men wheeling away the turves. The pared sods in time consolidate, so that the rough grazing of the bog is preserved at a lower level. Conditions vary considerably from one bog to another, and so do the methods of working and the shapes of the tools. The minutiae of the craft are so perfected that a team of diggers works with the rhythm of a machine. Strong arms are required—a single turf may weigh up to 20 lb. when cut—but experience and a good eye are necessary for speed, and skilled 'slanesmen' are becoming scarce. Great importance was attached to 'keeping a straight face', that is keeping the cutting face vertical, and a poor digger was referred to as a 'clod-cutter'. To break a turf was almost a crime: in the old days 'they'd have thrown you out of the bog'. Not only do broken turves double the handling each time they are lifted or turned, but they tend to break adjacent turves when stacked, and the stack will show by its shape if the turf has been badly cut. At the end of the bank it is customary, in the north, to leave three steps of turf uncut. They enable one to scramble out on to the uncut bog above, but one suspects that behind the custom there lies the widespread notion that a task should never be completely finished and that a small portion of anything taken by man should be left for luck or the fairies. You will be told that the steps are cut to avoid the curse of Columbkille, for it is said that the saint was once trapped in a bog hole and laid a curse on all who did not cut the three steps.

There are two methods of cutting, vertically or 'underfooting' and horizontally or 'breasting', and they tend to be used respectively on thin upland and deep lowland bogs, though these have to be cut underfoot if badly drained unless a platform or 'footgo' of flow turf can be built up for the breaster to stand on. Also, the upper layers of brown turf which preserve some of the tough plant fibres are easier to cut vertically. Breasting not only imposes less strain on the back but speeds up the work, since the turves can be retained on the slane and placed directly on the barrow. (The vertical digger can do this only if his spade has a lift, that is bends forward.) In consequence the breast-cutter's turf-barrow will be designed for his convenience, for example it commonly has no legs so that he can swing it into position laterally by hooking the wing of his spade over the handle. Slanes, as well as barrows, will be found to vary in some slight degree from one bog to another, and a seemingly trivial difference can generally be explained in terms of differences of local conditions and techniques: the human ecology of the bogs is no less interesting than the plant ecology. In essentials the turf slane is a narrow straight-shafted steel blade with a wing set at right-angles after the manner of a cheese-knife, which is said, indeed, to owe its origin to 'an ingenious cutler of Dublin' who borrowed the idea from the slane.[1] The purpose of the wing is to detach a complete turf at a single stroke of the spade. The breadth and length of blade and wing are variables depending on many factors, but mainly on the size of turf required, and this in turn is determined to a considerable extent by the nature of the bog. If it is a very wet bog, for example, the turves must be cut larger than normal to allow for greater shrinkage on drying. When absolutely dry peat will shrink to less than one-eighth its original volume, and though air-dried peat still contains

[1] Thomas Campbell, *A Philosophical Survey of the South of Ireland*, 96.

about 25 per cent water, when cut it may have 90 per cent or more. Again, some kinds of peat come away easily so that the turves can be cut somewhat larger than the dimensions of the slane, which for ease of working is naturally made as small and light as possible.

Increasingly in this as in every other department of rural labour, standardized implements are gaining ground, but the Irish spade factories still cater for scores of different tastes. When slanes were smith-forged almost every turf-cutter had his individual tool, made to measure. The factory-made slane weighs about 3¾ lb., but the old-style slane was merely a thin sheath of steel wrapped around a wooden blade and weighing about 1½ lb. It comprised four parts, blade, spade-tree, shaft and hilt, though shaft and spade-tree were sometimes in one piece, the shaft flattening out to enter the blade in a long 'web' (Fig. 62, 1). The thick round shaft, which had to be truly centred in the blade, was polished smooth as a piston with peaty sweat rubbed in. The two-piece haft, with separate spade-tree (No. 2), gave a certain springiness which eased the work. In the same

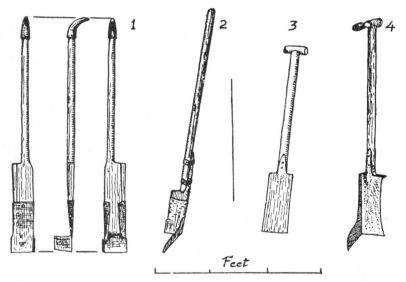

Feet

FIG. 62. Slanes old and new. Nos. 1 (Co. Antrim) and 3 (Co. Down) are breast spades; Nos. 2 (Co. Galway) and 4 (Co. Londonderry) are underfoot.

way a separate hilt, frequently a cow's horn well polished by use, saved the strain on the palm of the hand, but many slanesmen preferred a handle shaped to their own taste and to the needs of the cutting technique required. In the Antrim Glens I have seen a bent piece of black sally carefully spliced on: this wood is said to have the virtue of absorbing sweat. The blade itself widens towards the cutting edge which is from four to six inches in width, the splay preventing the spade from sticking in the wet peat. The cutting edge of the wing is anything from four to seven inches long, and the top edge is finished in a variety of pleasing shapes and is often notched with the proprietary marks of the owner.

A breast slane can as a rule be distinguished from the underfoot by the upward slant of the cutting edge of the wing as viewed from the side with the spade held vertically, whereas the wing of the underfoot slane slopes down. This ensures that the face of the bog which is left after cutting shall be vertical when breasting and horizontal when underfooting, for the strokes are naturally made with a slight downward slope in the former case and a forward slope in the latter. Another difference is that the underfoot slane is normally provided with a foot-step on one side or the other, depending on whether the user is left or right handed. In practice the foot is not used, however, unless the peat is very tough and little humified. Bits of fibrous matter (called fog, cat or 'old wife's tow') clogging the cutting edge are troublesome, but it is kept clean by a quick preliminary jab into the peat, which reminds one of the rhythmic anvil-tapping of the blacksmith. Modern slanes tend to have the blade made all in one piece, riveted to the haft with straps and fitted with a narrow foot-plate on the side away from the wing. (Fig. 62, 4.) The breast slane has been partly replaced, especially in wet bogs, by a short-handled flat spade which cuts larger peats (Fig. 62, 3). They are of a good shape for stacking and for transport on the canal-boats and, latterly, the lorries which supply Dublin with turf.

For taking the cut peats to the spread-field two wheelers and turf barrows are the minimum needs. The severed turves may be placed directly from the spade on to the waiting barrow, but a loader is more often required, lifting two turves at a

time: his finger marks can still be seen when the dried turves
are burning in the fire. In deep bogs the lifter may use a long-
handled fork (Fig. 66, 2) or shovel, pitching the turves for the
barrowman to load. A barrow load is anything from ten to
twenty peats. Apparently crude and artless, the turf barrow is
well designed for its purpose, and it shows many adaptations
to local conditions and traditions (Fig. 63). It is slatted for
lightness and is made almost entirely of wood, yet it must be
strong enough to take heavy loads over rough ground: it should
be low and flat for convenience in loading and unloading, yet it
needs a large broad wheel for pushing over an uneven surface.
Legs may be dispensed with, reduced to lugs or swept back to
serve as runners. Again the shape of the handles and the slope
of the front board depend on the method of loading and tipping,
over the side or over the front. Every detail of the design is in
answer to a general or local problem. If the ground is very
rough or soft the barrow must be pulled, not pushed, and in
extreme cases its place is taken by a slipe. In Antrim alone there
are several varieties of turf slipe. All are slatted lengthwise—
because the peats are loaded transversely—and are fitted with
short corner posts and tipping handles. An interesting variant—
the roller slipe—has been recorded but is no longer seen: it had
two rollers fitted under the body of the sledge.[1] The dried peats
also may be transported, if the bog is soft, on a slipe (Fig. 58, 5)
or in a carrying basket (Fig. 57).

Despite ingenious shifts towards greater speed the spreading
and drying of turf are inefficient because of the time taken in
wheeling and handling and the great difficulty of drying turf
which is spread on almost saturated surfaces. In exceptionally
wet summers the peats do not dry out, and tragedy may follow
if the winter is severe. It is then that the countryside is stripped
of what little timber it can provide, and before coal was obtain-
able anything from furniture to fishbones and cowdung was
utilized to boil the pot. In bogless districts dung was quite
regularly used: there are several accounts of it in travel records
of the seventeenth and eighteenth centuries. Indeed in the treeless islands dung was until recently carefully harvested, gathered
in piles in the fields in spring, and sometimes worked with the

[1] E. E. Evans in *Aspects of Archaeology* (Ed. W. F. Grimes), plate 2A.

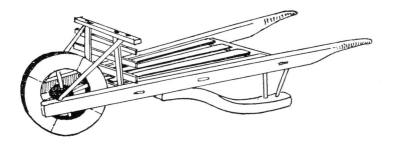

FIG. 63. Turf barrows from Cos. Meath, Donegal and Antrim.

hands into cakes and piled against a wall until dry enough to carry home.[1]

After lying spread on the ground for a week or two the turves are footed, that is a dozen or so are put to lean together in the shape of a pitched roof, to catch the wind (Fig. 64). This is work for women and for children, who are, in some districts, given a week's holiday from school. Through the months of June and July and often into August there is constant coming and going as the peats are turned and built into larger and larger piles, turn-foots, castles, rickles, lumps and clamps— the names and the shapes show considerable regional variation —until they can be ricked or stacked on the bog ready to be carried to the farms as opportunity offers. The wind is the main drying agent, and once dried the peats acquire a waterproof skin. A well-built stack will throw off the rain, but it is usual in the west to thatch with rushes and add a coping of sods or stones against the wind. Open-sided turfsheds specially built of wood or stone are the exception rather than the rule. A favourite place for the stack is against the house gable, where it provides a protective warmth even before the turf is burnt. The fuel is taken into the house in baskets, creels or wights, and a small supply is kept handy by the fireside or stored, as in the Aran Islands, on the kitchen loft (Pl. 9, 2).

Fig. 64. Stages in the drying and stacking of turf (not to scale; the stack, right, is about 9 feet high).

Some lowland bogs are too waterlogged to be cut into turves, and if no slane-turf is available the black turf-mud is moulded by hand into bricks or balls which are stacked to dry. In some counties, for instance Meath and Cavan, mud turf is highly prized and its preparation follows a well-ordered routine. After

[1]C. R. Browne and A. C. Haddon, *The Aran Islands.*

removing the sods over a rectangular area the turf is dug over to a spit's depth and worked into a slush with forks and bare feet, water being added if necessary. The slush is shovelled into box barrows and spread out to dry in a layer about nine inches thick. The process is repeated, a spit at a time, until the bottom of the bog or the water table is reached. After a few days, when the layer of black mud is hard enough to bear a man's weight, it is marked out in criss-cross grooves made with the edges of the hands, the bare-footed 'baker' or 'runner' walking backwards during the process and dipping his hands from time to time in water to clean them (Plate 10). The turf bricks marked out in this way are separated with a sharp spade, much as the Romans are said to have cut out their bricks, and they are then laid on end, footed, clamped and stacked in the ordinary way. Gerald Boate's description of the making of mud turf in the first half of the seventeenth century shows how little the methods have changed. 'They fall to the business, dividing it so among the labourers, that one part of them do dig out the earth, or rather the mud, and by spadesfull cast it on a heap, either by the side of the pit or somewhere within the same, where others stand, who very well work it, turning it to and fro, and then with their shovels fill it into certain wooden trays, amongst the English in Ireland peculiarly called lossels; the which being full, another part of the labourers draw the same, with great cords fastened to them, to some dry place within the bog . . . where having poured out the mud, they go back to fetch more, and so go to and fro all day long. On that dry place . . . sit certain women upon their knees, who mould the mud, using nothing else but their hands . . . the turf is fashioned flat and broad beneath, growing narrower towards the top; which being done, the turf is let lie upon the ground the space of a week or more . . . and being reasonably well dried, it is piled up in little heaps, leaving everywhere empty spaces between, that the air and the wind passing through them, they may dry the sooner.' He adds that two women moulders were sufficient to keep twenty men at work.[1]

From time to time the worker in the bogs comes across objects lost or buried there as the bog was growing, and we saw above

[1] G. Boate, *Ireland's Natural History* (1652), 155.

how these are used by the pollen-specialists to build up a bog chronology. Some, like the magnificent gold ornaments of the Bronze Age, were deposited in the bogs, or in lakes where the bogs later grew, for magical purposes. Other objects were sometimes hidden in the hope of being recovered, and still others were thrown into a bog hole when they were worn out. All have been almost perfectly preserved by the peat, whether made of metal or organic material such as wood, leather or clothing. None of the discoveries which occasionally astonish the turf-cutter and relieve the monotony of his labours is more mysterious than the 'bog butter' which is found in wooden vessels or baskets, occasionally in containers of cloth, bark or skin, in quantities ranging from a few pounds to as much as a hundredweight (Fig. 65). During the first half of last century,

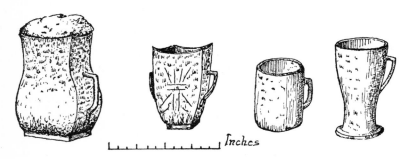

FIG. 65. Methers and wooden cups (Belfast Museum). The first example, from Co. Londonderry, contains bog butter. The cups are from the Aran Islands.

when the pressure of population and industrial needs led to immense inroads on the turf bogs, an astonishing number of finds was made. The 'butter' was a perquisite of the finder, and there are records of its being taken to the fair to be sold as grease for wheel-cars, which, like the 'singing carts' of Spain, were very noisy. In fact it resembles lard rather than butter and analysis shows that its composition has changed, but there can be no doubt that it was originally butter. There are many references to the practice of burying butter in bogs in the seventeenth and eighteenth centuries, and the explanations offered are also many. Petty thought it was done in order to make the butter rancid, since the Irish, he says, preferred strong butter.[1] An eighteenth century writer states that some of the buried butter was

> So strong, a dog with help of wind,
> By scenting out, with ease might find.[2]

Others have claimed that it was buried to mature and purify it, and one writer has seen an explanation in the need to have butter available at Lent. It is reasonable to suppose that the surplus butter of summer would be stored in this way once the preservative properties of peat were known, but the practice is certainly pre-Christian in origin. None of the Irish finds has been securely dated—the majority of the wooden containers have an ageless 'medieval' appearance—but a discovery in Skye was satisfactorily dated to the very beginning of the Christian era (it contained not only cowhairs but some strands from the head of a fair-haired dairymaid).[3] I am inclined to think that a practice which came to be generally adopted for utilitarian reasons had its origin in magic, and that deposits were originally made in the hope of appeasing the powers of evil and inducing an abundant flow of milk from the pastures.[4] The custom may well have originated during the crisis of the climatic deterioration in the last centuries of the pre-Christian era. Surviving folklore is full of the magic properties of butter, and in the west of Ireland it is known that lumps of butter were thrown into loughs and springs through which cattle were driven in order to restore them to health. It seems from the accounts of discoveries in the bogs that some of the butter containers had been thrown into a bog hole rather than buried. Later, no doubt, it became the practice to bury butter in order to preserve it, but if this had always been so I cannot think that there would have been so many unclaimed deposits left to await the slane of the turf-cutter. It should be noticed that the custom of preserving butter in bogs or in moist earth is found also in Scandinavia, Iceland, India and Morocco.[5] It is interesting that bog butter

[1]Sir W. Petty, *The Political Anatomy of Ireland*, 82.
[2]W(illiam) M(offatt), *The Western Isle*, Canto 2.
[3]J. Ritchie, *P.S.A.S.*, 75, 5–22.
[4]E. E. Evans, *U.J.A.*, 10, 59–65.
[5]ibid., 59.

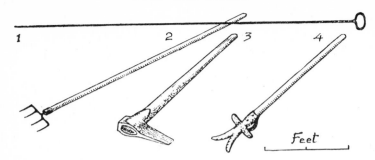

F<small>IG</small>. 66. Some tools used in the bog. (1) Trying iron for locating buried timber, Co. Cork. (2) Turf fork, Co. Armagh. (3) Fir-hatchet or 'finhow', Co. Armagh. (4) Fir-rooter, Co. Galway.

contains no salt, but the explanation may be that it was difficult to obtain and that its addition was not necessary when the butter was preserved by burying it. This is confirmed by the following quotation which shows also that the custom of preserving butter in a bog-hole was still remembered a generation ago in Co. Limerick. Lady Carbery writes: 'In their grandfather's time, butter, flavoured with wild garlic and unsalted (salt cost too much to buy except in small quantities) used to be put in a bog-hole and left to ripen.'[1]

[1]M. Carbery, *The Farm by Lough Gur*, 128.

XV

HOME-MADE THINGS

UNTIL the agrarian and industrial revolutions broke up economic self-sufficiency nearly every material need on the small farms was satisfied by the work of the family and the local community. Houses, furniture, food, clothing, simple implements and tools were home made or home produced. The most important specialist was the maker of edged tools, the blacksmith who thus occupied a special position in the community. His forge, customarily placed at a cross roads near running water, was never locked and became a rallying centre for idle men on wet days and for dancing in the evenings. His strength and skill were proverbial and magic powers were attributed to him and to the forge water. The smith was the first person to be invited to social functions. Not being a food producer he was, like the seers and later the priests, entitled to tribute of corn and first fruits. When a beast was slain the head was the perquisite of the smith. The ancient laws prescribe in detail the allotment of the various parts of the carcase to different offices, and the smith's right was maintained down to recent times. George Petrie, the nineteenth century antiquarian, is reported to have said that he remembered the time when a smith might have 50 or 100 heads of cows and pigs pickled in his kitchen.[1] Other craftsmen were itinerant because they could not be supported by the work available in any one district, and the last

[1] See Stephen Gwynn, *The Fair Hills of Ireland* (1906), 219. The method of dividing a carcase is thus described about the year 1600: the head, tongue and feet to the smith, the neck to the butcher, two small ribs that go with the hindquarters to the tailor, the kidneys to the physician, the udder to the harper, the liver to the carpenter and sweetbread to her that is with child. *C.S.P.* (*I*) (1601–3), 684. Dr. Johnson refers to the custom in the account of his journey to the Western Isles: cf. Martin Martin, *The Western Isles*, 171.

survivors of these wandering folk are the tinkers, sworn enemies of the farmers but useful in many ways to the farmers' wives. Though miscalled gypsies they are of native Irish stock and have little, if any, Romany blood. Numbering between 5,000 and 6,000 but declining, they now find little scope for their traditional skill as white smiths but subsist mainly on collecting scrap metal and dealing in horses. Down to recent times their services were in demand for making and repairing the stills in which home-made whiskey (poteen) was manufactured. Weavers and tailors as well as tinkers were despised by farming folk as 'travellers', whereas the smith was held in high esteem.

Most of the home industries depended on wood and other plant products, natural or cultivated, and on the skin and hair of animals. Nearly all these crafts are now dead or dying and their products, perishable by nature, are either gone or fast disappearing. A few skills live on, others survive in children's pastimes or in the memories of old people. The unwritten lore of the countryside included a vast store of information on all the varied trees, plants and animals, birds and fishes which in times past played their part in the lives of the people. Nearly every species had its practical, medicinal or magical uses, and through careful observation, empirical knowledge and a wealth of poetic fancy, a vivid interest in the world of nature was maintained and passed on from one generation to another. Much of this lore has been lost with the decline of the Gaelic tongue and the spread of formal education and book-learning. The country school must conform to a clerk-breeding curriculum designed to meet urban demands. The destruction of woodland and the debasement of standards of living which followed the adoption of the alien potato and the consequent famines had serious consequences on home crafts. Then mass-produced goods came to drive out many products which depended on a discriminating knowledge of local materials. Thus barbed wire has taken the place of its rustic prototype—a hay-rope strung with thorns—and binder-twine has killed a dozen varieties of home-made ropes and thongs. The economist might think of them as bonds tethering rural communities to the soil, but to the sociologist they imply spiritual as well as physical links with mother earth.

By far the most versatile of home-produced rope-making materials is straw. Rye straw is longer, softer and more flexible than any other, but very little rye is now grown save along the west coast where it is still the most popular thatching material. Wheat straw is the best substitute, but in fact most farmers must now depend on oat straw, thus 'tying up' some of their fodder. Straw rope (súgán) not only had many direct uses but served as the basis for such crafts as the making of mats, baskets, bee-skeps, mattresses, hen roosts, pigeons' nests and horse harness. It was used for seating chairs and making arm-chairs, and for a great variety of hobbles and tethers for animals and ties for holding down thatch. The fondness of the Irish for tethering and hobbling their livestock must be seen in the light of inadequate fences and the conditions of partnership farming in open fields. Not only the larger animals, but hens, turkeys, and geese were commonly restrained in this way. 'All livestock of the poorer man is in this sort of thraldom' wrote Arthur Young.[1] One may still see a tethered hen with her chickens that might have stepped out of the illuminated pages of the fourteenth century Luttrell Psalter. A straw rope stretched across the kitchen made a serviceable clothes-line. Torches were sometimes made from twisted straw; on the other hand, when suitably coated with mud, straw ropes made a fireproof smoke-canopy. Chopped straw or layers of straw ropes were also used in constructing mud walls, and it is possible that, as in Sweden, stakes wrapped in straw rope daubed in clay were once an alternative to 'wattle and daub' for wall building. It has been stated that the fowlers of the Mayo coast would let themselves down the cliffs on straw ropes,[2] which must have been exceptionally well made; ropes made from the fibres of bog fir were more reliable. In Co. Antrim fowling ropes were of horse hide, but bent ropes are also recorded.[3] I have seen countrymen on a windy fair day wearing an improvised belt over their long coats in the form of a straw rope, and in the early nineteenth century children in Co. Cork were described as 'clad in nothing except a coarse woollen shirt that came half way down the thighs and

[1]Arthur Young, *Tour*, 2, part 2, 37.
[2]P. Knight, *Erris in the Irish Highlands*, 55.
[3]R. Dobbs, *County Antrim in 1683*.

was bound about the waist with a suggan of straw.' The Rev. Philip Skelton was said by his biographer 'in cold weather, to go through Pettigo with a straw rope about him, to keep his large coat on.'[1]

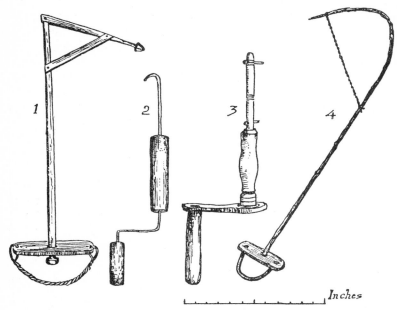

FIG. 67. Rope-twisters. (1) Co. Kerry. (2) Co. Antrim. (3) Co. Armagh. (4) Co. Down. Nos. 1 and 4 are the old-style 'thraw-hooks'.

Short lengths of rope ('thumb-ropes' of hay or straw) are skilfully twisted by hand or, if the material is fine, made by wrapping it round a stick and pulling it out, but a simple tool of ancient lineage, the throw-crook or thraw-hook, is employed when long ropes are needed: it is known also in England and in Scandinavia. A twister of cranked wire resembling a carpenter's brace has, however, largely replaced the wooden hook; it is more tiring but requires less skill (Fig. 67). I have seen a wooden hayrake serving as an improvised thraw-hook. The prepared ropes are wound into golden balls (clews) up to two

[1]S. Burdy, *The Life of Philip Skelton*, 131.

fcet in diameter. (Small, carefully made clews of hay rope, with a centre of rags or corks, are occasionally used as footballs; similar coils of rope in England seem to be oval in shape and would serve rather as balls for Rugby football.) Laying by a stock of clews was a useful occupation for a wet day. The man of the house chose the sedentary end of the rope, sitting under cover in the barn among the thrashed straw and feeding it evenly into the rope as the other end was twisted by a retreating youth armed with a thraw-hook. As the rope grew, the boy had to withdraw into the rain away from the shelter and the sociability of the barn, and this simple scene is the theme of one of Douglas Hyde's Irish plays, *Casadh an tSugáin* (The Twisting of the Rope). A rival suitor makes love to a girl in the barn while the unfortunate twister is forced by his unco-operative employer to watch the proceedings from the end of a lengthening and apparently endless rope.

Hay ropes are both softer and stronger than straw and were used, for example, for parts of the harness where straw ropes would have chafed and broken. They were naturally employed for securing large cocks of hay (tramp cocks, Fig. 52) against the wind; and tethers for young animals were often made of hay rope. A Donegal landlord writing of the early nineteenth century tells of cabbages tethered against the wind with three hay ropes.[1] The shearing rope, four or five feet long, by which the legs of sheep were tied together when clipping the wool, was also made of hay or marram grass. Here we may take note of the curious practice of piecemeal shearing, recorded from Mayo[2] and Donegal[3] and possibly to be attributed to ancient usage rather than to indolence. It seems that the women were in the habit of clipping bits off the sheep at any season, as they needed the wool. Stronger than ropes of straw or hay are those made of rushes or sedges, and stronger still those of fir, heather, birch twigs, willow bark, horsehair or rawhide. Bog fir ropes were still being twisted in north Antrim, a few years ago, for securing thatch and making bed-frames. Ropes were made even from seaweed, as we shall see in the following chapter. Many

[1] J. Hamilton, *Sixty Years Experience*, 19.
[2] C. R. Browne, *Garumna and Lettermullen*.
[3] Lord George Hill, *Gweedore*, 24.

of these rope-making materials had other uses as well, not forgetting their functions in ceremony and magic as represented by Briget's crosses, harvest knots, the blaeberry baskets of Lammas and the rush ladders of Hallowe'en. Better known, though no longer made, are the rushlights whose feeble glow, in the words of Gilbert White, made 'darkness visible'.

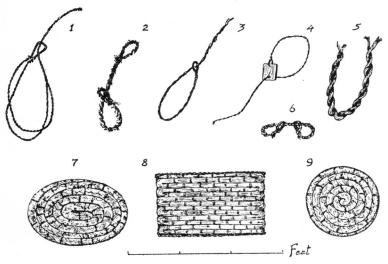

FIG. 68. Ropes and mats. (1) Rush burden rope, Co. Donegal. (2) Tie of cow-hair, Co. Kerry. (3) Willow bark burden rope, Co. Roscommon. (4) Grass burden rope, Aran Islands. (5) Tie of fir-rope, from roof, Co. Down. (6) Sheep's langle of oat straw, Co. Down. (7) Plaited mat of marram grass, Co. Wexford. (8) Coiled mat of rye straw, Aran Islands. (9) Coiled mat of oat straw, Co. Donegal.

Examples of ropes and mats of various kinds are shown in Fig. 68. The burden ropes, carefully made in two or three ply, enabled quite heavy loads to be carried from inaccessible places. A correspondent in Co. Cork has sent me the following account of one method of lifting the burden, in this case of furze (gorse, whin) which was harvested both for bedding and for fodder. 'Passing his rope round the bundle, the carrier would throw himself on his back on top of the bundle, kick his heels in the air and jerk himself to the vertical, walking away completely concealed beneath a moving mountain of furze.' Where tracks were poor and there were no wheeled vehicles, or where there was no horse for a slide-car, the burden rope was all that was required to carry home the harvest; distances were mercifully small on the tiny farms. Rushes for rope making were cut when fully grown, beetled with a mell and broken by hand to rid them of pith. They were then spread to dry and afterwards tied in bundles ready to be fashioned into ropes when wintry weather brought indoor leisure. Ropes made of cowhair as well as horsehair, sometimes mixed with seasoned sedge (sprit) once found many uses about the farm. Horsehair fishing lines and snares for seabirds are described elsewhere, but we may refer here to snares for small birds which in south Armagh, for example, are laid on the grass in hard wintry weather over a scattering of grain or breadcrumbs. Inside the frame of a pegged string or a bent sally rod are tied a dozen or more snares made of single or double horsehair. By this means blackbirds, thrushes, sparrows, and finches are caught by the feet, nowadays for sport but, no doubt, once as a welcome addition to the food supply. Similar horsehair snares for catching small birds are known from England and, further afield, from the Sudan. Reins of horsehair are said to have been common quite recently in Donegal, and I would hazard a guess that horsehair nets, such as were made in Harris (Martin Martin tells us) for catching seals, were formerly made there.

Mats and baskets of many kinds were fashioned from straw and other materials such as marram grass. This tough grass is harvested in places all around the coast and put to many uses, including thatching. It is cut below the surface of the sandy dunes, and in Donegal I have seen a toothed sickle used for the purpose. The techniques of constructing mats and baskets of these materials are closely related and seem to fall into three classes, sown plaits, built-up plaits and coiled work. Coiled basketry is best represented in the once universal bee-skep, in the seed-baskets of the south, the seats and armchairs of the west, and in the food-carrying baskets of the Aran Islands (Fig. 69). It is an interesting detail of their construction that a bone pin is used to insert the ties, which are usually made of split briar. The conical hens' nests hung on pegs on the kitchen walls (Fig. 16) are also constructed in a coil technique, but

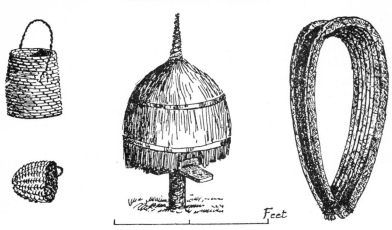

Fɪɢ. 69. Coiled food-basket, Aran Islands; calf muzzle, Co. Clare; beehive and horse-collar, Co. Antrim; all of straw except the calf muzzle.

some large rectangular examples seem to be made of built-up plait as described below. The distribution of coiled basketry in western Europe suggests that it is an extension northwards from south European and African regions where it is a richly developed art. A straw underthatch from Co. Down—the only one of its kind I have seen in the north—was made in a simple weaving technique, using straw ropes. But the commonest method of making mats was by what I have called built-up plaiting; beginning with a straw rope twisted on itself, wisps of straw are inserted in every third twist and their ends worked into plait in combination with the combined ends of the previous wisp. Fresh handfuls of straw are regularly inserted into the plaits. They are given different names in various parts of the country; for example, tates in Antrim, kets in Down, and gleogs in Meath.

Such mats can be made of any desired size, and in the past they served many purposes, as hangings to mark off bedrooms or bed alcoves, as linings for the wattled doors of houses, and as mattresses. Their long-continued use with wattled doors on houses of mud or stone carries the suggestion that wattled houses of the better class may once have been lined with straw mats serving as draught screens and taking the place of the

206

hanging skins, carpets or tapestries of other cultures. Today the most familiar use of the plaited mats is as creel mats on the backs of asses (Fig. 56). When creels are dispensed with and the load is placed directly on the ass a simple 'sugan' is some-times made—a ring of straw some fifteen inches in diameter bound with a fine straw rope. This is a variant of the head-wreath once widely worn in western Europe as a carrying pad. Straw collars—made entirely of straw and not merely straw-stuffed—have so recently gone out of use that I have seen several decayed specimens on hill farms in the north, and the art of making them is not forgotten. In their construction several oval rings of three-strand straw plait are stitched together (Fig. 69). Unlike the ordinary Irish horse collar, they are, of course, not made to open; they were carefully shaped to hold flattish wooden hames.

Many varieties of baskets of straw rushes and other pliant materials which were once made in the homes are now known only by name: for example, the puckan of built-up plaiting which held seed potatoes in Co. Down, or, hung in the stable, served as a nest for pigeons. They had short lives, and few specimens have survived, so that we shall never know the full range of such domestic skills. On the other hand fancy basket work, using both whole and split fine sally rods, has probably long been a specialized craft, and has clung to certain districts such as the shores of Lough Neagh and the Suir Valley. As in these areas so all around the coasts of the island it is a craft which accompanies fishing skills. The long-line fishermen of the sea coasts have traditionally made their own line and fish baskets, but it is only inland communities such as those mentioned who have become commercial basket-makers, possibly because their fishing was more seasonal than that of the sea folk. Their products are now mainly baskets for carrying potatoes or turf (Fig. 71). In a special class are the large creels and carrying baskets made of hazel or black sally which were generally employed for farm transport before wheeled carts were adopted. In many districts these were made by itinerant creel-makers who were held in very low esteem, next above the hackler and the tinker. The method of construction, in which the standard rods are stuck upright in the ground, stamps the craft as being of ancient origin. We shall see that it is the way the Boyne curraghs are built, and it is said that the African pygmies make their carrying baskets in similar fashion. For lightness and to facilitate lifting one or more rows of open 'windows' are left in the sides of the creels. Those used for seaweed were sometimes quite open in construction, and like the manure pots they were generally fitted with hinged bottoms for unloading (Fig. 56).

Besides their utilitarian uses, rushes, grasses and straw have long been playthings for young folk who fashion out of them, for love or for luck, many varieties of decorations and emblems. We describe the Briget's Crosses elsewhere (Fig. 85). Harvest knots, twisted out of the ripe straw of harvest, seem formerly to have been in truth love tokens, though now worn merely as buttonholes for the harvest fair (Plate 13). As one might expect, the girls' knots were the more ornate and they differed from those worn by the boys in having the ears left attached. Some exceptionally fine specimens are fashioned out of flax or fine wild grasses. Star-shaped emblems in these materials are also made (Fig. 70). More complicated knots have four or six strand work, but the ordinary knots are in two ply, made by bending the straws sharply over each other at right angles. Before being knotted they make tolerably strong cords: I have experimented with these on unbaked clay pots and find that when impressed in the soft clay they make very good imitations of the 'cord impressions' seen on Bronze Age pottery. I have heard that in Nigeria the same two-ply technique is employed in making roulettes, from the fibres of the wine palm, for decorating the native pottery. Among the many toys and playthings made of rushes we find baskets for wild strawberries and blaeberries, rattles, butterfly cages, fishing nets, caps, bracelets, belts, hatbands, mock-ceremonial whips, canes and swords and imitation birds' feet and flowers, some of which are shown in Fig. 70. Many of them are associated with particular occasions of the year, for example the imitation flowers with Easter and the blaeberry baskets with Garland Sunday (Chapter XIX) but in general they are the products of the infinite leisure of long summer days of cattle-tending in field, bog or mountain. Probably a number of these objects once had a practical value

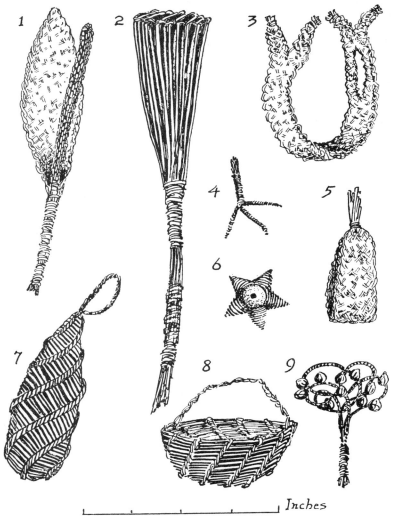

FIG. 70. Rush, grass and straw-work. (1) Cuckoo pint made of rushes, Co. Armagh. (2) Butterfly cage of rushes, Co. Down. (3) Rush bracelet in nine-strand plait, Co. Armagh. (4) 'Hen's claw' of grass, Co. Mayo. (5) 'Briget's rag' of oat straw. Tory Island charm. (6) 'Harvest star' of flax, Co. Antrim. (7) Rush rattle, Co. Mayo. (8) Blaeberry basket of rushes, Co. Down. (9) Harvest knot of flax, Co. Armagh.

209

and others were ceremonial; some may be no more than simple pastimes prompted by fancy. Rush baskets were in fact made until recently in some of the Hebridean islands for carrying the fishermen's bait and for holding fish. Baskets of birch twigs, dock stems, ragwort and thistles have also been recorded, and it should be recalled that several examples of grass, sedge, and even moss, made in a similar cross-twisted technique have been recorded from Bronze Age burials in Scotland. The cone-shaped hat of rushes or straw made by children (Fig. 86) recalls in shape at least the traditional headdress of the leprechauns, and it may be noticed that tall steeple hats and helmets seem to have been popular among the Irish down to the seventeenth century.[1] In Co. Kerry the rush hats are worn in mock fights and seem to be regarded as helmets.

Of all these rush toys, none is stranger than the butterfly cage (Fig. 70) which is deftly made by bending long rushes, held upright between the fingers, over others placed transversely. One side of the cage may be left open and a dock leaf inserted as a door. The ends of the rushes are bound together to make a handle. This pastoral plaything can be paralleled in many parts of the world: in the cages in which Spanish shepherd boys carry insects, in the little baskets of dried grass which the Indian herd children make for grasshoppers, in the locust traps which Greek boys, Theocritus tells us, used to weave out of asphodel stalks, and even among the nomads of the Gobi Desert, where, when the cicada begins to call in the great heat, 'every child cuts the desert grass to make a tiny cage to hold one of the fascinating tree-hoppers . . . The Gobi baby's rattle, too, is a hollow ball of twisted grass enclosing a large bead.'[2] The Irish rush rattle is provided with two hazel nuts. Some of the leaves and bracelets are plaited with four, six, nine, or even twelve strands, and a nine strand plait is also seen in one variety of three-cornered Briget's Cross (Fig. 85, 3; Pl. 13, 7).

The conical straw masks and the capes worn by strawboys (Chapter XX, Fig. 88) stripped of their gay ribbons, have been compared with the straw dresses of peasants in Spain or China, and, no doubt, they had their practical prototypes in Ireland.

[1] H. F. McClintock, *Old Irish and Highland Dress*, 88.
[2] M. Cable and F. French, *The Gobi Desert*, 100.

The straw cape placed over the bee-skep (Fig. 69) is a humble relation. Straw masks are worn also by Biddy Boys on St. Briget's Eve, and by the Christmas Rhymers. On St. Briget's Eve, too, a small straw doll (Brideóg) was dressed up and carried from door to door in the south-west of Ireland. A charm of plaited straw known as Bratóg Brighde (literally, Briget's Rag) is carried by the fishermen of Tory Island as a protection against storms (Fig. 70, 5). There was also Briget's Girdle, a two-strand straw rope, a circle with crosses attached, which was passed over the body as a protective charm, by inserting one leg and then pushing the head through on the Saints' Feast Day (Fig. 85).

Before the Irish live-cattle trade developed there had been for some centuries a great export of hides and skins, and if one goes back earlier it becomes clear that these products must have found a multitude of uses about the farm. For a number of purposes where toughness and durability are specially needed animal skin has remained a traditional material, and in old-fashioned mountainy areas the countryman makes a habit of curing the skins of wild and domesticated animals on the principle that 'you never know but what they'll come in useful'. On analogy with the Hebrides, with which Donegal in particular shows close cultural affinities, skin mealbags should have had a place in cottage economy in north Ireland. When grinding corn, a skin was laid on the floor under the quern to catch the meal. Seal skin served many purposes, from plough traces, in Harris, to the covers of curraghs in Donegal. We have descriptions of cured sheepskins serving as windows,[1] and (from St. Kilda) of fowling ropes bound with strips of salted cowhide to prevent them from being cut by the rocks.[2] But it is in the skin tray, the wecht or wight, that one is most likely to see tradition maintained (Fig. 71). The well-scraped skin of sheep, or sometimes of goat, is stitched on to a rim of ash, bog fir or, in the naked islands which have exhausted even their bog timber, a ring of sugan. To secure the skin free of wrinkles is skilled work, and the finished product is not unlike a tambourine: in fact, it closely resembles the Eskimo caribou drum. Irish wrenboys

[1]Lord George Hill, *Gweedore*, 25.
[2]Martin Martin, *The Western Isles*, 315.

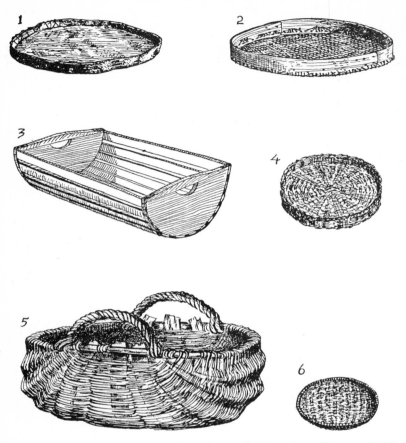

Fig. 71. Skin-tray, split-ash riddle and potato baskets. Approximate scale 1/9 (No. 5, 1/6). (1) Sheep-skin tray or wight. (2) Split-ash riddle. (3) Potato 'basket'. (4) Potato skib. (5) Potato basket. (6) Potato skib. (All Co. Antrim.)

carried a skin tambourine which they beat when hunting the wren on St. Stephen's Day, and one wonders whether the drummers from whom the Orange performers on King William's Day inherit their wild rhythms were trained on ceremonial wights. (There are also sieves, riddles and shallow baskets of split ash or sally, but these, for example the flat round potato skib—a communal self-service plate—should properly be classed as the work of specialists (Fig. 71). The pampooties of the Aran Islands deserve mention here. Made of calfskin, but formerly of sealskin,[1] these one-piece shoes were once doubtless widely worn and have kept their hold in Aran because of their suitability for wet rocks and frail curraghs. The rivlins of Scotland and the Highland *bròagan* were very similar and I have seen rawhide shoes of the same type from Norway and the Pyrenees. They all have the hair outside and are secured by lacing back and front.

The wight serves both to hold corn, in filling a sack for instance, and to convey peats from the stack to the fireside: perforated it becomes a meal-sieve (boran) for sifting the skins (seeds) from oatmeal, or a buttermilk sieve for taking out the last grains of butter from the churn. The winnowing tray or dallan is a larger version, and it, too, may be perforated to allow the wind to pass through as the corn is shaken out on to a spread cloth. There are, up and down Ireland, many bold windy Shilling Hills where the 'shellings' (husks) were, in past times, separated from the grain in this way (Pl. 7).

This brings us to the flail and its 'hanging' (the mid-kipple, hooden, gad, middling, or tug) which was commonly a thong of cow-, horse-, sheep, or goat-skin, though sometimes of rabbit- or eel-skin or a cord of flax. The flail, the proverbial 'stick-and-a-half', consists of a three to four feet long helve or hand-staff, usually made of ash, and a shorter beater, swingle or souple of hazel or holly. There are two principal methods of 'hanging' the parts together. In one variety, the tie passes through two leather caps lashed over the ends (Fig. 72, 1). This appears to be a variant of the common English flail-hanging, where, however, the cap is made of steamed ash or yew and there is no linking piece. Its distribution in Ireland, down the east coast, points to derivation from England. Modifications, occurring as far west as Donegal (Fig. 72, 1a, b), have the linking thong passing through a hole made either in the helve or in the beater. Kevin Danaher states that the capped flail is characteristic of central Europe: it is believed to have first appeared in north France in the early Middle Ages.[2] The

[1]O'Flaherty, *H'Iar Connaught*, 59 (footnote).
[2]*J.C.H. and A. Soc.*, 60 (1955), 6–14.

other method of hanging has a somewhat peripheral distribution in Europe (Scandinavia, Poland, Yugoslavia, Switzerland, the Pyrenees) and also in Ireland, and as its simplicity as well as its distribution suggest, it is the older type. The tie passes around grooves cut in both hand-staff and souple (Fig. 72, 2) though again there are variants, one end of the tie, for example, being passed through a hole (Fig. 72, 2a). The grooved hanging, it is claimed by its users, is superior to the capped because the join is almost universal and there is no need to turn the halve in the hand when flailing. The holed fastening may be the most ancient method of all: it is found in parts of Atlantic Europe and the Baltic lands, but in Ireland is apparently restricted to Ulster (Pl. 6, 2).

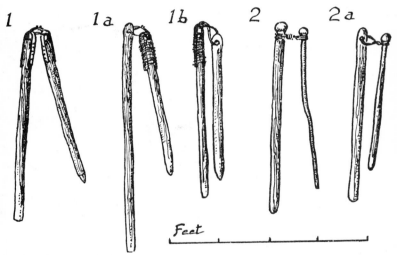

FIG. 72. Flails. (1) Co. Meath. (1a) Co. Armagh. (1b) Co. Donegal. (2) Co. Cavan. (2a) Co. Antrim.

Ancient and rudimentary as the flail is, requiring for its making no tool save a sharp knife, there are some thrashers who dispense with it, 'scutching' the corn instead with a stick or 'lashing' it over a barrel, a stone or a board (Plate 4). Many a small farmer in the north of Ireland harvests his seed grass in this way. The scutching method is used also in the

Pyrenees and in Africa, but the flail, apparently spreading through western Europe in post-Roman times, in time replaced it almost everywhere, to be in turn displaced by the mechanical thrasher. Thus the sound of the flail has almost gone from the countryside. The best thrashing place is the floor of the barn above the byre, with its opposite doors to draw the wind and advertise the flailer's industry. Such barns, however, were not built outside the planted districts before agrarian changes and improvements spread in the eighteenth and nineteenth centuries. Ireland knows nothing of the carefully built thrashing floors of England and Scandinavia. At best on the farms lacking a barn a thrashing board was sometimes kept, a square wooden platform raised a few inches off the ground. A good thrashing floor should bend to meet the flail, and in Scandinavia, for instance, great pains were taken in the old days to construct floors which would make the flails sing. They were occasionally strung with wires, and to magnify the echo of clay floors a horse's skull was buried under each corner.[1] It has been thought that this purpose was secondary to the luck it was hoped would follow from what was originally a foundation sacrifice. In Ireland traditions of the burying of horses' skulls under the floors of dwelling houses are both widespread and well authenticated. The usual explanation again is that this gives the house an echo, but it is also said to be lucky, and Sean O'Sullivan concludes that the custom of burying skulls began as a substitute for foundation sacrifices.[2] In Armagh 'the frontal bones of a horse's head are regarded as being peculiarly sonsie; they were often buried in barn floors and under the thresholds of dwelling houses for that reason.'[3]

In time, the expressed object came to be to magnify the music of the singing flails as well as that of the ballad-singing and dancing before the fire. The space between the doors of the old style kitchen-byre, it will be recalled, was a favourite thrashing place in times past. The Briget's Crosses above the door would have blessed the thrashing as well as the cattle. It

---

[1]Albert Sandkelf, *Singing Flails* (Folklore Fellows Communications, Helsinki, No. 136), (1949).
[2]Seán Ó Súilleabháin, *J.R.S.A.I.*, 75 (1945), 45–52.
[3]J. Donaldson, *Upper Fews in 1838*, 77.

is worth noticing that symbols in the form of a swastika, but including also circles, pentagrams and horses, were formerly cut as protective devices in the beams of barns in Scandinavia. Some of the designs are reminiscent of the art of the Bronze Age.

An Irish verse giving the four essentials of a good thrashing, collected in Co. Armagh, runs in translation:

> A hand-staff of holly,
> A souple of hazel,
> A single sheaf,
> And a clean floor.

This is where the besom of heather or bent comes in: it is still preferred to the sweeping-broom for a clay floor or to get into the joins of boards or cobbles. Thrashing was a daily job, carried out on well-run farms night and morning before the cattle were fed. It was held that the cattle throve best on freshly thrashed oats, and the storage of grain would anyhow have been difficult where there were no barns.[1] For this reason, too, the level 'street' in front of the house, or even the public road was often the most suitable floor available. The thrashing was usually done on a strong linen sheet. Publicity as well as a steady echoing beat seem to have been the desired aims. Everywhere prestige has attached to a noisy thrashing, and partly no doubt for self-aggrandisement a solitary thrasher would beat with his feet to make the noise of two. Everywhere too the sound of the flail has been turned into jingles and rustic rhymes. They did not accompany the work itself because it was too noisy and too exhausting to allow talking or singing. The flails' beaters made their own merry music; was it, one wonders, originally intended to drive away evil spirits from the precious food supply?

In this chapter we have confined ourselves to some of the things that were made at home out of materials that lay to hand. To describe the utilization of all the lesser plants that have

[1]Mr. A. T. Lucas, however, has described traditional outdoor granaries, now restricted to west Cork, constructed of thick straw ropes, which when completed resemble round stacks (*Gwerin*, I (1956), 2–20). Mr. V. B. Proudfoot calls my attention to the similar 'corn bykes' of Caithness (*P.S.A.S.* (1932), 136–7).

figured in the economy of the farm or in medicinal and magical lore would be an almost endless task. One recalls that a group of Californian Indians practising a food-gathering economy is said to have made use of 176 species of wild plants for satisfying almost all their needs. A few examples of the survival of a collecting culture in Ireland may be given, taken from various sources such as Wood-Martin's pioneer work, but also from folk-memory. From the roots of ferns were extracted oils used in weaving, from those of the water lily, a cherished red dye, a substance for tanning from tormentil roots, and ink from the roots of flags (saggins). Bracken and wood ash were kept for making soap, and the ashes of thistles were the perquisite of the herdsmen. Large lake rushes provided materials for caulking boats and churns, and phragmites stems for winding yarn in the shuttle. Lady's bedstraw besides being rubbed on bee-skeps to attract a swarm, produced both dye and rennet. For cures we have the carrageen or Irish moss as well as the moss growing on crosses and other special stones, and a great number of flowers and herbs. Yarrow, in Irish, is called 'the herb of the seven cures'. But the sovereign remedy was the essence of all wild flowers contained in what was euphemistically known as 'all-flower water', i.e., cow's urine.[1] We shall return to these topics in Chapter XXI.

[1] W. G. Wood-Martin, *The Elder Faiths*, 2, 183.
Note. Mr. A. T. Lucas has recently published accounts of hurling balls made of cowhair (see *J.C.H. and A. Soc.*, 57, 99–104; 59, 78–81).

XVI

WRACK AND WRECK

NO part of Ireland is more than sixty miles from the sea and its most populous districts have for ages been strung along the shore. This is as true today for Co. Donegal as it is for Co. Dublin. Yet we think of the seashore as the most natural part of our scenic heritage, the zone least affected by the hand of man which, inland, has wrought massive changes and turned forests into bogs and farmlands. True the great headlands must have presented to ancient man much the same majestic outlines as we admire today, but the lowlying stretches of coast, unstable in the face of erosion and deposition, have been considerably modified also by human interference. Deep in the ancient beach deposits and layer upon layer in the sand-hills where we picnic and play lie the relics of ancient shore dwellers. It was here of necessity that man found his first foot-hold on the island, to it he has clung and to it inlanders have returned to satisfy a variety of needs. Here by the shore man has gathered cockles and mussels, dug for bait and reaped the harvests of wreck and wrack, here he has built weirs and traps for fish, slips and shelters for boats, racks for drying nets and kilns for burning seaweed. Here too he was wont to hold festival with rites and games in seasonal gatherings long before port cities blocked the estuaries and holiday crowds thronged the open beaches. Easter and Harvest were the old times of festival, when the moon was full and the tides ran low.

A teeming population of shellfish was the shore's first attraction, a steady supply of food supplemented at the nesting season by seabirds and their eggs and in summer by the ana-dromous fish seeking fresh water. In hard winters and late springs when fodder was scarce cattle, sheep and horses found edible seaweed on the shore. Scottish planters in Co. Down found that their sheep 'kept fat and wholesome all winter and spring by feeding on the oare.'[1] This is nowadays one of nature's neglected resources partly, no doubt, owing to enclosure and the loss of grazing rights. It has been claimed as the result of experiments that the feeding value of *Ascophyllum nodosum* (knob wrack), which grows towards high tide mark, is almost equal to that of meadow hay. Certain species of seaweed are still, however, gathered for human consumption—carrageen or Irish moss (*Chondrus crispus*) sloke or laver (*Porphyra*), dulse (*Rhodymenia*) and dulaman (probably chanelled weed)— whether as medicine or 'kitchen', that is a tasty morsel to be chewed between meals, or boiled to be eaten with potatoes. In lean times the kitchen might become the staple, and a writer in the 1830's stated that when the potatoes gave out 'hundreds of the people may be seen going to the seaside to gather dulaman.'[2] Carrageen, besides being made into a jelly possessing many virtues, was used as a thickener for milk.

The most profitable way of exploiting seaweed down to recent times was for the burning of kelp, which became a considerable business among shore-dwellers in the eighteenth century as the growth of industry stimulated the production of soap, bleaching materials and glass: more recently kelp was chiefly in demand for the preparation of iodine. But there are dimly remembered ways of utilizing seaweed ashes in the home which would make kelp-burning a traditional occupation. In the Western Isles of Scotland kelp-burning is said to have been introduced from Ireland about 1735, but there too it must have been an ancient custom, for Martin Martin tells us at the end of the seventeenth century that seals, seafowl and fish were preserved in 'the ashes of burnt seaware'.[3] (Cheese, we learn, was preserved in the same way, or 'lapped in tang'). Kelp was made by burning the thick stems of tangle (*Laminaria*) or other coarse weeds—to which, as well as to the ashes, the name kelp is applied—which are thrown up in the winter storms or

[1]W. Montgomery, *Description of Ardes Barony* (1683), 139.
[2]J. Binns, *Miseries and Beauties*, 1, 50.
[3]Martin Martin, *The Western Isles*, 135, 159.

cut at low tide. The weeds were dried on low stone walls and
ricked and thatched until ready for the kiln on summer days.
Rain rots the weeds, so that in wet weather the heavy kelp
had to be shaken and turned repeatedly until it could be safely
ricked. The half obliterated ruins of drying-walls and kilns
made of sea-boulders can be seen on stormy beaches all around
the coast (Fig. 73). In the early decades of the century the

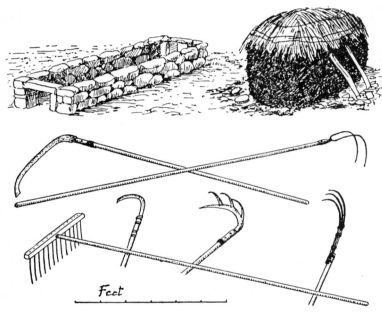

Feet

FIG. 73. Kelp harvest. Kelp kiln and stack. Co. Galway. Hooks, knives and
drags, west and south coasts (See Pl. 11).

dense oily smoke from the kilns drifting far inland was a familiar
sight, each kiln burning for many hours and consuming several
tons of weed, which was fed in a little at a time. It is said that
60 tons of weed are required to provide 1 ton of kelp, and the
work was both arduous and filthy. If the supply of drift-weed
failed the heavy tangles were laboriously dragged ashore or
cut with knives mounted on handles up to twenty feet long to
reach the best weeds, free of sand, growing in deep water. A

combined knife and drag found in Connacht has three heavy
hooks attached to a strong sickle-shaped blade mounted on a
12-ft. pole (Fig. 73). Powerful long-handled scythes and great
hand-rakes with teeth a foot long were used on the south
coast. In Donegal the men would wield their long knives from
curraghs while the women dragged the weed ashore.

In the Rosses of west Donegal around 1750 the rents were
paid in kelp: any surplus was bartered for 'the two luxuries,
spirits and tobacco, enjoyed by men and women alike.'[1] For
the lesser weeds growing in shallow water ordinary sickles
were employed when the tide was low, but these species made
inferior kelp. Yet in some areas, for example Strangford Lough,
stones were planted on the shore to grow wrack for kelp
burning: Arthur Young commented on this practice in 1776.[2]
Old seaweed beds may be seen also in Lough Swilly, Clew Bay,
Achill Sound and probably elsewhere.

Today the most remarkable area of cultivated weed is near
the mouth of Carlingford Lough in County Down, where at
low tide a wide stretch of mud and sand is exposed in Mill Bay.
It is grown solely to supply fertilizer for the potato crop.
Wrack rights are mentioned in grants of land in County Down
as far back as 1506, but the earliest reference I have found to the
cultivated weed in Carlingford Lough is in a guidebook of
1846. As we have seen, however, Arthur Young refers to the
growing of wrack for kelp-burning in Strangford Lough, and
since the best species for kelp grow in deeper water the planting
of seaweed beds is not likely to have originated with the kelp
industry. Through the second half of last century some 1,100
beds, covering well over a square mile in area, were maintained
in Mill Bay, and it was not until the depression between the
two world wars that they began to be neglected. Today the
use of wrack has almost entirely given way to artificial fertilizers, with a great easement of labour but a loss of annually
renewed organic matter in the soil. The wrackbeds, or 'plans',
are half-acre rectangles set with rows of boulders a foot or so
in diameter, but many beds are subdivided into small 'cuts' for
sub-letting, and the Estate Map showing the beds has the

[1] A. B., *The Rosses in 1753*, 201.
[2] A. Young, *Tour*, 1, 194.

minutely fragmented appearance of land held in rundale. Rights
of access, by narrow lanes between the beds, were often dis-
puted, and there were occasions for fights when as many as a
hundred carts from forty townlands might converge on Mill Bay
at low tide. I first heard of the seaweed beds from an Air Force
pilot who brought me air photographs of what he thought was
submerged farmland: the little rectangular fields of Mourne
seemed to march out beneath the sea.[1] In fact they were necessary adjuncts to the arable land, and the rents of up to twenty
pounds an acre were often higher than those paid for the fields
of coarse sand and gravel which the wrack enriched. An auc-
tioneer told me he had sold a wrackbed of one Irish acre for
£145 not many years ago. Nearly all of the several hundred
farmers who had wrack rights here held two or three beds,
and each man's plans were scattered so that he had different
kinds of weed growing on them: 'knob wrack' close inshore,
then 'bladder wrack' and farther out still the 'lazy wrack' whose
fronds are submerged at high water even at neaps and which
therefore grows faster than the other species.

The crop was harvested with knives and sickles between
March and June, the bare-footed reapers at the same time
lifting, turning and re-setting the heavy boulders which tend
to get buried in the sand. Carts too are liable to sink, and when
the going is too soft the weed is rafted ashore. It is allowed to
float on the incoming tide and a boat dragging a rope pulls the
load together and tows it ashore. Very large rafts, secured by a
rope of seaweed, used to be floated ashore on the tide in Mayo.
Patrick Knight, describing Ballycroy about 1830, observed that
the steersman, armed with a pole, might be seen 'sitting on
the heap, roasting his potatoes and shellfish'.[2]

The great bulk of the wrack taken all round the coast for
manure was driftweed thrown up during storms, but the supply
was often supplemented by cutting or pulling weed from the
rocks, and in some places there were complicated methods of
regulating and distributing the harvest. On a stretch of coast
familiar to me in south Down one can pick out strips running
out into the sea, demarcated by marked boulders. They were

[1]E. E. Evans, *Mourne Country*, ch. 15.
[2]P. Knight, *Erris in the Irish Highlands*, 99.

formerly allotted to tenants in proportion to the acreages of their farm holdings. The weed had to be carried away among the slippery boulders in back-creels and hand-barrows and stacked on the beach ready for the carts and creel-asses. The driftweed cast up by the storms of winter was more accessible but its division gave rise to endless disputes and was often regulated by careful procedure and the casting of lots, though some beaches were subdivided by standing stones. In Donegal I was told how at low tide, by the light of lanterns, men would dash into the sea up to their necks to drag out the floating weed. It is an interesting example of manorial privilege that on one beach, below the Norman castle at Greencastle, County Down, all the wrack blown in after 17th March goes to the farm which occupies the ruined castle. Every little bay where the weed collects has its wrack road leading down (Fig. 4), and fields near the shore may have a seaweed gate giving direct access. From Christmas onwards a careful watch was kept on the weather, and a spirit of excitement spread inland from the shore as the wind rose. Every bay has its own particular wind, blowing from 'the right art', for a good yield of wrack. (For kelp, however, an offshore wind was needed, because it is the returning undertow which brings the deeper weeds ashore). There are many accounts of the extraordinary zeal of the wrack gatherers and their feats of endurance. Even English visitors were forced to admit that 'it would be impossible to witness a scene of greater industry than was being enacted by these lazy Irish'.[1]

As on other occasions when men left their lonely farms and gathered together there was much merry-making and noisy recollection of past wrack harvests. One cannot doubt that the harvest of the fields, its 'luck' as well as its bounty, was felt to depend on success in this first step in the farming year. The desire to be first and the intense rivalry were prompted by motives stronger than the wish for material gain. In Scotland one reads of the great anxiety that was shown to secure the first load of wrack on New Year's Day, and on that day a portion of seaweed was laid at the doors of the farmstead and in each of the fields.[2] In Jersey the *vraic* (wrack) harvest is

[1] J. H. Tuke, *A Visit to Donegal and Connaught*, 54.
[2] M. Banks, *British Calendar Customs: Scotland*, 2, 97.

described as a gathering of the whole people, a time of feasting and festivals and courting. That there was magic as well as manure in the golden weed is apparent from the urge to possess some share, however small, of the harvest. In the kingdom of Mourne 'men would walk three miles to be present at the division of the wrack and were content to take back a single creelful on their backs. They would gather the bits of wrack on their knees, scraping them up with their hands as though it was gold dust.'[1] Here the division was by lot following a given signal— in one case a bush hoisted on a tall pole—for the farmers concerned to assemble. Wrack rights and ways of access are sometimes still bitterly fought over though they now have little meaning.

Spring was also the season for gathering other gifts of the sea, the shellfish and the shell sand which was carted inland and even taken on horseback for distances of up to thirty miles. Prized because 'it cut up the clay', it also provided much needed lime for acid soils. In South Donegal boatloads of mussels used to be scraped off the rocks with spades and distributed in creels for spreading on the potato ridges. In Dundalk Bay, Mr. H. G. Tempest tells me, mussels for the table and for bait are scraped up from boats with long-handled rakes (Fig. 74). Easter and Good Friday in particular were times for visiting the shore. Of the now deserted Blasket Islands Thomas O'Crohan writes: 'it has always been the custom here to go and get kitchen from the strand to eat on Good Friday.'[2] Winkles (willucks) were the favourite food on these occasions, but after St. Patrick's Day, they say, limpets are better eating than winkles. Shellfish were boiled in milk to give food for children and for calves. Sandeels were pulled up with a bent iron rod or a blunted sickle: in Mayo 'they are taken on moonlit nights by considerable gatherings of young people, the object being as much the amusement as the sandeels'.[3] In Donegal 'for scallops and oysters, when the tide was out, the young women waded into the sea, some of them naked, and by armfuls brought them to the shore.'[4]

[1]E. E. Evans, *Mourne Country*, 144.
[2]T. O'Crohan, *The Islandman*, 29.
[3]C. R. Browne, *Ballycroy*.
[4]A. B., *The Rosses in 1753*, 201.

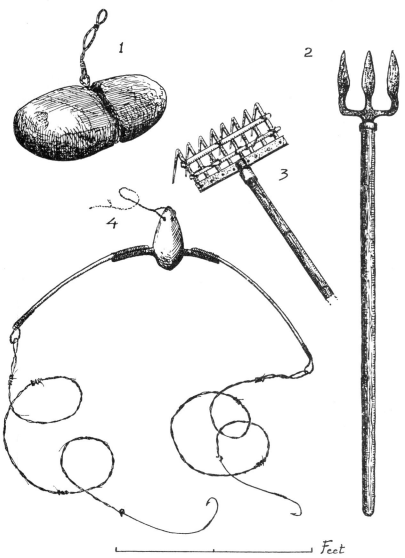

FIG. 74. Fishing gear. (1) Stone sinker for long lines, Co. Antrim (scale ×3).
(2) Fork for digging lug worms, Co. Down. (3) Mussel rake, Co. Louth.
Handle 15 ft. (after H. G. Tempest). (4) 'Frog' with horsehair crops for codling
fishing, Co. Down (scale ×3).

225

Scallop shells were put to many uses and were often a substitute for the iron oil-pan of the open-wicked crusie. Seashells were also burnt to make lime for whitewashing the houses.

In late summer the sprat come ashore in vast numbers on the west and south coasts, so that in Donegal 'they constituted the chief food of the peasantry during three or four months of the year.'[1] They were taken from the water in buckets and sieves, and the mackerel pursuing their prey close against the rocks might be caught almost as easily. In Waterford harbour there were specially erected wickerwork head weirs to take the sprat; and Dr. Went has described a wattled sprat-weir in working order in the estuary of the Blackwater.[2] Fishing from the rocks, too, is most popular in harvest time and though now little more than a pastime it once provided a reserve of food for the winter. About hay-harvest the ballan wrasse is at its best, 'when the flags (wild iris) are in bloom', they say. Known as bavin, byan, morran and by other names, it is now despised nearly everywhere, as is the coalfish which was salted and dried and which has different names in Gaelic for every stage of its growth to demonstrate its former importance and popularity. 'Glassan' oil was the luminant for the crusie lamps in Rathlin Island. On the north coast you may see anglers 'frassing' for small coalfish, that is attracting them by spitting into the water chewed potatoes or limpets. Formerly ground bait was made by pounding limpets in rock basins of the type known as 'bullauns' (Fig. 90). Occasionally you may come across a fisherman casting a feather lure for pollack with a line made wholly or in part of horsehair. One method of twisting these lines, with quills, will be described in the following chapter. For short lengths next the hook—the fine foot-lines—white hair is preferred, and I have seen it made in County Down by twisting the hair between the bare thigh and a hand dusted with wood ash, a method practised by 'primitives' in many parts of the world. Two strands of from fifteen to twenty hairs are twisted on each other. (The anglers in the Seine at Paris are also said to prefer a 'crop' made from a grey mare's tail.) To

[1]'Kinnfaela', *The Cliff Scenery of South-Western Donegal*, 19.
[2]A. E. J. Went, *Antiquity*, 25 (1951), 32–35.

watch rock-fishing from the great limestone cliffs of the Aran Islands is a memorable sight, the 300 foot line being flung out weighted with a large grooved stone.

Inshore net fishing, which will be considered in the next chapter, has probably taken the place of other methods of catching fish close to the land. In some river estuaries and across the mouths of little streams in many shallow bays curving lines of boulders are all that is left of fishing weirs in which salmon and flatfish were once trapped (Fig. 75). I first noticed an example in Belfast Lough some years ago, and later came across a seventeenth century reference to their occurrence in Strangford Lough. The 'wares and fishyards' are described as being built of loose stones which allowed the tide to flow through, and fish seeking food from the fresh water were carried over the weir at the flood to be trapped as the tide ebbed. They were then netted or speared. The weirs were said to have decayed 'since fish days were neglected',[1] but the remains of many of them can still be seen around the lough. Such 'tidal fishing engines', to judge from their world-wide distribution, are an extremely ancient fishing device. More elaborate are the V-shaped wickerwork weirs of which Dr. A. E. J. Went has made an historical study.[2] One or two are still worked but they became obsolete over a century ago when the Scotch stake net was introduced for salmon fishing, and they were later condemned as obstacles to navigation. In Waterford harbour alone no less than forty-four were destroyed. These head weirs were operated by holding a conical net below a platform which crossed an opening placed at the apex of the V. Large weirs of this kind required considerable capital to keep in repair and were owned by the privileged classes but they have no doubt

---

[1] E. E. Evans, *U.J.A.*, 14 (1951), 48.

[2] A. E. J. Went, *J.R.S.A.I.*, 76 (1946), 176–94; 78 (1948), 1–4. Professor C. M. Yonge (*The Times*, 10th November 1955), in an article on the mussel industry of La Rochelle in the Bay of Biscay, attributes it to a resourceful Irishman, Patrick Walton, who is said to have been wrecked there in the year 1235. He is given credit for erecting a tidal head weir which also served as a *bouchot* or mussel bed, and for devising a net for catching sea-birds and a narrow plank-boat pushed by one leg over the soft mud. 'The French naturalist, Quatrefages, writing about 1850, reported that a direct descendant of Walton was then engaged in mussel culture and took a natural pride in the name he bore.' No doubt Patrick Walton derived some of his ingenious ideas from his native land.

Fig. 75. Fishing weirs and curragh pens. *Above:* wattled head weir in River Bride, Co. Waterford (after Went). *Centre:* old stone fishing weirs at Newcastle, Co. Down. *Below:* curragh pens, Achill Island, Co. Mayo (after Piggott).

developed from wicker constructions which, like the stone weirs, were once built by shore dwellers for their own needs. But weirs were not the only structure built in tidal waters. The inquiring visitor will observe along many stretches of coast straight lines of stones running out to sea which are the remains of little piers alongside which small boats could lie. Back of them beyond the reach of the tide there may be the ruins of a boat shelter which might never have been more than a rectangular pen of stone walls or earth banks. Such pens are still used to protect the curraghs of the west coast from the wind which is their worst enemy.[1] The vessels are in addition weighted down with stones (Fig. 75), and to this end the gunwales often project at the rear of the curraghs to give purchase for the boulders (Fig. 78).

On the lonely and now abandoned island of St. Kilda the portion which a woman took to her husband on marriage is said to have been 'a pound of horsehair to make a gin to catch fowls'.[2] Martin Martin in his account of the island also tells us that the 200 inhabitants yearly killed and preserved above 20,000 birds, and in addition prodigious numbers of seabirds' eggs were consumed. The killing of seabirds and the taking of eggs for export to England during the worst period of food shortage in the second world war brought about a temporary revival of old skills on many parts of the Irish coast. Down to times still remembered fowling was a seasonal activity on most of the islands where seabirds assemble to nest. Birds of the auk family were caught in horsehair 'dulls' (snares) pegged to the ground. For other birds such as rock pigeons the snares were baited. July was the busy month, and the birds not eaten in this 'hungry month' were salted down for the winter. On Rathlin Island the cliffs and sea-slopes were apportioned in strips and demarcated by spikes driven into the rocks. It is remembered that single men in search of eggs would let themselves alone down ropes attached to iron pins in the cliff edge. Traditions of other ways of catching the birds have been lost but one may be fairly sure that the various methods described by Martin Martin and more recently by Kenneth Williamson for the

[1] S. Piggott, *Antiquity*, 28 (1954), 19–24.
[2] Martin Martin, *The Western Isles*, 317.

Faeroe Islands[1] were practised in a region which has so many culture parallels with the northern isles.

Down to recent times coast-dwellers also took their toll of seals and porpoises. 'We thought more of a seal in those days', wrote Thomas O'Crohan of the Blaskets, 'than of the very best pig.'[2] They were valued too for their skins, which as we have mentioned made covers for the curraghs and shoes for the rock-climbers. Seal hunting was dangerous work, sometimes involving swimming into the underwater caves where they breed. The seal catchers in County Cork wore 'bags quilted with charcoal' on their arms, for the animals let go their hold when they bit on the crunching charcoal.[3] In the Blaskets porpoises were slaughtered after being driven ashore by boats, and then 'everyone was crimson with the blood of the sea-pigs'.[4] The meat was salted down.

Crabs and lobsters, like so many other seafoods, are now neglected and even despised, though there are commercial fisheries in areas accessible to markets. Apart from creel fishing they were formerly taken from the rock holes where they lie, either by hand or with an iron hook. In County Kerry one man would hold another under the water with an oar while he searched the holes. The old-style pots or creels are circular, with a flat weighted bottom, sometimes hinged: the principle rods are of hazel or even whin, the woven sides of sally, laurel or heather stems. They vary in pattern from one district to another, as do the round-topped rectangular net-creels which have taken their place almost everywhere (Fig. 76). The lobstermen are a hardy breed, many of them having turned from long-line fishing, and they have kept up the feuds and rivalries to which the long-liners were addicted. In both types of fishing the search for bait is an exacting occupation. I illustrate a special fork used for digging lug worms, and also a mussel rake (Fig. 74).

If it is difficult to obtain information about the history of such tools and activities as these, which have been the concern

[1] K. Williamson, *The Atlantic Islands*, ch. 6.
[2] T. O'Crohan, *The Islandman*, 99.
[3] E. Wakefield, *An Account of Ireland*, 2, 127.
[4] T. O'Crohan, op. cit., 12.

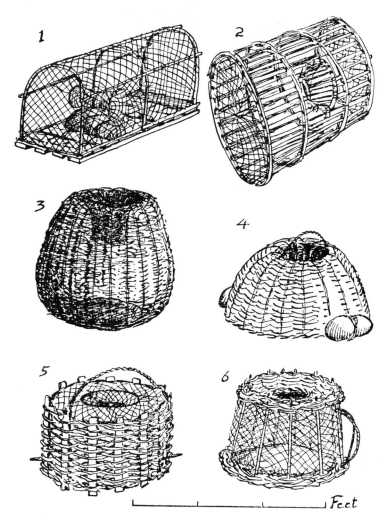

FIG. 76. Creels and pots. (1) Lobster, Co. Antrim. (2) Crayfish, French pattern, south and west coasts. (3) Lobster, Co. Mayo. (4) Crab, Co. Antrim. (5) Buckies, Co. Down. (6) Crab, Co. Down.

of the common people and have not been caught in the net of written records, it is still harder to throw light on some of the darker aspects of shore life. Both smuggling and wrecking have almost everywhere at one time or another been regarded as legitimate methods of obtaining food and acquiring goods from the sea. A dread harvest from ships sunk by enemy action was reaped with seeming callousness during two world wars by coastal dwellers who would risk their own lives in the process. Driftwood has always been an acceptable gift, and many a fisherman's cabin is roofed with ship's timbers and its fittings augmented with ship's furniture. Nearly all these varied shore activities demand a measure of co-operation, and one finds that communal schemes of one kind and another and old ways and beliefs live long among folk who have to deal with the sea. Collective effort is necessary in hauling boats and handling nets, and while there are traditional rivalries between different coastal settlements each one tends to be a closely knit community displaying a strong spirit of independence. They were often able to resist the repressive hand of landlords and they still remain suspicious of the efforts of government bodies to improve their lot.

XVII

BOATS AND FISHING

THE lower reaches of the River Boyne, celebrated among archaeologists as the setting of one of the most remarkable groups of chamber tombs in western Europe, have another claim on our interests as the last refuge of a venerable craft. This is perhaps the only place in Europe where the phrase 'the skin of a boat' preserves its literal meaning. The lath or wickerwork coracle is known on several of the Welsh rivers, but only in the Boyne curragh (Ir. *currach*) is the covering still made of hide. The ox-hides now used are imported: the one I examined during a recent visit to the salmon fisheries near Drogheda had been tanned by a specialist in the dressing of beaver skins. Each hide may outlast several 'baskets' or boat-frames, for these quickly rot with repeated wettings and dryings, and on the average two frames of doubled hazel wands are required each season, which lasts from 12th February to 12th August. A few other Irish rivers kept their curraghs into recent centuries— the curragh was certainly known on the Shannon and the Erne and possibly on the Bann—but on most of the inland waters dug-outs seem to have been traditional, and if we knew more about the two distributions important cultural inferences might be drawn. Dug-outs have been found, however, in nearly every part of the country, including the River Boyne.

The curragh is not likely to survive much longer and its lore should be fully recorded. Netting salmon in fresh water on all Irish rivers has been illegal since 1st January 1948, so that the curragh's last legal refuge is the tidal portion of the Boyne. But it has been long a-dying. I was told that no more would be made after the death of that fine craftsman Michael O'Brien

233

some twenty years ago, but it was not so. I find that W. F.
Wakeman was informed that the two curraghs which he sketched
on the Boyne in 1848 were 'probably the last which would be
constructed for use on those waters'.[1]

Fortunately James Hornell has published a careful study of
British Coracles and Irish Curraghs,[2] and the following account is
based on his book, supplemented by personal observation. On
the level sward—his rustic shipyard—the boat-builder first
marks out, with string and pegs, two semicircles of 2 ft. radius,
their centres being about twenty inches apart. This will give
the basket a mouth measuring 6 ft. by 4 ft., a size determined
by the average size of a hide. Joining the two circles into an
ellipse, he thrusts into the ground along this line, at intervals
of about nine inches, long pointed hazel rods which have been
cut the previous autumn after the leaf-fall and allowed to
season (Fig. 77). They are pushed about six inches into the
ground, at an angle so that they slope outwards somewhat. At
one end, the bow-to-be, an extra rod is inserted on either side
to give strength where the weight of the kneeling paddleman
will fall. Against the ground a strong gunwale of withies is
woven on to the rods, and above it a skirting of lighter withies.
Opposite rods on each side are now bent over and their thin
ends pushed into the ground to secure them temporarily. The
fore-and-aft rods are similarly bent over and heavy stones
placed on the basket, their weight distributed so as to make a
symmetrical frame with the top (that is the bottom of the curragh) as nearly flat as possible. At this stage two or three days
are allowed for the frame to set. Then the crossings of the rods
are lashed with a continuous twine and again the frame is left
weighted. The thin ends of the rods are now broken off at the
last lashings in such a way as to leave the bark projecting to
prevent the ends from damaging the hide. This, which has
meanwhile been softening in the river, is sewn on to the gunwale with twine, the basket having been pulled out of the ground
and inverted. The thwart is fixed in position amidship, its
ends suspended from the gunwale with withy ties, and withy
braces are laced across the stern portion to form a rest for the

[1] W. F. Wakeman, *J.R.S.A.I.* (1872), 76.
[2] J. Hornell, *British Coracles and Irish Curraghs* (1938).

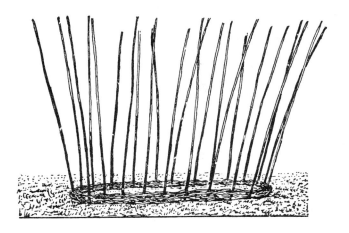

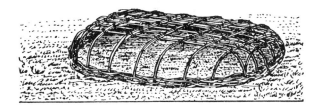

FIG. 77. The Boyne curragh: construction of basket.

235

net. Sitting on the thwart, the boat-builder now drives in the projecting rod-ends to tighten the skin, and trims them to within an inch of the gunwale. Finally he weaves on a protecting mouth of hazel rods which he binds to the gunwale and covers, behind the thwart, with canvas to save the net from damage as it is played out.

The curragh was well adapted to the draft-net salmon fishery at the Oldbridge weir on the Boyne. The following account is based on notes made at Oldbridge in 1947: 'Every half hour of daylight during the season, the curragh makes its brief trip with a draft-net around the pool of water where the salmon lie below the weir. Its virtue lies in its lightness and ease of handling—though not for the novice—in the method of paddling over the bows which allows it to keep close to the banks, and especially in the shallow draught which enables it to pass right under the weir without being swept down by the under-current. The paddler kneels in the deep bows and draws the boat along with rapid strokes alternately to left and right. The net-man sits on the thwart facing backwards and plays out the net, the end of which is held by a third man on the bank. Having reached the far end of the weir the paddler races downstream and returns across the current to join the third man and close the net. The salmon are dispatched with a heavy 'priest' here called the killing-stick.' The fishermen still operate two rectangular fishtraps below the weir, one near each bank, composed of iron gratings which have probably replaced wicker traps since they are known as 'hurdles'. The salmon are taken out with a landing net. A weir has probably been worked continuously at this spot since the Middle Ages, for the monks of Mellifont Abbey operated a weir here.[1]

It comes as a shock, after seeing the little basket-curragh of the Boyne, to recall that the legendary histories tell of much trafficking across the seas in splendid curraghs which carried sails. *The Voyage of Teigue* was made in a curragh constructed of forty oxhides and fitted with twenty-five thwarts.[2] Allowance must be made for picturesque exaggeration, but there is no doubt that the monks of the Irish Church went far afield in

[1]A. E. J. Went, *Co. Louth Arch. Journ.*, 13 (1953), 18–33.
[2]Standish O'Grady, *Silva Gadelica* (1892), 386.

their skin boats and almost certainly reached Iceland before the Norsemen. An account of the legendary voyagings of St. Brendan speaks of the hides of his curragh as dressed with butter. Port-na-Curaich, on the island of Iona, commemorates the landing of another Irish saint, St. Columba, though one hesitates to accept the tradition that the long mound which may be seen there is the place where he buried his curragh so that he could not return to Ireland. The sea-going curraghs were ideal craft for the Irish raiders who plundered west Britain during and after the Roman occupation: light in weight, of shallow draught and capable of flying over the waves. Probably the plank-built longboats of the Vikings drove the curraghs from the Irish Sea, but its descendants are still to be found in the rowing curraghs of the west coast from Donegal to Kerry. The Boyne curragh is a fossilized relic of an earlier form, if indeed it is not, as Hornell thought, a degeneration product.

But besides the rowing curraghs up to twenty-five feet in length there are also, in Donegal, smaller paddling curraghs eight or ten feet long which seem to stand between the oval river baskets and the sharp-pointed rowing curraghs. In an account of the Rosses in the 1750s we read of the funeral processions to the island of Aranmore in Donegal which comprised as many as sixty or eighty curraghs covered with seal skins.[1] We learn from a description of their construction written nearly 100 years later that the frame of sallies and laths, at that time 'skinned with a hide or tarred canvas' was lashed together with cords of horsehair.[2] The same writer tells us that cattle were transported in them by lifting an animal into the curragh on its back, with its legs tied, and carrying the loaded vessel into the water. He gives the following example of 'the reckless daring of these islanders. A man and his wife coming out of the island of Aranmore, in a little boat filled with turf, had a horse standing on top of it; with the roll of the sea, the animal was thrown out, and as they were a long way from land, must have been drowned, had not the man cleverly succeeded in getting him into the boat again!' It seems from what records are available that the hides used for covering the vessels,

[1] A. B., *The Rosses in 1753*, 202.
[2] Lord George Hill, *Gweedore*, 31.

whether seal-skin or the hide of a cow or horse, were untanned. I can add little to the historical account given by Hornell, but it should be noticed that the paddle curragh, covered with horsehide, was common in Erris, Co. Mayo, around 1830[1] and that, to judge from an entry in a Rathlin Island account book of 1760—'paid for one mare's hide for the boat, 1s. and 6d.'— the paddle curragh was used there also.

The long rowing curragh with its high pointed nose is widely distributed on the west coast from Donegal to Kerry, and its seaworthy qualities are known to many from its dramatic participation in such films as *Man of Aran* and *Shark Island*. This vessel too is built bottom upwards, but the frame is pegged, not into the ground but into a strong wooden gunwale frame, single or double, which Hornell believes was borrowed, along with the fixed thwarts which give lateral rigidity, from plank-built boats. Yet the method of pivoting the oar on a single tholepin, originally perhaps a strong projecting rib of the curragh frame, rather than in a rowlock, suggests that the rowing curragh has native forerunners. There are many variations in constructional details from one district to another but nearly all the vessels are now built of laths and all are covered with tarred canvas. An emergency repair is contrived by an operation which, if you are a timid passenger, looks like 'burning your boats': the curragh is inverted, the tar around the hole is set alight and a calico patch stuck on when the tar has run. The curraghs are rowed by two, three or four men, and the largest are said to have a carrying capacity of two tons. In Kerry they are masted to carry a small lug sail. A feature of many curraghs is a small bottle of holy water, a protection against misfortune, suspended on a string in the bows.

The looms of the long narrow oars overlap so that the oarsman pulls cross-handed. A heavy wooded counterweight, the bool, is attached near the loom, and the oar pivots by means of a round hole in the bool on a single wooden peg, the tholepin, driven into the gunwale (Fig. 78). This method of rowing is found on many lake and river boats in Ireland, perhaps especially in those areas, such as the Shannon and Lough Neagh,

[1]P. Knight, *Erris in the Irish Highlands* (1836), 56. See also *Pococke's Tour* 1752, 64.

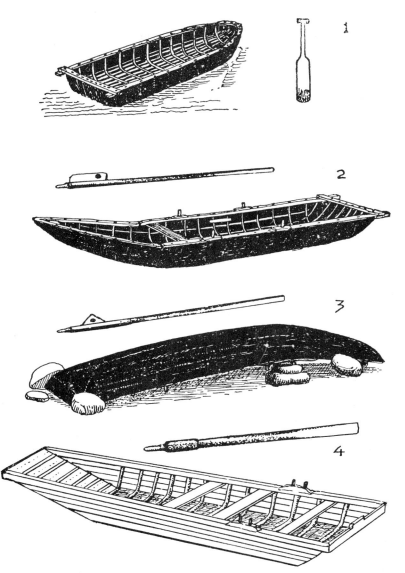

Fɪɢ. 78. Curraghs and cot. (1) Paddle curragh and paddle, Bunbeg, Co. Donegal.
(2) Rowing curragh and oar, Sheephaven, Co. Donegal. (3) Rowing curragh
and oar, Spiddal, Co. Galway. (4) Cot and oar, Lough Erne, Co. Fermanagh.

where curraghs were formerly known. But it is also characteristic of Scottish cobles and the boats of some English lakes.
The inshore fishing boats of Co. Antrim also had booled oars,[1]
and farther afield the single tholepin is said to typify the rowing
boats of Madeira, the sardine boats of Portugal and some
vessels of the Upper Nile. These often use a grommet, as do
the boats of the north-east coast of England.

Sea-going curraghs are put to many uses, for inshore net
fishing, for setting lobster pots or long lines, for gathering
kelp and for carrying freight, livestock and passengers. But
the most spectacular purpose to which they have been put is for
hunting the basking shark or sunfish from whose liver, before
the advent of paraffin, oil for lighting was obtained. A single
fish will yield from seven to ten barrels of liver. Measuring
up to forty feet in length, the basking shark is one of the world's
largest fish and though harmless—its diet is minute copepods—
its bulk makes it a formidable adversary. These fish move
down the west coast in summer, and in early May they haunt
the Sunfish Bank thirty miles off Achill Island, where they
come to the surface in the morning and evening. The bank is
remarkable for the break of the tide on it, although it lies between seventy and ninety fathoms near the edge of 'soundings'
—the continental shelf—and a heavy swell makes conditions
difficult for small boats. Here and elsewhere the sunfish used
to be harpooned from curraghs, but the advantage lay with
decked vessels which could stand by for several days. In the
early nineteenth century as many as thirty or forty fish were
sometimes killed on the Sunfish Bank in a single day of fine
weather. Nowadays the sharks are taken in strong nets fixed to
island headlands around which they swim. They are occasionally
seen off the other Irish coasts, where they cause great havoc if
they get involved in the fishing nets.

Of the small open clinker-built boats of traditional type which
takes the place of the curragh on the north, east and south
coasts, no systematic study has been made. Some of them betray
their Norse inheritance in their lines or their names, for example
the Wicklow skiff and the drontheim (Trondhjem) of the
north coast. These boats are double-ended—unlike the cur-

[1] S. McSkimin, *The History and Antiquities of Carrickfergus*, 276.

raghs—and would not be out of place in the fiords. In fact during the nineteenth century, and perhaps from earlier times, many yawls were imported unfinished from Norway, carrying only the bottom (garboard) strakes hollowed from a thick plank. Local materials, always scarce in Ireland in recent centuries, were utilized where possible, holly for the keel (it wears smooth and slides well on beach gravel) ropes of bog fir, and a 'whin root' for the tiller. In Kerry the entire vessel was sometimes built from bog fir: for this purpose as for making roof-frames it had the advantage of impermeability.[1] For off-shore fishing in the Irish Sea the lugger—a name now applied to the motor drifter which has taken its place—developed in the nineteenth century under the influence of visiting 'nickies', the Manx name for Cornish lug-sailed herring boats, said to have been given because so many of their crews were named Nicholas. On the west coast the Galway hookers are now, despite their name, used almost entirely for carrying turf and live-stock. The lug-sailed pookhauns used for fishing are a variant of the Irish Sea yawl, of clumsy construction thanks to limited resources and unsuitable building materials.

On many inland loughs and larger rivers dug-out boats not much different from those of the Bronze Age seem to have continued to be made into the seventeenth century and probably even later in places. The most serious problem to be solved in hollowing out a solid log is how to keep the sides and bottom of the vessel of even thickness. Some of the ancient dug-outs recovered from the Irish lakes and rivers show that their makers had availed themselves of a method which is practised today in parts of Indonesia. The method is to bore holes through the shell and plug the holes with pegs of the right length to serve as gauges. The plugged holes observed in the bottom of many an Irish dug-out have been explained as drainage holes, but the pegs would in that case have been left protruding, and one hole would surely have sufficed. As the country lost its forests it must have become difficult to obtain trees of the right size and kind, especially oak, for boat making, and by the eighteenth century, it seems, plank boats retaining some features of the dug-out were substituted. Around 1800 the salmon-fishing cots

[1] A. Young, *Tour*, 2, 89.

of the River Nure were described as 'flat narrow boats equal at both ends and propelled by paddles'.[1] Earlier, about 1645, Gerard Boate described the cots as 'things like boats, but very unshapely, being nothing but square pieces of timber made hollow.' 'They are very common throughout all Ireland . . . even upon the great rivers and loughs'.[2]

To judge from the numerous discoveries of small dug-outs at river crossings their last surviving use was for ferrying purposes. They were replaced locally by flat-bottomed cots built with wide planks laid edge to edge, such as serve the eel-fishers of the River Bann. These are propelled with a pole. The punt-like cot is also the old craft of the River Shannon. A number of dug-outs are found to have been adapted for propulsion with oars, using the single thole-pin of the rowing-curragh. The large rowing boats of Lough Neagh also use the single thole-pin: to give greater leverage for the heavy oars the iron thole-pin is set out from the gunwale on an outrigger or 'bolster'. In the cots of Lough Erne the oar is worked between double thole-pins (Fig. 78). The maze of lakes which make up the Lough Erne group have yielded many ancient dug-outs of varied types, some of them spoon-shaped, others rectangular and provided with carrying lugs. Others again seem to be both boat and sledge, an alternative to the portable curragh in a land strewn with little lakes. But the strangest vessel, apparently misnamed a curragh, was a kind of raft which is said to have survived until a hundred years ago, 'composed of wreaths of bull-rushes tied upon a frame or raft made of rough branches of trees'.[3]

Methods of fishing in river and lake include not only legitimate forms of angling and netting, but many ways of killing fish which game laws and other vested interests have made illegal, but have not extinguished. The spearing of salmon, prohibited since 1714, is now left to poachers, but well into the last century it was openly practised in the city of Galway.[4] On Lough Neagh yellow (feeding) eels are caught illicitly on long lines by fisherfolk whose claims to ancient rights have not

[1] W. Tighe, *Statistical Observations, County of Kilkenny*, 150.
[2] G. Boate, *Ireland's Natural History*, 64, 136.
[3] W. F. Wakeman, loc. cit.
[4] A. E. J. Went, *J.R.S.A.I.*, 82 (1952), 110

been recognized by the courts. 'Bobbing' for eels with a ball of worms attached to a string is practised on dark stormy nights, and on the River Bann a vicious-looking eel-rake is used to jab among the river weeds. Its teeth of sharp steel, often discarded hackle-pins, are set an inch apart in the end of a long pole. Bone pins of prehistoric date recovered in quantities from the bed of the river may have been put to a similar use, and this method of catching fish, probably of ancient origin, is widely distributed. There are specimens of eel-rakes in the Danish museums (Fig. 79). A very similar eel-comb is known in China, and a herring rake, used by the native fishermen of north-western America and mounted with sharp bone teeth, was first described by Captain Cook in 1778.[1] For taking salmon, poachers in the River Barrow use a staked net fashioned into a conical trap, and trout are taken in the north of Ireland in home-made 'loop nets' large enough to bridge small streams (Fig. 80). Salmon are also 'strokehauled' with naked hooks, and gaffed when within reach of the river banks. Trout are taken not only by 'ginling' (tickling) but also with a 'dull' or horsehair noose.

Dr. Went has made a careful study of Irish fish spears and the interested reader may be referred to his paper.[2] It may be mentioned that two of the three classes of eel-spears which he describes have been recovered from crannogs of the Dark Ages: they are the barbed spears known as rock- or sun-spears, so named from the conditions which are required for the eels to be impaled, and the more common mud-spears, which are within the law and of which excellent specimens can still be seen in parts of the country. They have flat tines, notched at the sides to prevent the enmeshed eels escaping. Spears of this type are plunged blindly into the mud. Consequently they are often very large and heavy, a seven-pronged example from the River Bann weighing over nine pounds and having a handle 30 feet long. Old specimens have a circular aperture at the junction of each pair of tines which facilitated the removal of the eels. The advantage of the mud-spear, which has a much wider distribution than the primitive looking rock-spear (which is apparently

[1] *Captain Cook's Third Voyage,* Ed. C. R. Low (N.D.), 395.
[2] A. E. J. Went, *J.R.S.A.I.,* 82 (1952), 109–34.

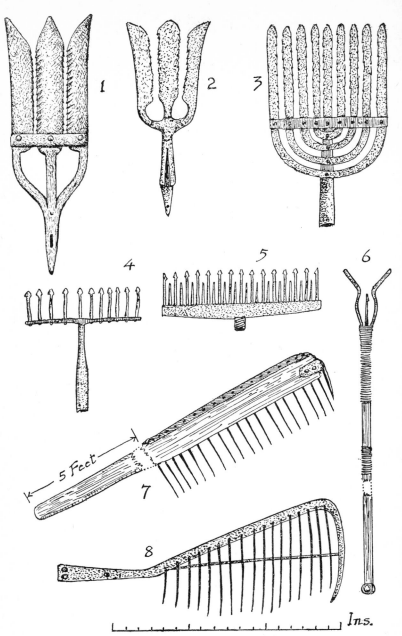

FIG. 79. Eel spears and rakes. (1) Mud-spear, Co. Antrim. (2, 3) Mud-spears, Co. Westmeath (after Went). (4, 5) Rock- or sun-spears, Co. Westmeath (after Went). (6) Wexford harbour eel-spear (after Went). (7) Eel-rake, River Bann (after N. C. Mitchel). (8) Eel-rake, Denmark (National Museum, Copenhagen).

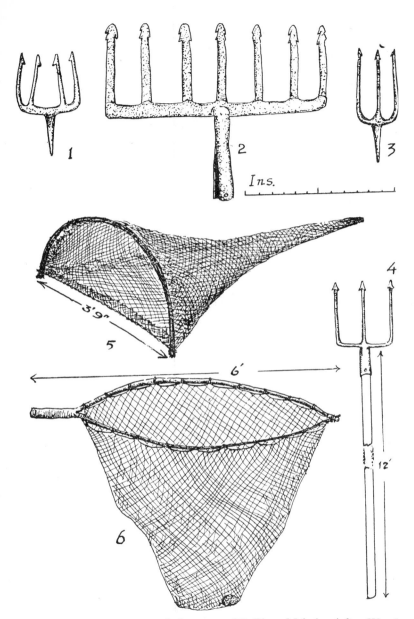

Ins.

3'9"

6'

12'

FIG. 80. Salmon spears and river nets. (1) River Mulcaire (after Went).
(2) River Suir (after Went). (3) Co. Down. (4) Co. Antrim. (5) Co. Donegal.
(6) Co. Tyrone (after E. N. Carrothers).

confined to Co. Westmeath) is that the eel was undamaged and its skin could therefore be utilized. Apart from their use as thongs and flail-hangings eel-skins were worn as charms against rheumatic pains. Eel fat, too, is esteemed as a cure for rheumatism. The third type of eel-spear is quite different in form and methods of use. It is confined to Wexford Harbour and would appear to be a relic of Scandinavian influence in that half-foreign south-eastern corner of Ireland comprising the baronies of Bargy and Forth. It consists of two splayed prongs between which is ingeniously mounted a single barbed prong on to which the eel is guided by the outer members (Fig. 79). When the tide covers the mudflats the fisherman lies in a punt with his head over the prow, and with a spear in each hand propels the boat until he spies an eel in the mud, when his punting pole becomes a weapon. At low tide the eel fishers wear yard-long 'scooches' or mud-shoes, wooden boards turned up at the front like miniature skis. We note in passing that boards were formerly worn by both men and horses in working on soft bogs in Co. Mayo.[1]

The salmon spear or leister, being illegal, is normally a light three-pronged instrument, but large specimens weighing up to eight pounds and made after the fashion of the Westmeath eel-spears are found on the River Suir (Fig. 80). The fish were attracted at night by 'burning the river' with resinous splits of bog-fir or lumps of peat soaked in oil.

Riverine weirs of many kinds have been the privilege of religious houses and landed properties through the ages, and many examples specially designed for the capture of migratory fish, salmon and eels are maintained. There are traditions of temporary weirs of heather stems weighted down with stones, into which trout were driven to be extracted when the bundles of heather were pitched on to the bank. Gerard Boate describes the weirs in his day as consisting of 'big stones set close together from the one side of the river to the other, leaving only one hole . . . before which hole a basket being laid, they take therein a great quantity of fish'.[2] 'Fish baskets' and 'weels' are referred to in many ancient fishing grants, but I have not

[1] J. McParlan, *Mayo*, 94.
[2] Gerard Boate, *Ireland's Natural History*, 70.

come across surviving examples of these ancient devices. The
iron 'cribs' associated with modern salmon weirs, however,
appear to derive from wattled traps. And the long conical
'coghill' nets in which the eels are caught in the weirs of the
Bann, the Shannon and (until recently) the Erne, are shaped
like weels and indeed they are sometimes built up of a series
of cones. The fine meshed 'tail' of the net is made to open and
the eels, nowadays, are poured directly into submerged tanks.
A detail suggestive of long custom is that the 'skiver' with
which the tail is closed in the coghills of the weirs at Portna
on the Bann consists of a perforated rib-bone of horse or cow.
The pin is attached to a cord, which is wound round the end
of the net and secured by thrusting the pin into the windings.
The walls of the weirs are often still built of wattles, and the
old style of weir on the Erne consists of a base of large stones
into which the wattled superstructure is thrust.[1]

The wattles are known on the Bann as *skeaghs*: of the six
weirs now fishing there four are of the traditional type and
two have been modernized. At Athlone on the Shannon there
were twenty-two eel weirs in the early seventeenth century,
and nearly all were still working in the nineteenth century: a
single weir is now fished there.[2] The eel weirs of the River
Erne had been reduced to five when they were abandoned
owing to the recent construction of a dam for the Ballyshannon
hydro-electric scheme. The Bann silver eel fisheries are probably
the largest of their kind in western Europe, and it is significant
that the Bann is one of the richest rivers in Europe for archaeological discoveries ranging in date from the Mesolithic to the
early medieval period. Both salmon and eels have now become
money-crops and the catches are exported. Already in the eighteenth century Irish salt salmon was exported in considerable
quantities to America. The ice-house in which salmon used to
be preserved is one of the many ruined buildings to be seen
about the decaying houses of the gentry, and most country
houses also had their fish ponds.

Among the common folk eels are esteemed only by the folk
who catch them, legally or otherwise, but they were formerly

[1] A. E. J. Went, *J.R.S.A.I.*, 75 (1945), 213–23.
[2] A. E. J. Went, *J.R.S.A.I.*, 80 (1950), 146–54.

sold fresh in the markets of the Bann Valley, and were salted down for winter use in place of herrings.[1] They have gone the way of most of the pre-famine 'relishes' which came to be despised as the threat of famine faded after the middle of last century. The elvers, too, used to be taken out of the teeming rivers in spring with sieves and pressed into cakes or boiled in milk and made into a kind of eel-cheese. In the River Bann the elvers are now trapped at the first weir, at the tidal limit, and transported upstream, up to 30 million a year being given an easy passage in this way. A marked reduction in the size of the silver eels netted on their return to the sea some ten years later has been interpreted as a result of this interference with nature. The bulk of the eels taken are sold live in the London markets. In addition to elvers salmon fry also was in former times taken for food and fed to pigs, and by an Act of Elizabeth's reign swine were prohibited from feeding on the shores of tidal rivers 'where they destroy a great quantity of salmon and eel fry'.[2]

Many traditional methods of fishing survive on the lakes of the Irish midlands. The otter board, now more often seen along the coast where fishermen trawl for flat fish in sandy bays, was formerly widely used in lake fishing and is considered to be 'an implement of very ancient origin in Ireland'.[3] Related to it is the 'pooka', a board fitted with mast and sail which carried out the baited long lines.[4] Fishing lines were until recently sometimes made of horsehair by an interesting and undoubtedly ancient method. The instruments employed are goose or swan quills, cut down to make open-ended tubes some three inches long, two or three being needed according to whether a two- or three-strand line is being prepared. From ten to twenty long hairs taken from a horse's tail are threaded through each quill and knotted together at one end, the other ends of the quills being plugged with short pieces of quill which grip the hairs yet allow them to slide through. The quills are now rolled one against the other in the fingers, and as the strands twist on one another they pull down the hairs which feed them. The

[1]G. V. Sampson, *Memoir*, 243.

[2]W. Tighe, *Statistical Observations, County of Kilkenny*, 153.

[3]C. R. Browne, *Ballycroy*. See also R. U. Sayce, *Montgomeryshire Collections*, 53 (1954).

[4]W. H. Maxwell, *Wild Sports of the West*, 77.

line grows as if by magic as the quills rotate in nimble fingers. A fresh supply of hairs is inserted from time to time by removing the plugs. I illustrate an example of this fascinating apparatus made for me by Mr. T. J. Barron of Knockbride, Co. Cavan (Fig. 81). Mr. A. T. Lucas has described the Cavan

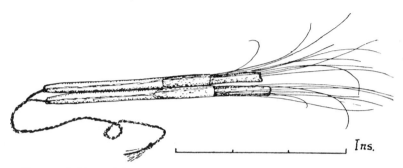

Ins.

FIG. 81. Quills used for making horsehair fishing lines, Co. Cavan. The quills are rolled between the forefingers.

specimens and others from Co. Mayo.[1] In Cavan the lines were made for bream fishing: the bream were both split, salted and dried and stored fresh in little ponds on the lake shores. Around the coasts—I have seen examples from the Aran Islands and from Co. Down—a more complicated machine was made for twisting long lines of hemp, three spindles being rotated by pulling on an endless cord twisted round each spindle.[2] A very similar device is employed in China for making bamboo ropes for raising coal in primitive mines. On the shores of Lough Neagh the long lines are manufactured in rustic rope-walks. These night-lines, which have tended to replace draft-nets, are set in lengths of up to four miles. The season of yellow (feeding) eel fishing runs from March to October. It is illegal, as we have mentioned, but shows no signs of being given up. The eel fishermen claim immemorial rights and are not deterred by the fines imposed when they are caught. Their vocabulary, like that of the men who work the eel weirs on the River Bann, has many words which have come down from Gaelic and perhaps from

[1] A. T. Lucas, *Journal of the Galway Arch. and Hist. Soc.*, 24 (1951), 111–14.
[2] E. E. Evans, *Mourne Country*, Fig. 63.

pre-Gaelic tongues, and there can be little doubt that the eel fishery is prehistoric in origin. The draft nets in which pollan are caught in the lake—the pollan is a fresh-water herring peculiar to some Irish and Scottish lakes—also display old features. The sections, known as webs, are sewn together with a bone needle into long nets, which are weighted with stone sinkers. The draft-net is widely used in the salmon rivers, as described on the Boyne earlier in this chapter, and references to draft-netting go back to the twelfth century. On some rivers tall towers are erected from which a watcher signals the presence of fish.[1]

We are not here concerned with the commercial offshore fisheries, but something must be said of the inshore fishing because it has been characteristically combined with farming all around the coast. This type of fishing was well suited to the Irish crofter economy, so that the comment frequently made by improving visitors and despairing Government officials was that the Irish would not go out to fish, but waited for the fish to come close inshore. The shore-dwelling farmer is knowledgeable about the ways of fish and knows all 'the signs'. He has been accustomed to keep a net to hand and watch for shoals of different fish at the right seasons. There are watching points on the cliffs overlooking many a small bay, and it was from such vantage points on the south and west coasts that the pilchard 'huers' directed the seine boats to the shoals that visit Ireland intermittently.[2] In the seventeenth and eighteenth centuries the Irish pilchard fishery grew to large proportions but it has now declined to something like its older local significance. When the industry was capitalized by promoters like Sir William Petty it was the train oil pressed out during the packing of the pilchards for export which found an Irish market. It was used both as a luminant and in the preparation of leather. The seine boats have now turned their attention to herring and mackerel, and Dr. Went has pointed out that the seine is used for catching salmon only in Kenmare Bay, where Petty introduced it for pilchard fishing about the year 1672.

In the Irish Sea the herrings come close inshore in September

[1] A. E. J. Went, *J.R.S.A.I.*, 85 (1955), 22–23, Pl. 3A.
[2] A. E. J. Went, *J.C.H. and A. Soc.*, 51 (1946), 137–57.

and are therefore known as 'harvest herrings'. It is then that the yawls or skiffs which lie half hidden for most of the year have their brief spell of activity, and the farmers who jointly own them find on moonlight nights a cool relief from the hot pressure of harvest. The fish are caught in trammel nets, and they were formerly in great demand not only locally but for many miles inland for salting down as winter 'kitchen'.[1] A more varied diet has lessened the demand, for the great days of the salt herring were the eighteenth and nineteenth centuries when a potato diet cried out for a tasty accompaniment. On the north-west coast the herring fishery extends through the winter, with consequent serious risks which the Donegal men have none the less been willing to take. Here, perhaps, is one explanation for the survival of the light rowing curragh down to the coming of powered vessels, for a small sail boat brings many hazards on this stormy Atlantic coast.

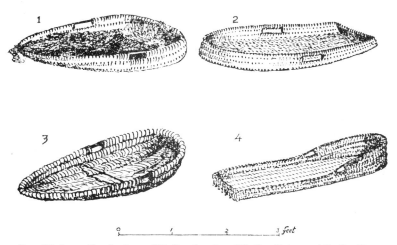

Fig. 82. Long-line baskets. (1) Co. Antrim. (2) Co. Galway. (3) Co. Down. (4) Aran Islands.

Long line fishing for cod, skate, ling and other big fish is almost certainly far older than the herring fishery, and it has preserved down to our own day many ancient practices and

[1] E. E Evans, *Mourne Country*, ch. 18.

types of gear. It used to be said that you should never risk taking a dog into some of the fishing villages on the north coast: their skins were in great demand for making the line floats or 'stookies'. Very probably seal skins were formerly used for this purpose, as among the Eskimo. The sinkers of grooved stones from the beach might well pass for prehistoric implements (Fig. 74). The beautifully made line-baskets of unpeeled willow have the graceful curves that one associates with the work of untouched 'primitives' (Fig. 82). And the division of labour was on a primitive level, for to the womenfolk fell the tedious labour of baiting and preparing the hooks. The long-line fishermen were exceptionally hardy and were regarded with awe and respect by the inshore fishermen-farmers. No doubt the timid and the weakly had been weeded out by continual stress. Their knowledge of the sea and of the fishing marks was a guarded secret, and the best banks were sometimes allotted, no doubt to avoid fights, by casting lots. In the Hebrides this was done on Bride's Day. There also, and possibly in Ireland, the banks were held in rotation in a kind of marine rundale.

XVIII

FAIRS AND GATHERINGS

THE Irish countryman enjoys nothing so much as 'a gathering' of people, and when he is forced to leave his native land he does not willingly settle down away from large urban centres. At home a crowd goes to his head like poteen. The daily routine of life on an isolated farm presents him with few opportunities for seeing people from outside his immediate neighbourhood, and on fine summer evenings his favourite pastime is to throw himself against a roadside ditch with a knot of companions and watch the passers-by. That the remarkably large attendances at rural churches and chapels owe something to the social needs of a scattered population is suggested by the phrase, applied to someone who arrives late at chapel: 'he missed the mass but hit the gathering'—he had something worth while for his trouble. In the Irish laws the freeman's rights of assembly were carefully defined: there were assemblies for transacting legal business (the oireacht), and others for commerce and games (the aenach) which came to be called fairs. With the coming of Christianity the traditional gatherings at sacred sites were transmuted into patterns (pardons), at which the new religion was quickened by practices of the elder faiths. In fact most gatherings served more than one purpose. The secret assemblies of Roman Catholics at 'mass rocks' in penal days no doubt also provided opportunities for social and commercial dealings, and the 'sacrament Sabbaths' of Presbyterian Ulster were great gatherings having something of the nature of fairs. Tents and booths were erected for the occasion, and indeed they were popularly known as 'holy fairs'.

Although the fair has lost something of its former significance in Northern Ireland, thanks to Government marketing schemes

253

and purchasing boards, it is still a powerful commercial and social force in the rest of Ireland. In fact the numbers of fairs have increased with the post-famine dominance of the cattle trade, though they have tended to be concentrated in fewer centres as many small fair-towns have been by-passed by improved means of communication. On the other hand the weekly markets have declined or disappeared, their place taken by shops which typically handle drinks as well as groceries, clothing as well as hardware. Thus the fair has retained and even strengthened its magnetic hold on the countryfolk, and though many of its subsidiary functions have been taken over by institutions of more recent origin, the fair itself retains a pagan aura. There is a widespread belief, by no means confined to Ireland, that fair days are always rainy days. This belief may well be justified by climatic averages, but I have heard it explained as a consequence of the lies and profanity, the fights and pagan ways of the fair. Many an ancient fair has become extinct, no doubt because it no longer fulfilled its economic functions, but the explanation usually given is that it was abandoned 'on account of the fighting'.

In Europe, north of the Alpine mountains, the fair as a means of exchange and social intercourse is an institution older than the town, and older far than Christianity. The periodic assemblies of early Celtic Ireland served as temporary towns, and it was probably these sites which Ptolemy marked as cities on his map of the second century A.D. They were held on hill-tops hallowed by an antiquity which archaeology has in some instances traced back to the Bronze Age, and the regions which they served were, we have suggested, already taking shape in the late Neolithic period. Ireland has a number of large enclosures of Neolithic date analogous to Windmill Hill in Wiltshire, which apparently functioned as seasonal meeting places where stock was rounded-up and sorted. An enclosure of rather different type but of similar age—the Giant's Ring near Belfast—was the scene of horse-racing down to recent centuries. On the cairn-crowned Cave Hill, too, overlooking Belfast, crowds used to assemble on Easter Monday 'in accordance with immemorial usage'.[1] We may see in the 'parles

[1] J. B. Doyle, *Tours in Ulster* (1855), 102.

upon hills', which the Dublin government found so obnoxious in the sixteenth century, the persistent efforts of the Irish to maintain their ancient rights and customs of public assembly. In the Anglo-Norman period and again during the plantations of the sixteenth and seventeenth centuries towns were deliberately established with the intention of bringing 'civilized ways of living to the wild Irish'. Many of them are characterized by a wide street or square—the 'diamond' in Northern Ireland— where fairs and other gatherings could be dominated and controlled from a castle which overlooked it. These urban settlements were known to the Irish, whose native 'towns' were rarely anything more than disorderly clachans, as 'street towns'. They are found scattered at fairly regular intervals all through the countryside, usually at some river crossing or hill gap where routeways meet. Some of them, well-placed in good fertile country, have expanded, while others have decayed or remained mere villages. Often one will find not far away the old Fair Hill from which the fair was attracted as the facilities of the town outweighed the traditional pull of the inconvenient hill-top. But for long the Irish kept to their own fairs which continued, according to an Act of 1431, to 'take great customs and profits to the depression of the boroughs and the trading towns'.[1] The old assembly places are not entirely forgotten, and it often happened that they were visited for games and horse-racing long after they had lost their function as places of commerce. They are celebrated in local ballads and their sites can still be traced by the grassy mounds which are the remains of booths and cattle pens. The lost fairs of Ireland deserve a study such as is being made of the lost villages of England, but the chief sources for such a study, in the absence of records, must lie in field work and the fast-fading memories of the countryside.

The fairs were formerly organized in a recognized sequence of goods and livestock, terminating in sports and horse-racing— and not infrequently in bloodshed. Several of them achieved a notoriety which made their names a byword, and among them none was more notorious, owing partly no doubt to its proximity to Dublin, than Donnybrook Fair. The Parliamentary Gazetteer of 1845 forgets its sober purpose in thus describing

[1] T. W. Freeman, *Ireland*, 95.

it: 'During the week, beginning on the 26th August, is held
the notorious Donnybrook Fair, professedly for the sale of
horses and black cattle, but really for vulgar dissipation, and
formerly for criminal outrage and the most revolting debauchery. It was for generations a perfect prodigy of moral horrors
—a concentration of disgrace upon, not Ireland alone, but
civilized Europe. It far surpassed all other fairs in the multitude
and grossness of its disgusting incidents of vice; and, in general,
it exhibited such continuous scenes of riot, bloodshed, debauchery and brutality, as only the coarsest taste and the most
hardened heart could witness without painful emotion.' This
was by day; 'the orgies of the night may be better imagined
than described'. An anonymous writer is quoted as saying:
'We venture to say that there is more misery and madness,
devilment and debauchery, than could be found crowded into
an equal space of ground in any other part of this our globe,
during five times the same space, which is spent at Donnybrook,
in one given year'. The *Gazetteer* then recovers itself and
offers excuses for 'describing what ought never to have been
described'. One regrets rather that the compiler was so over-
come by horror as to forget his statistical duties.

The absence of moral restraint which led to extremes of
lawlessness at Donnybrook and elsewhere was a normal and
characteristic accompaniment of these periodic folk-gatherings.
Such moral holidays are a feature of many societies which have
not been greatly influenced by urban ways and values. Their
purpose appears to be cathartic, but that there is a lingering
fertility magic underlying the excitement is suggested by such
strange rituals as those which mark the 'Puck Fair and Pattern'
of Kilorglin at the head of Dingle Bay in Co. Kerry. The fair
is unfortunately not mentioned in the *Parliamentary Gazetteer*,
though the village of Kilorglin is described as 'an unprosperous,
sequestered, and almost squalid seat of population; and appears
to have acquired marvellously little profit from the advanta-
geousness of its position for both inland and seaward trade'.
Puck Fair, held every August, is the great event of the year in
West Kerry, and lasts three days. 10th August is 'Gathering
Day', the 11th is 'Fair Day', and the 12th 'Scattering Day',
terms which have no doubt been handed down from days when

'the order of the fair' was prescribed and the business lasted several days. On the evening of Gathering Day a procession assembles at the bridge and makes its way to the central square carrying (nowadays in a large cage mounted on a lorry) a billy-goat bedecked with ribbons. He is chained by the horns on a high platform erected for the purpose and, supplied with a liberal stock of cabbages, he presides over the fair. Tradition says that the goat used to stand, 'garlanded by greenery' on the old castle which was erected here by the Geraldines in the thirteenth century. The business of the fair is the sale of live-stock, and as with many another large fair it is a traditional gathering place for the tinkers who in Ireland take the place of the gypsies. On the evening of Scattering Day the Puck is borne triumphantly back to the bridge. The popular explana-tion of the custom is that it commemorates an occasion when the noise of goats warned the Irish of advancing English forces, but it is more reasonable to see Puck as a symbol of fertility and good luck. 12th August is Old Lammas, and Lammas Day, the 1st August, was known to the Irish as 'Lewy's Fair', in memory of a pre-Christian deity. This season of high summer has many associations with the pastoral freedom of the hills, with young people and with dancing and courting. There are traditions of other Puck Fairs in the south of Ireland, and there were certain fairs at which a white horse was paraded through the assembled crowds and then tied up to preside over the proceedings.

Another celebrated gathering place was the great fair of Ballinasloe, which brought such fame to this Galway town that the *Gazetteer* describes it as 'the cynosure of much the larger part of the western province of Ireland', so prosperous that even its poorer quarters, 'a segregation of lanes, and houses, and cabins, aggregately repulsive', were yet 'greatly less haggard than what constitutes the whole of many a third or second rate town in Ireland'. The fair was held from the 5th to the 9th of October, and during the first half of the nineteenth century the average numbers of sheep and cattle offered for sale were respectively 90,000 and 12,000. Ballinasloe Fair served the west of Ireland in much the same way as the great trysts of Crieff and Falkirk served the Scottish Highlands in the days of the famous cattle droves.[1] The town lies on one of the sinuous gravel ridges (eskers) which lead eastwards from the limestone grazing grounds of east Galway to the crossing of the Shannon and then thread their way through a maze of bogs to reach the headwaters of the Irish Sea rivers. The eskers provide dry footing for roads some of which are routeways of great antiquity, and down to the coming of railways they served as drove roads along which cattle and sheep were taken to the fattening pastures and markets of the eastern lowlands. The date of the great fair of Ballinasloe, in early October, corresponds with that of the largest trysts at Crieff and Falkirk, and would have allowed time for the movement of livestock to eastern Ireland or to the English fairs by All-Hallows or Martinmas.

No study of the Irish drove roads has been made as for those of Scotland and Wales, but it seems probable that the movement of livestock along routes from west to east has been developing since the Middle Ages, when its logical outcome was the export trade in hides from the Irish Sea ports. In the seventeenth and eighteenth centuries exports largely took the form of salt beef and butter, but since the early nineteenth century the store cattle trade has been so dominant that it has latterly accounted for half the total export trade of southern Ireland. It involves a movement of cattle not only from west to east but from small farms to large, and from scanty grazings to the lush fattening pastures of Meath or the English lowlands. Apart from small strings of beasts on their way to local fairs, the cattle droves are today most in evidence in the crowded dockside streets of the ports where they are herded on to the cross-channel boats, but until quite recently donkeys and goats purchased at fairs in the west still travelled to the ports on the hoof. The drover-dealers who accompanied them were colourful characters whose experience stood them in good stead in the wider world. These dealers in the unwanted residues of the countryside—in rags and scrap as well as asses and goats—have often set up as rag-and-scrap merchants in the large towns along their routes from Belfast and Dublin to the English fairs, and one of them became Lord Mayor of a Scottish city. Others made big money as pedlars of cloth in America or Australia. Most of these 'pahvees',

[1] A. R. B. Haldane, *The Drove Roads of Scotland.*

as they are called, were born in the mountain country of Slieve Gullion in Co. Armagh, adjoining the rich plains of the Pale where their ancestors sharpened their wits on the English settlers. Many stories are told of the tricks by which 'the goatmen' disposed of their animals before they reached their goal at Barnet Fair, of billy-goats sold to the innocent English as good milkers or as an infallible means of keeping a garden free of weeds. 'Every guy who comes here selling cloth', said a Canadian rancher, 'tells me he is from Slieve Gullion. It must be some city.'

Although the export of live cattle from Ireland was prohibited, in the interests of British farming, through most of the seventeenth and eighteenth centuries, the short sea-crossings from north-east Ireland enabled dealers to ship them to southern Scotland. The embargo was lifted in 1765, and by the early nineteenth century many thousands of cattle were reaching Portpatrick and being driven to the fairs at Dumfries and Carlisle, and farther afield to Barnet in Hertfordshire and St. Faith's near Norwich. Many Irish harvesters and other summer migrants followed the trails trodden by Irish cattle and their drovers, but after 1830, with the coming of the steamship, Glasgow, the Mersey and Holyhead became, as they remain, the chief points of entry for both animals and men.

Before the agrarian revolution and the import of feeding stuffs made it possible to keep stock through the winter, the months of October and November were critical for the farmer, who had to dispose of many of his animals at this time. The trade is now better distributed through the year, but although monthly fairs have become general since the famine, the sales vary a good deal from month to month, and the important fairs still fall at the turning points of the pastoral year, particularly in May and November. The spring fairs of February and March and the Lammas fairs of July and August were to a large extent concerned respectively with horses and with sheep and wool, but those of May and November were the great cattle fairs and also the hiring fairs. We are reminded that the Celtic year in pre-Christian times had only two seasons, winter and summer, and that the first days of November and May are still the Irish gale-days, the times when rents fall due.

One may readily see how this came about, for these were the times when the stock was gathered and sorted, and dues were paid to the overlords in cattle. In the ordinary business of the fair exchange and barter gave way in time to money transactions, but one has only to visit a cattle fair to sense that the noisy ritual of assessing values and the prolonged bargaining have come down from a time before the use of money was general. The vigorous hand-slapping by which bargains are sealed in tight-lipped silence could derive from the days when different languages were spoken at the fairs. Apart from the difference between English and Gaelic it should be remembered that in many districts pockets of non-Gaelic speech, perhaps even of non-Aryan tongues, survived well into the Christian era. Another interesting accompaniment of the concluded bargain is the piece of money, the luck penny, which the seller hands back to the purchaser as a gesture of independence when a price has finally been agreed on. Many a fight has begun because a buyer has been dissatisfied with the amount of his luck money. Similar bargaining took place when a servant was being hired for the half year, and he received his earles or earnest money as a sign that the contract was concluded, handing over to his employer his bundle of clothes in return.

The countryman will find any excuse for going to the fair, and it is his proud boast that he has seen so many fairs. It is by the fairs, and not by the calendar, that he measures time and dates important events in the life of the community. 'Their whole thought seems to be going to fairs and selling or exchanging', it was written of the Mayo peasantry in 1836,[1] and in the seventeenth century we find this comment on 'the inferior rank of husbandmen' in Westmeath: '(they) are very crafty and subtile in all manner of bargaining, especially in their dealings in fairs and markets'.[2] Your luck at the fair might depend on the colour of the hair of the first person you met on the road, and it was unlucky to be passed on the way, so that horsemen riding at full gallop were not merely trying out their paces for the races which followed. For good luck you should carry with

[1] P. Knight, *Erris in the Irish Highlands*, 104.
[2] Sir Henry Piers, *West-Meath*, 115.

you some borrowed article made of steel, an old shoe should be thrown after you, and special charms recited. A knot should be tied in the tail of a horse which is to be sold. If a tinker takes a fancy to your horse you will be wise to sell, for 'he will take the good out of it whether or no'. And if you buy an animal you should put a handful of earth on its back to ensure that you have also purchased 'the luck of the beast'. It was at the fair that a man proved his adult status by his ability to hold his own at buying and selling, and a favourite theme of the stories which raise a ready laugh at the fireside concerns the simpleton who exchanged his cow for a worthless trifle.

The old countryman is not ashamed to try out, often with success, his age-old bargaining methods when making purchases of standard-priced goods at a shop. For the shop has taken over some of the traditions of the larger less personal world of the fair. Not only is a certain amount of haggling expected—and enjoyed on both sides of the counter—but there is a communal interest in the outcome. Thus it is held that you should never be alone when making a purchase. And there is an old belief that money earned in a particular way should be spent on some special purchase, for example there should be some 'egg money'—normally the woman's earnings—in the cash set aside to buy a horse in spring. Reference has already been made to the tradition that if you sell a hide you should buy something made of metal with the money. In parts of the country there were certain things which it was thought should never be sold though they might be given away—a kid for example. And in Mayo milk might be given away but would be sold only in secret, and it used to be an indelible disgrace for a woman to sell butter: it was regarded as a sign of abject poverty.[1]

It is perhaps because of the anonymity which the bustle of the fair confers on the buyer that certain classes of goods tend to be purchased there rather than at a shop. One of the remarkable features of an Irish fair is the quantities of old clothes and boots on display, and I am told that there is a considerable export of second-hand clothes from Scotland to the country fairs of Northern Ireland. Sir Walter Scott commented on this

[1] P. Knight, *Erris in the Irish Highlands*, 77; C. R. Browne, *Ballycroy*.

trade in 1825.[1] Formerly it was at the fair that country folk
purchased the specialized goods that could not be home-produced—edged tools, vessels of wood and metal, pieces of delph,
and such colourful trivialities as beads and ribbons. The pole-
lathe on which wooden vessels for the dairy were turned was
known in early Christian times if not before, and a few examples
are still in use. It seems probable that the turners once utilized
a living branch as a spring-pole, like the bodgers of the Chil-
terns. At any rate we read of Co. Meath, early last century,
that 'turners and wooden dish-makers generally build a hut in
a wood that is being cut, and reside there while the timber is
felling, buying and working those kind of trees most suited to
their purpose and paying for them as the manufactured goods
are sold'.[2] Today the turner selects and fells his own trees,
preferably sycamore, and works them up in his own yard.

The churn-maker also had his stand at the fair, and there
were the noggin-weavers and sieve-makers, the carvers of
ladles, wooden spoons and butter prints (Fig. 83), and the
makers of baskets and creels. Here also forgathered the beggars
and ballad-singers, fiddlers, pedlars, gamesters, and the trouble-
makers and the match-makers. It was a recognized practice for
a bachelor to be on the look-out for a mate, or for a match-
maker if things had gone far enough, and for the men of one
parish to seek to settle old scores with enemies from another
parish. There is some evidence that trial marriage contracts,
binding for a year, were at one time an accompaniment of the
fairs. Like the Scottish hand-fasting, the system allowed the
husband to test the usefulness and fertility of the wife. Nor
should we forget the games and horse-racing, and into the
nineteenth century the cock-fighting and bull-baiting, which
have long been associated with the great fairs.

Down to fairly recent times all the fairs were held on saints'
days or at the movable feasts of Easter and Whitsun, and if
the saint was a local one the fair, as at Kilorglin, was also a
pattern, that is a festival associated with the patron saint.
Unless the church has been able to keep a firm hold on the
proceedings, these patterns have degenerated until many of

---

[1]See also De Latocnaye, *A Frenchman's Walk through Ireland, 1796–97*, 250.
[2]R. Thompson, *Statistical Survey of the County of Meath*, 253.

them have had to be suppressed: they became occasions of law-lessness and bloodshed. Like the fairs they drew their adherents from several rival neighbourhoods and therefore brought feuding clans together. The following is a typical comment of the early nineteenth century: 'On these patron days, which

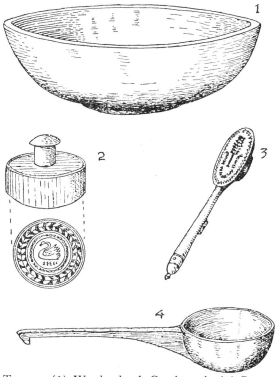

FIG. 83. Turnery. (1) Wooden bowl, Co. Armagh. (2) Butter stamp, Co. Fermanagh. (3) Butter stamp, Co. Antrim. (4) Ladle, Co. Antrim.

generally fall out on Sundays, great numbers of young persons of both sexes assemble, tents are erected, music, dancing, drink-ing and every kind of excess takes place, and the revel not infrequently terminates in battery and bloodshed, from the contention of adverse factions'.[1] Sir William Wilde's description

[1] W. Shaw Mason, *Parochial Survey*, 3, 245 (of Listerling, Co. Kilkenny).

of the Pattern of Glendalough in Co. Wicklow was written later in the century. The fights would begin early on the eve of the patron's day, on 23rd June; 'the scene was remarkable, an immense crowd had bivouacked among the ruins (of the seven churches of Glendalough) and were cooking their evening meal, gipsy-wise, throughout the space of the sacred enclosure. Dancing, drinking, thimble-rigging, prick-o'-the-loop and other amusements continued even while the bare-headed venerable pilgrims and bare-kneed voteens were going their prescribed rounds. Towards evening the fun became fast and furious . . . the crowd thickened, sticks were brandished and the faction fight began. It was an unsafe locality unless a stipendiary magistrate and about 100 police could keep the combatants, the Byrnes, Tools and Farrells, etc., separate'.[1]

Some of the most notorious patterns were connected with holy wells named after a saint but not necessarily located near an old church site. Reading the accounts of witnesses in the early nineteenth century it is hard to believe that religious devotion could be associated with such profanity, but granting that social conditions in the decades before the great famine must have contributed to scenes which the church itself described as 'drunkenness and debauchery', there was, as with the wakes for the dead, a vestige of innocent paganism in the rituals. Some patterns survived their banning by the church and have persisted, stripped of their grosser elements, to this day. The celebrated wells of St. Patrick at Struell in Co. Down, which are still visited by a few pilgrims on St. John's Eve, were the scene of the gathering of great crowds of people and of strange rites until a few years ago. Here as often happened the chief celebration was on the Eve of the Feast of St. John the Baptist and not on the patron saint's day, so that it was not strictly a pattern. Another Midsummer gathering which has often been described is that of St. Ronogue's Well near Cork, which has changed beyond recognition since Mrs. Hall, in 1824, described it as an assembly of 'the worthless and dissipated of the whole county. To the superstitious rites of the morning succeeded the saturnalia of the evening;—the having drunk of the water being considered as a licence for every sort of debauchery . . .

[1]Sir William Wilde, *J.R.S.A.I.* (1873), 449.

FIG. 84. Portable crucifix ('penal cross'). Found at Hilltown, Co. Down.

dancing, shouting, fiddling, courting, drinking and fighting'.[1]

In some celebrated instances the holy wells are associated with lakes and islands, for example Gouganebarra at the source of the River Lee, and the most famous of all Irish pilgrimages

[1]Mr. and Mrs. S. C. Hall, *Ireland: Its Scenery, Character Etc.*, i, 281.

is that of St. Patrick's Purgatory, on a small island in Lough Derg in Donegal. Still a powerful attraction, it has been maintained since the early middle ages and has been described, with piety or derision, by innumerable writers since one of the earliest accounts was written by Giraldus Cambrensis, about 1185. The pilgrimage became very popular in the early nineteenth century, when the numbers of visitors are said to have averaged 10,000 annually. Mr. A. T. Lucas has shown that this pilgrimage resulted in the distribution through the country of certain portable wooden crucifixes popularly known as penal crosses.[1] Carved from the solid in a characteristic style, they bear dates between 1700 and 1830 (Fig. 84). It seems that they were sold to pilgrims at Lough Derg and taken home as souvenirs after being used in the devotional ritual. They were a local development, no doubt initiated by some peasant woodcarver, of simple crosses, consisting merely of two sticks tied together, such as are still made at some patterns and occasionally at the festivals of St. Briget and All-Hallows. In this way, as in sanctifying the gatherings themselves, Christianity has taken over the symbols and strength of the elder faiths.

The pilgrimage of Croagh Patrick, in Co. Mayo, is the most celebrated of those held at the end of July, involving the ascent of high mountains and marking, by tradition, the close of summer and the beginning of harvest, as discussed in the following chapter. Here we may quote once more the *Parliamentary Gazetteer* for 1845: 'No place in Ireland is the scene of more superstitious observances, or a more popular resort of pilgrims and devotees, or the site of more numerous small memorials of superstition, or the subject of more generally credited legends of hagiology. Vast crowds of miserable human beings . . . swarm all over its summit and sides and skirts; one grand current legend is almost everywhere believed in the teeth of all credulity, that St. Patrick gathered hither, and swept hence all venomous creatures in Ireland.'

[1] A. T. Lucas, *Co. Louth Arch. Journ.*, 13 (1954), 145–74.

XIX

FIXED FESTIVALS

THE great fairs, patterns and pilgrimages were attended by people who travelled considerable distances and included strange folk from the outside world, 'beyond the mountain men'. It was partly for this reason that they earned a reputation for lawlessness, especially where 'the gatherings' had outlived their original purpose and their real business had become subordinate to pleasure. A Nottingham Goose Fair or a Marlborough Mop Fair may still be conducted with propriety, but in Ireland they would probably have become Donnybrooks. Having little opportunity for regular social contacts as compared with the villagers of the ploughlands, a pastoral people makes the most of the periodic pauses in the cycle of the seasons.

For climatic reasons these great gatherings have been largely confined to the summer half-year between May and November. The winter festivals have been more local, involving the family and the townland rather than rival groups from different parishes and baronies. The feast days of both St. Briget and St. Patrick fall in early spring and their associations are more intimate and have more local colour than those of the saints of high summer such as St. John the Baptist. But the entire round of the year is liberally sprinkled with days of festival, and if we begin with St. Briget it is not merely because she was Irish-born but because her feast marks the beginning of the pastoral year. The blessed Bridie was a cowherd and is therefore associated with cattle and with such flowers as the dandelion—the Plant of Bride—yielding a milky juice which was believed to nourish the young lambs in spring. St. Briget's Feast was very popular and many superstitious practices, more or less

FIXED FESTIVALS

Christianized, cling to the preparations made on St. Briget's Eve, the last day of January. On that day rushes are fashioned into protective charms known as Briget's Crosses, a name which illustrates how the church has won over pagan symbols, for the 'crosses' take the form of either swastikas or lozenges, and comparative evidence suggests that they are magic symbols of suns or eyes (Fig. 85). A three-legged swastika, presumably an old form, is reserved for use in the byre: its shape may be compared with the Celtic triskele. The lozenge-shaped charms have their counterparts in many parts of the world. The Huichols of Mexico make similar charms of wool mounted on a bamboo frame: known as a 'god-eyes', they bring good health and long life to children.[1] A Californian Indian charm made of grass or rushes is very similar. In the Old World similar magic 'squares' have a wide distribution, in Europe, Africa, Tibet, Burma, Assam and Indonesia, and farther afield in Melanesia, Polynesia and Australia. Among the Nagas of Assam the squares, made of coloured thread, are placed on the graves of women and protect them against evil spirits.[2] In Sweden and Estonia straw squares are strung up as Christmas decorations and tied to the straw masks worn during Christmas games (Fig. 85).

Briget's Crosses are believed to protect the house and the livestock from harm and from fire. No evil spirit could pass the charm, which was therefore hung above the door of house and byre. The rushes must be pulled, not cut, on St. Briget's Eve, and care must be taken to fashion the crosses from left to right, with the sun. As a rule they are left in position until replaced the following year, though I have seen byres with many crosses thrust into the underthatch, the decaying accumulation of annual offerings. In Co. Galway similar crosses made of wood or straw were also placed in the rafters at Hallowe'en, and the discovery of a partly burnt rush cross which had been deposited in a megalith in Co. Limerick points to a more general cult of the 'cross'.[3] A 'love-knot' of similar shape, fashioned out of sedge leaves, is known from South Wales.

[1] F. Toor, *A Treasury of Mexican Folkways* (1947), 72.
[2] H. E. Kauffmann, *J.R.A.I.*, 73 (1943), 101, 106.
[3] S. P. O'Riordain, *North Munster Antiquarian Journal*, 1 (1936), 36. For a study of Briget's Crosses in Co. Armagh, see T. G. F. Paterson, *U.J.A.*, 8 (1945), 43–48.

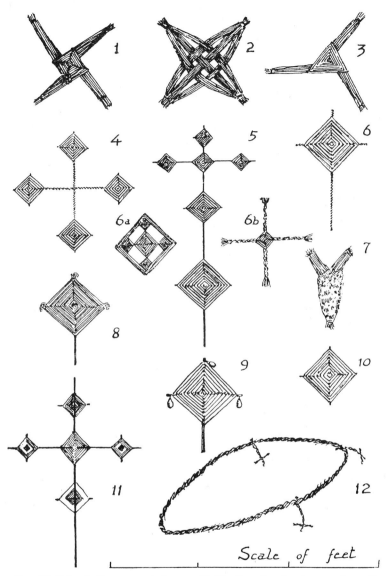

FIG. 85. Briget's Crosses and charms. (1–7) all made of rushes, are from Co. Armagh (in County Museum, Armagh). (8) is a Naga thread-square (after Kauffmann). (9) is a Wailaki charm of rushes (after Kroeber, *Handbook of the Indians of California*). (10) is an Estonian straw-square, worn as decoration on straw hats at Christmas (see Fig. 88, 5). (11) is a Mexican 'God-eyes' made of woven wool (after Toor). (12) is a Briget's Girdle (in National Museum, Dublin).

It was popularly believed that the saint wandered through the countryside on the eve of her feast day. Bread was left on the doorstep, and in some districts it was the custom to prepare a small bed of rushes or birch twigs and place it by the fire so that Bridie might come in and rest. Sometimes the last sheaf of harvest was used for the purpose. In south-western Ireland a doll made of straw—or decorated churn-staff—was carried from house to house by 'Biddy Boys', wearing straw masks such as are used by mummers and by strawboys at weddings, and singing songs in honour of the saint. They would solicit gifts and end the day in jollification. The evening was celebrated by a supper of pancakes taken from a plate laid on a rush cross, and as on the other quarter-days prognostications were made. A ribbon or piece of cloth exposed on St. Briget's Eve became endowed with curative powers. It was believed that no worl which involved the turning of a wheel should take place on the saint's day. The placing of a periwinkle in each corner of the kitchen likewise hints at a remote pre-agricultural origin for the festival, but it came to be associated with the pastoral promise of spring, of warmth, new grass, lambs and milk. It is said that the saint placed her foot in water on her feast day so that on that day it begins to warm up each year.

St. Patrick is credited with carrying the process a stage further by putting a stone in the water, or alternatively 'turning up the warm side of the stone'. 17th March marks the end of winter and the starting-point of work in the fields. The country-man likes to have his first ridge of potatoes planted on that day, and he is not greatly moved by the patriotic celebrations which are anyhow more in evidence in New York and Boston than in Ireland. Traditionally the cult of St. Patrick is strongest in Ulster, where hundreds of churches and holy wells are named in his honour, and according to legend he was reluctantly accepted as patron saint in some of the other Irish regions. They say in Ulster that Connachtmen speak with husky accents because their forebears stole and ate St. Patrick's goat. Like Columbkille, Patrick is remembered for his curses as well as his prophecies, for instance he cursed the rushes that pricked him when he rested, so that every green rush has a brown tip.

To refer to all the associations of the movable feasts of

Easter would take us away from our present subject but mention must be made of some of the folk practices connected with Shrove Tuesday, Ash Wednesday, Easter and Whitsuntide. Shrove Tuesday (Shraft) was a time for hunting the hare, and for feasting in preparation for Lent. A portion of the meat was not eaten but hung in the rafters. It was the great day of the year for marriages, and on that night tricks of many kinds were played on unmarried adults and on courting couples who had not fulfilled their promise. They were serenaded with horn-blowing; animals were tied to the doors of their houses, and cart wheels were rolled down hill. At Ardmore in Co. Waterford a piece of symbolic horseplay was performed by the young men on Ash Wednesday. A hollowed stone with a hole in the centre was the scene of the play. In the hole was stuck a wattle with a handful of tow tied to its top, and unmarried women were made to dance around the stone, holding the tow and spinning while they danced. 'The youths then terminated their amusements by dragging them through the village seated on old logs of wood.'[1]

Good Friday was an important day in the farmer's year, the luckiest day on which to begin the sowing of corn. There was an aversion to the use of iron and to the shedding of blood on Good Friday, which was a favourite day for visiting holy wells and the graves of the dead. Shell-fish were eaten, and visits to the shore were enlivened with games and horse-racing. On Easter Day the young folk would be up early in the morning to see the sun dance, and during the day vast quantities of eggs were consumed. The colouring and rolling of eggs are customs kept up by children in many districts. A special Easter Day dance, for which the prize was a large cake exhibited on a garlanded churn-staff, is popularly supposed to have given rise to the expression 'taking the cake', in the sense of beating all comers. If Easter was a lucky time, ominous superstitions attached to Whitsuntide, for example persons born at that time were supposed to have the evil eye, to be fated to die a violent death, or to take a life. A chicken would sometimes be killed in the hands of a Whitsun child to serve as a substitute slaughter. To cross water or go to sea at Whitsun was to invite death by drowning.

[1]E. Fitzgerald, *J.R.S.A.I.* (1856), 43.

271

The May Festival, the Gaelic Beltane, remained almost untouched by Christianity, and an astonishingly rich growth of magic beliefs and superstitious customs accumulated around it. They were concerned with the safety of the familiar things which supported life, and especially the milk cows whose 'whitemeats' were to provide the main food-supply until harvest came round once more. It was a matter of pride to have a last formal dish of stirabout on May Day, 'for if they can hold out so well with bread they can do well enough . . . for then milk becomes plenty, and butter, new cheese, and curds and shamrocks are the food of the meaner sort all this season'.[1] It was considered most unlucky and unwise to give away salt, water or fire on May Day lest the luck and 'profit' of the farm went with the gifts. Witches and fairies were unusually active at this time, and many tales are told of the wiles they adopted to outwit the unwary and gain admission to house or byre to do their mischief. It was a wise precaution to pour milk on the threshold, or at the roots of a fairy thorn, and the many protective charms against the stealing of cattle and milk were augmented by others special to the occasion. 'On May Eve the peasantry used to drive all their cattle into old raths and forts thought to be much frequented by the fairies, bleed them, taste their blood, and pour the remainder on the earth'.[2] It was said that the ghosts of cattle that had been lost could be seen in such places.

Portents, prognostications and protection were sought in the familiar flowers of field and hedgerow, in the weeds and shrubs which had followed in man's footsteps and were associated with his secular struggle for survival, especially in those that carried the promise of butter in their golden cups and a free flow of milk in their bounteous white blossom. May flowers, primroses and gorse gathered before sunrise were scattered on the threshold of the house and garlands of 'Summer', as the flowers were called, were hung on the doorposts and even tied to the cows' tails. In the Antrim Glens the mayflowers were crushed to provide a juice with which the cows' udders were washed, and elsewhere buttercups were used for the purpose. Cow dung, if less hygienic, had similar protective power, presumably in

[1]Sir Henry Piers, *West-Meath*, 121.
[2]*U.J.A.* 3 (1855), 165.

the belief that it contained the essence of the flowers of the fields. Sprigs of rowan were stuck in the midden, placed over the door of the byre and hung on the cows' horns. Flowers were also put around the well, for it was supposed that a milk-thief could steal your summer's milk and butter by skimming the water at this time, or by dragging a rope across a field to collect the dew. Boundary streams were also potent in this connexion, and I was told in Donegal that the milk churn had to be washed on May Day in 'three landlords' waters', that is the meeting place of three properties.

Besides these family rites there were public ceremonies, the lighting of bonfires and parades of May Babies, of May Boys and the May Queen. One of the rhymes sung by May Boys in the west of Ireland runs, in translation:

> Summer! Summer! the milk of the heifers,
> And ourselves brought the summer with us,
> The yellow summer, and the white daisy,
> And ourselves brought the summer with us.[1]

The May Baby parades link the festival with the fertility of the family as well as the fields. I give an account of the ceremonies as described in Co. Louth in the early nineteenth century: 'On May Day, the figure of a female is made up, fixed upon a short pole and dressed in a fantastic manner, with flowers, ribbons, etc. This figure they call 'The May Baby' . . . Around this figure a man and woman (generally his wife) of the humble class, dressed also fantastically with straw, etc., dance to the sound of a fiddle and entertain the people with indecent shows and postures . . . These exhibitions cause great merriment among the assembled populace; women who have had no children to their husbands also attend to see this figure and performance, which they imagine will promote fruitfulness in them, and cause them to have children.'[2]

The May Day bonfires and the May Queens are now little more than children's games and excuses for begging. The burning of bones—whence the word bonfire, which in Ireland keeps its original pronunciation—and in particular of horses'

[1] Lady Wilde, *The Dublin University Magazine* (1849), 541–60.
[2] J. Donaldson, *Upper Fews in 1838*, 70.

273

bones, were formerly considered proper to the occasion. There were dances round the fires, performed with great dexterity and precision by youths armed with cudgels. The May-pole, however, and the May-bush observances seem to go with areas of strong English influence and do not seem to have been generally adopted by the Irish, perhaps because May-trees, which are not given this name in Ireland, are likely to be fairy thorns and therefore should not be damaged. The May Eve assemblies are thus described in eighteenth century Kilkenny: 'Bloody battles and much confusion and uproar is the mischief that follows from the barbarous and unheeded custom of collecting *May-balls* among the new-married folks . . . The hedges and fences, in the outlets of our city, are stripped of full-grown hawthorns, whose late blooming pride and fragrancy is now miserably dying away on dunghills before cabin doors, by way of *May-bushes*, no longer, alas! to afford a nuptial bed to the new-married linnet and his mate, but fastened in the ground for the vilest purpose—to hang filthy clouts upon'.[1] The gold and white balls which were hung on maypoles have been regarded as symbols of sun and moon—or it may be of butter and milk. Another May Day custom was the licence allowed young boys to run about stinging people with nettles, a privilege which in my youth in Shropshire was permitted only on 29th May, the victims being those who did not wear an oak-apple.

If the May Day fires are now more in evidence in the back streets of Belfast than on the high hills, the Midsummer fires still burn strongly in some country districts and their pagan flames have not been so easily quenched. I saw dozens of them in Co. Galway on Midsummer Eve in 1956, mostly at country crossroads. Old men in Donegal have told me that they remembered the time when they had counted from their hilltop fire nearly a hundred others. Young men would show their mettle by jumping to and fro through the flames, and girls by doing so hoped to marry early and have many children. We recall that leaping is in folk tradition a widely approved method of making the crops grow high, and the fires, it is conjectured, were meant to encourage the sun, now at its turning point, to shine on through the harvest. Midsummer was a time when evil influ-

[1] *Finn's Leinster Journal* (4th May, 1768).

ences affecting human beings and the animals and crops were usually potent. It is remembered that 'the oldest woman in the town' would go round the fire three times on her knees, reciting prayers. To walk three times sunwise round the fire was to ensure a year without sickness, and as the flames died down the cattle were driven through the embers and their backs were singed with a lighted hazel wand: the sticks were preserved and utilized for driving the cows. By tradition everyone carried home a burning stick from the fire, and whoever was first to take it into the house brought the good luck of the year with him. A glowing turf from the fire was carried three times sunwise round the dwelling house, and others were thrown into the growing crops. Yarrow was hung in the house to ward off illness. Fernseed was gathered for its magic powers and divinations made from the roots of bracken and lilies. We have already noticed the custom of retaining some of the ashes from the Midsummer fires to mix with the following season's seed corn.

The third fire-festival of the year is associated with St. Peter's Eve on 28th June, but I have not come across many traditions of St. Peter's bonfires except in Armagh and Wexford: it may thus be mainly restricted to areas where English influence was strong. More widespread and better known, because they have been caught up in many patterns and in such popular pilgrimages as that to Croagh Patrick, are the celebrations of Lammas, originally 1st August, now held on Lammas Sunday, the last in July, which is also known as Garland, Bilberry or Height Sunday. This marked the end of summer and beginning of harvest: it was a first-fruits festival into which the alien potato has been fitted, and no potatoes were dug before this time. Offerings of flowers and fruits were made at holy wells, and in some places cattle were made to swim through streams and loughs into which lumps of fresh butter had been cast:[1] 'They think no beast will live the whole year through unless they be thus drenched'.[2] In hilly districts Height Sunday is observed by climbing to a recognized picnic place where bilberries are gathered and games and dancing were formerly enjoyed. In Co. Down a large prehistoric

[1]Wood-Martin, *Elder Faiths*, 1, 282.
[1]Sir Henry Piers, *West-Meath*, 121.

cairn on the summit of Slieve Croob was until recent years the scene of a great gathering on the first Sunday in August. The fiddling and dancing are no more, though numbers of young people still assemble there and frolic in the heather. Blaeberries (bilberries) were picked into little rush baskets made on the spot (Fig. 70) and that the occasion was recognized as a legitimate time of courting is shown by the comment that 'many a lad met his wife on Blaeberry Sunday'. The name Garland Sunday derives from the hoops decorated with ribbons and flowers which were made by unmarried girls and, latterly, carried to church before being set up in the graveyard to preside over the dancing with which the day terminated. Rites in honour of the dead seem to have marked the old Lammas festival, so that again we notice the association of ancestral spirits with the fertility of farm and family.

By St. Bartholomew's Day, 24th August, harvest is well under way and the first-saved corn is ready to be thrashed. By tradition the flails were made ready on this day, and if the high harvest winds are blowing it is said that the saint is testing his flails. Next comes Michaelmas, 29th September, linked closely with the sea, with horses, and, strangely, with the ceremony of killing a cock or a goose, originally as a sacrifice in honour of the saint. In some parts Michaelmas was regarded as one of the most important feasts of the year, but I have not found any districts where it was, as in Uist, 'much the most imposing pageant and most popular demonstration of the Celtic year': nor have I come across any tradition of the rites of digging up and making presents of wild carrots which was associated, in the Hebrides, with the eating of cakes made of mixed flour baked before a stone flag, with the killing of a lamb, visits to graveyards, and a night of 'dance, song and love-making'.[1]

Throughout Ireland these lesser feast days pale in comparison with the culminating festival which marks the end of the dying year on All-Hallows Eve. An astonishing amount of lore still clings to Hallowe'en, and we must restrict ourselves to picking out some of the main elements of this crowded occasion. The crops should now be all gathered in and no fruit should be picked

[1]A. Carmichael, *Carmina Gadelica*, I (1928), 198.

after this date, for the *púca*, a supernatural being, is busy befouling unpicked fruit at Hallowe'en. Here again we notice superstition acting as a stimulus towards the completion of routine tasks. The return of the livestock from their summer grazings, once accompanied by their herders, made the occasion one of family reunion, and this is a strong element in the present festival. But it was also a reunion with the ancestral spirits of the family: for Hallowe'en was preeminently a commemoration of the dead, a time when ghosts and fairies were unusually active, the whole of the world of the supernatural astir and the dead returned to their earthly homes. On that night the grass-grown homesteads—the fairy raths—were wide open and the fairies were on the move to winter quarters, surely a folk memory of a former transhumance. It used to be thought unlucky not to make preparations for the return of the dead by leaving the door of the house open, putting out tobacco and traditional dishes such as sowans—a kind of porridge—and setting seats around the fire. The games and amusements which alone survive have commonly degenerated into pranks and horseplay, but one can detect in them echoes of magical observances. The many divination customs may well have begun as rites to avert evil or to secure the benefits which they now pretend to forecast. Among the things involved in these games and divinations are apples, nuts, oatcakes, cabbages, a ball of yarn, articles made of straw and rushes (Fig. 86), and herbs such as yarrow. The wearing of straw dresses and the breaking of pots are certainly archaic elements. In Co. Cork there survived well into last century a Hallowe'en ceremony similar to the well-known Mari Lwyd of South Wales: a procession was led by a figure clad in a white shirt and carrying a horse's head. This 'white mare' was followed by youths blowing cowhorns, and as they stopped to levy toll from farmhouses they recited a long string of verses 'savouring strongly of paganism'.[1] Hallowe'en bonfires and noisy demonstrations remind us that these features of Guy Fawkes' Day have, in England, been stolen from the older festival.

In certain districts, especially in Connacht, north Munster and south Leinster, strange customs have been associated with

[1] *J.R.S.A.I.* (1853), 303—19.

the Feast of St. Martin on 11th November. On St. Martin's Eve the blood of a farm animal or fowl was spilled and sprinkled in the corners of the house, on the door-posts and windows, and in the byre and stable. In some areas the blood was also used to make the mark of a cross on the forehead of each member of the household. The flesh was eaten on St. Martin's Day, which is by tradition one of the feast days on which flesh meat is taken.

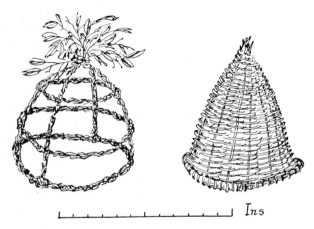

Fig. 86. Hallowe'en caps. *Left:* of plaited straw, Co. Down. *Right:* of woven rushes, Co. Kerry.

We recall that in Scotland a mart was an animal killed at Martinmas to be salted down as winter food, and it may well be that this very practical custom grew out of the cult, which was intended 'to exclude evil spirits for the year'.[1] It seems that seabirds were sometimes killed for the occasion, and there are many superstitions relating to the ill luck which attended anyone who went fishing at Martinmas. Wheel-turning of any kind, whether on cart, mill or spinning wheel, was prohibited. These sacrificial offerings and tabus must be of great antiquity and relate to the preparations for winter. St. Martin's Summer was regarded as the last spell of fine weather before the gales began in earnest. There are hints in folklore that ailing children were

[1] I. Weld, *Roscommon*, 553.

sometimes killed at this time, so that the animal slaughter may be a sacrificial substitute.

Although Christmas is the outstanding Christian festival of the year its traditional 'Twelve Days' of holiday are steeped in pagan lore and in folk practices relating to the winter solstice and the new year. In Co. Cavan I came across a custom known as 'blowing the Christmas horns' by which youths heralded the festival by blowing horns from hilltops. The burning of candles on Christmas Eve is a ceremony which involved divination as well as devotion. 'Each district seems to have its taste in colour. For example, in Limerick and Clare white candles are mainly used, while red and green are popular everywhere. In the Midland areas pink candles are sought, and in some parts of Dublin only blue candles will be taken. In Killarney nothing less than a 6-lb. candle will suffice for the occasion'.[1] On Christmas Day traditional ball-games were played, often between parishes, and near the coasts these meetings took place on the strands.

St. Stephen's Day is in many parts of the country associated with the hunting of the wren, and the sport is not entirely extinct. It seems that some details of the ceremony, such as the rhymes which are sung, are of English origin, but the wrenboys often wore straw masks in the native tradition, and occasionally animal skins or horns. The wrens were killed beforehand by noisy and excited bands of youths, and carried on a holly bush or a decorated wooden tray on St. Stephen's Day (Fig. 87). The procession, shouting and singing the prescribed songs to the accompaniment of home-made skin tambourines, made its way from house to house demanding money or drinks. The wrenboy processions, despite their English rhymes, appear to be a degeneration of more elaborate performances of native origin which had affinities with the mummers' plays and which like them may have been attracted by the powerful prestige of the Christmas festival from their proper season of spring. At one time the wrenboy ceremonies involved much fertility symbolism and were attended by men disguised as women.[2] The robin, linked with the wren in superstition, was also the object of persecution in south-western Ireland, but in this case the tail

---

[1] *Ireland* (Bulletin of the Department of External Affairs) No. 303 (1955), 10.
[2] E. R. R. Green, *U.J.A.*, 9 (1946), 3–21.

was pulled out and the bird's life spared: 'In severe winters a robin with a tail was rarely seen.'[1] Another popular Boxing-Day pastime was bull-baiting, though in Kilkenny, where it was officially supported by the town officials and was presumably an English introduction, it was held on the following day, St. John's. In several parts of the country bull-baiting continued well into last century, in Kilkenny down to 1837.[2]

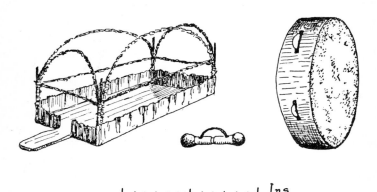

Fig. 87. Hunting the wren. Wren Box for carrying dead wren, and wrenboys' tambourine and stick, Co. Clare. (National Museum, Dublin.)

New Year's Day similarly has attracted to itself some of the portents proper to the older year's beginning on 1st November. The prosperity of the individual and the household is felt to depend on the events of New Year's Day. The fairies are active on New Year's Eve and it is well for people to stay indoors that night. First-footing ceremonies appear to be confined to families of recent Scots origin, but the idea behind them is widespread. In parts of Co. Down it is customary for youths to prepare little 'wisps' of straw or dry grass and go from house to house distributing them together with New Year's greetings in the expectation of a gift. In the west on the last night of the year (or alternatively on the eve of Twelfth Night) a large 'Christmas Loaf' specially prepared for the occasion was taken

[1] W. R. Le Fanu, *Seventy Years of Irish Life*, 41.
[2] J. G. R. Prim, *J.R.S.A.I.* (1853), 326.

by the head of the house and hammered against the barred doors and windows to the accompaniment of an Irish rhyme which warned famine to retire.[1] This too has parallels with the banging of doors and the 'pounding away of hunger' at Hallowe'en.

[1] *J.R.S.A.I.* (1853), 146.

XX

WEDDINGS AND WAKES

THE average age of marriage among Irish countrywomen, about 28, is said to be higher than in any other country in the world: that of the men is higher still, and in addition there are many who never marry. These are among the demographic consequences of the economic and social changes which followed the Great Famine of 1845–47, for down to that time the mass of the population had nothing to lose and everything to gain by marrying young. Among the economic factors which led to the postponement of marriage may be mentioned the rising standards of living, the prohibition of the subdivision of holdings so that only one son could inherit, and the need for larger farms consequent on the decline of subsistence farming and the increase of pastoral husbandry, which meant that the peasant had to look and plan ahead. Equally important, I believe, was the effect of the crisis of the famine in breaking down patterns of behaviour which had continued with little change since prehistoric times. The elder faiths were rudely shattered so that today we have only the broken remnants left, stray survivals which have lost their meaning in a modern setting. The scattering of the fairy hosts is the constant lament of old people for whose parents they were a reality. Over large parts of the country, down to famine times the fairies (among them the ancestral spirits), and the powers of nature in sun and stone, tree, flower and welling water were ruling forces whose malice must somehow be averted, and whose beneficence must be courted by magical acts. Nature's reproductive surplus on which human life depended could best be assured by breeding children to capacity.

The Irish birthrate remains high, and despite delayed marriages the population would continue to increase were it not for emigration, latterly to Britain instead of America. Moreover, sterility is still regarded as a disgrace, and superstitious practices find one of their last pathetic appeals in attempts to be cured of 'the sterile curse'. Among a peasant people a childless marriage is an economic and social tragedy. There is some evidence that, in the north of Ireland at least, trial marriage or bed-fellowship (bundling), as in Wales, the Hebrides, Norway and Holland was an accepted preliminary of marriage and a means to which the fertility of a prospective partner was tested. The reliability of the notorious Richard Twiss as a witness may be impugned, but in this instance his account of the custom in Co. Fermanagh is likely to be true[1] since there are living traditions of trial marriages in Counties Antrim and Londonderry.

For the most part, these immemorial attitudes did not survive the crisis of the famine and the watchfulness of a now well-organized priesthood. The fertility rites of wakes for the dead and the unashamed courtships which were carried on at patterns and at the great seasonal festivals find a plausible explanation in the fact that they occurred at times and places where the spirits of the dead were waiting to be reborn. The gatherings at hill-top burial places attested by tradition and the legendary histories were similarly drawn together by the pull of ancestral spirits. The name Dermot and Grania's Bed which is applied to many megalithic graves gives these ancient monuments a reputation which is evident in a belief recorded by Hely Dutton in Co. Clare early in the last century: 'If a woman proves barren, a visit with her husband to Dermot and Grania's Bed certainly cures her.'[2] And the Saints' Beds associated with many ancient church sites have taken over some of the megalithic magic, for they have the power of curing of barrenness a woman who spends the night there.

If the youthful marriages of pre-famine days seem far removed from the carefully arranged matches of the present-day peasantry, it should not be concluded that they were casual and

[1] R. Twiss, *A Tour in Ireland in 1755*, 103.
[2] H. Dutton, *Clare*, 318.

283

not subject to recognized laws of marriage. Romantic unions there must have been, but among the farming population they would have been followed by prolonged arguments and arrangements as to the bride-price. An unusually detailed account of marriage customs in County Armagh in the early nineteenth century is worth quoting at some length:

'The acquaintance and courtship of the parties often commence and are carried on at fairs, patrons and other public places of rural sports and amusements, and at wakes, funerals, etc. from whence they run away together—that is, the male brings the female to one of his friends or relations house. This was heretofore sometimes accomplished by force . . . Shortly after the running away, as it is termed, some of the female's relatives follow her and negotiations commence respecting the match, which often terminate by the female's unhappy father being obliged to promise more portion than his abilities will allow, in order to preserve the reputation of his daughter. The match being agreed upon and the day appointed for the wedding, the intended bride is permitted to return to her father's house, where a scene of preparation commences for the wedding dinner, which generally consists of bruised potatoes and flour . . . and large quantities of oatbread and butter.

'On the day appointed for the wedding, the bridegroom's party, from ten to twenty of his relations . . . mount their horses, the women behind the men, except a few of the latter that are single and intend running for the bottle, and advance towards the bride's residence, where they are met by a few single horsemen belonging to the bride's party. When the parties meet, those of them that are single-mounted then contend for who will be at the bride's house first; where, when the parties arrive, the bridegroom and bride are presented . . . with a plate of oatmeal and salt, of which each of them take three small mouthfuls; probably to prevent the power of witchcraft or the effect of an evil eye. After this the parties . . . mount their horses, and the whole then join in one grand cavalcade, the van being led by the bridegroom; the bride riding behind the bridesman, until they reach the ale-house most convenient to where the priest lives. (Here it should be explained that there were few Roman Catholic places of worship at that time and that the ceremony presumably took place in the priest's house.)

'Whichever of the new married couple first rises after the nuptial benediction, will, it is considered, live longest . . .; after this scene is over they again adjourn to the public house . . ., after which the company again mount their horses, the bride being then changed behind the bridegroom's man, and scamper away towards the bride's house, whilst numbers of people are collected on the hills and eminences to behold the race for the bottle. The winning of the bottle is frequently contended for between the bridegroom's and the bride's parties; the first person that arrives at the bride's house is victorious. The victor then receives the bottle and again returns to the main body of the wedding, where he hands it to the bridegroom, who first drinks of it and hands it to his bride, who also partakes, it then goes the round until nearly finished, when . . . the bridegroom flings it with the remaining contents away. On their arrival at the bride's house a cake of oatmeal or flour, which is called the bride's cake is broken over the bride's head, and is greedily seized upon by young people of both sexes for the purpose of placing a portion of it under their pillow, in order that they may dream of their future partners in life. Another scene of noisy festivity and drunkenness then commences, which often terminates in riot and bloodshed between the different parties; there being frequently a kind of rivalry between them in supporting the dignity of the bridegroom and bride, particularly if they do not happen to be of one line of ancestors.'[1]

No doubt where land and livestock were involved such marriages were not so uninhibited as it might appear. Physical attraction was not a prime consideration. The normal course was for a peasant to marry a girl whose capabilities were known or could be fairly judged, preferably 'a far-out friend', who lived close enough for family visits and exchanges of labour to be made. We know from other accounts of marriage customs in the early nineteenth century that the order of events as described above was sometimes reversed: 'The marriage is agreed upon by bargain, and the theft or abduction follows as a concerted

[1] J. Donaldson, *Upper Fews*, 64–66.

matter of form to make valid the marriage.'[1] After the famine, at least, the mutual attraction of the suitors themselves was a secondary consideration. An ill-favoured girl could be made pretty with a dowry of cows or its equivalent in cash, known in the west as 'dry-money'. A marriage between near relatives was not unknown if it meant keeping the name on the land or enlarging the patrimony: 'a blanket is the better of being doubled,' it was said. 'We are all related one way or another' is a comment one hears in isolated mountain districts. In general romantic love was the luxury of the landless, but whatever the motives of marriage there were many charms and omens to be taken into account in winning a person's affections, and some of the magic devices to which a girl might resort are listed in one of Bryan Merryman's poems of the late eighteenth century:

Up the chimney stuck the flail
Slept with a spade without avail,
Hid my wool in the limekiln late
And my distaff behind the churchyard gate;
Flax in the road to halt coach and carriage,
And haycocks stuffed with heads of cabbage.[2]

To this day the marriage or remarriage of old men to young women is regarded as unnatural and wrong, perhaps because it complicates the question of succession. In Co. Wexford, and probably elsewhere, unpopular marriages of this kind are marked by noisy gatherings of young men who serenade the married couple with horn-blowing. A similar custom, the *vito*, is well-known in Andalusia, where it includes the ringing of cow-bells and the singing of scurrilous songs. One of the strangest traditional features of Irish weddings is the visitation of 'straw-boys', that is youths wearing straw masks who attend as uninvited guests and disport themselves at the dance which normally follows a wedding (Fig. 88). I am told that they may still be seen occasionally in Co. Cavan and parts of the west. Formerly the visitors also wore straw suits or white shirts and red petticoats decorated with coloured ribbons. The leader

[1]Wood-Martin, *The Elder Faiths*, 2, 32.
[2]*The Midnight Court*, translated by Frank O'Connor (1945).

Fig. 88. Straw hats and dress. (1) Strawboys' wedding mask, Co. Mayo. (2) Strawboys' straw suit, Co. Kerry (National Museum, Dublin). (3) Biddyboys' straw hat, Co. Londonderry. (4) Mummers' straw hat, Co. Fermanagh. (5) Estonian straw hat, worn at Christmas games.

of the strawboys claimed the right to dance with the bride, and they were all well entertained. It seems that they would sometimes claim to be shipwrecked sailors, and whatever the origin of the custom it is evident that disguise was an important element in it.[1]

[1]C. R. Browne, *The Mullet*.

287

The good luck of the bottle race referred to above may be associated with the 'agreement bottle' of whiskey which was drunk, according to a seventeenth-century account, when the parents and relations of the young couple had reached a marriage agreement.[1] To this day in parts of Co. Down 'running for the broth' is a feature of country marriages, a bowl of broth being the reward given to the person who reaches the bride's house first after the wedding. Until recently, also, the young couple were expected to appear at the Bride's Show on the first Sunday after their marriage: they were accompanied to a special sloping field where they ran hand-in-hand to a stone near the bottom of the field, followed by pairs of linked boys and girls, each boy kissing the stone. Games and what was described to us as 'general carrying on' followed the Bride's Show.[2]

In more remote parts of the country match-making is still a recognized procedure. The professional match-maker is a well-known figure, usually a shrewd elderly person well versed in the arts of rural diplomacy, and his role has been fully described by Arensberg. He acts for the farmer who is ready for his son to marry—the son being often well into middle age— by negotiating with the parents of the girl whom the farmer has selected. In the prolonged bargaining as to the amount of the 'fortune' which the girl is to bring with her the values of peasant living stand clearly revealed.[3] Marriage is not so much a personal relationship as a union between groups, reinforcing relations which extend far beyond individuals.

There was a popular belief that the curse of sterility could be placed on the bride by any ill-disposed person who tied knots in a string during the marriage ceremony. A more obvious example of magic was the custom of tying a hen which was about to lay an egg to the bed-post on the marriage night. There are widespread traditions of the days when landlords exercised the *jus primae noctis* over their tenants' wives, and one hears of leases which contained clauses governing the right. During pregnancy it was lucky to do certain things and to avoid

[1]Sir Henry Piers, *West-Meath*, 1, 122.
[2]E. E. Evans, *Mourne Country*, 193
[3]C. M. Arensberg, *The Irish Countryman*, ch. 3.

doing others; and there is simple symbolic magic in the act of blowing the bellows in a forge to ensure safe delivery. In Mayo a ploughman would be called in to lift and shake a woman in difficult labour,[1] and there are hints of the *couvade* in the custom of wearing the husband's jacket during childbirth in the belief that he will then bear some of the pain. Mothers and babies were thought to be especially liable to be abducted by the fairies, and protective charms were hidden in a baby's dress or placed in the cradle. When children were taken to be baptised, too, special preparations were made and precautions taken, for example, a Co. Antrim clergyman reported that his parishioners would place a piece of bread and cheese in the child's clothing.[2] The old custom of dressing boys in girls' clothes, in long frocks, until they were ten or eleven years of age has been explained as a means of deceiving the fairies, who were always on the lookout for healthy young boys whom they could replace by feeble 'changelings'. For the same reason it is unwise to praise a child without adding a saving 'God bless him', and young boys are still half jocularly referred to as 'rogues and tories'. The belief in 'changelings' may have arisen as an explanation of the high mortality rate among baby boys as compared with girls.

When we come to the topic of the omens and rites of death and burial the supernatural world is ever-present. The custom of opening windows and doors to let the spirit of the dead depart is well known: in addition a hole was sometimes made in the roof thatch. Of Co. Sligo early last century we read: 'As soon as the breath has departed from a sick person, the bed is carried out, and if there be high ground near the house, it is there set on fire and consumed to ashes, while the air resounds with doleful cries.'[3] When death was imminent the sick person was laid on the floor, for this was believed to ease the escaping spirit. Two persons of the household should take part in every necessary task at this time, and two persons were sent out to carry news of the death, traditionally to the livestock and the bees as well as to the neighbours. Great care was taken to

[1]C. R. Browne, *The Mullet*.
[2]Wood-Martin, *Elder Faiths*, 2, 39.
[3]W. Shaw Mason, *Parochial Survey*, 2, 368.

observe the correct procedure in laying out the corpse, generally on a table or a door. A plate containing tobacco or salt was placed on the corpse and sometimes a turf, which was believed to prevent decomposition, a transference from the observed preservative qualities of the bogs.

Although a great deal of information on the wakes which followed has been collected, it is difficult to obtain precise details about the wake games because of their apparent obscenity. Some of them survive as innocent games in districts where wakes have not been entirely suppressed, but it should be stressed that the full ritual of the traditional wake games was carried out in innocence: 'the peasantry who practised them had no idea of outraging propriety or religion in their performance, holding an unquestioning faith that such observances were right and proper at wakes, whilst under any other circumstances they would shrink with horror from such indelicate exhibitions'.[1] Moreover, they were generally 'reserved for the deaths of old people who had survived the ordinary span of life, or young children who could not be looked upon as an irreparable loss.'[2]

Apart from a great variety of informal amusements which were traditional at wake gatherings—riddles, jokes, singing, dancing, horse-play, tricks, feats of strength or agility, wrestling and so on—a list of 130 specific wake games has been collected by Seán Ó Súilleabháin, and it is 'of necessity incomplete.'[3] Some of them were dramatic performances of considerable complexity; and one recalls the Irishman's traditional skill in dramatization. In Kilkenny the principal game was the *frannsa*, a mock ceremony during which several young folk were 'married' by a mock priest, usually a weaver or a tailor, who was dressed in straw and wore a huge straw rope as a stole. 'After each couple was married, he put them to bed in a corner of the room, sprinkled them with water and gave them plain advice about their future conduct as man and wife.'[4] We need not be surprised that, after this initiation, in the words of

[1] J. G. A. Prim, *J.R.S.A.I.* (1853), 334.
[2] J. G. A. Prim, loc. cit.
[3] S. Ó Súilleabháin, *A Handbook of Irish Folklore*, 662.
[4] J. O'Donovan, *J.R.S.A.I.* (1858), 31.

Maria Edgeworth, 'more matches were made at wakes than at weddings.' The most frank account of the nature of the games I have come across reads as follows: 'They were placed under the conduct of some peasant of the district who excelled in rustic wit and humour, who went under the title of "Borekeen", and whose orders were carried into force by subordinate officers, all arrayed in fantastic habiliments. The "game" usually first performed was termed "Bout", and was joined in by men and women, who all acted a very obscene part which cannot be described. The next scene generally was termed "Making the Ship', with its several parts of "laying the keel", forming the "stem and stern", and erecting "the mast", the latter of which was done by a female using a gesture and expression, proving beyond doubt that it was a relic of Pagan rites. The "Bull and the Cow" was another game strongly indicative of a Pagan origin, from circumstances too indelicate to be particularized. The game called "Hold the Light", in which a man is blindfolded and flogged, has been looked upon as a profane travestie of the passion of our Lord; and religion might also be considered as brought into contempt by another of the series, in which a person caricaturing a priest, and wearing a rosary, composed of small potatoes strung together, enters into conflict with the "Borekeen", and is put down and expelled from the room by direction of the latter . . . "Turning the Spit" and "Selling the Pig" are the names of two others of those games; in that called "Drawing the Ship out of the Mud" the men engaged actually presented themselves before the rest of the assembly, females as well as males, in a state of nudity, whilst in another game the female performers attired themselves in men's clothes and conducted themselves in a very strange manner.'[1] From other sources we learn that boys and girls, in some games, wore hides and appeared representing bulls and cows.

Parallels to these practices can be adduced from the so-called simple societies in many parts of the world, and as in Ireland Christian missionaries found it very difficult to suppress the rituals enacted between death and burial. The keening of the corpse likewise carries us through time to the earliest emotions of human societies faced with the mystery of death. The liberal

[1] J. G. A. Prim, loc. cit.

distribution of food and drink on these occasions, and the provision of tobacco or snuff—a magic substance in Negro Africa—are widespread practices. In an Irish wake the distribution of tobacco and clay pipes follows a well-established routine. Curative properties were attributed to snuff left over from a wake, and the pipes were sometimes buried, apparently often in or near a prehistoric burial place, for quantities of old pipes not infrequently turn up in archaeological excavations of such sites. Among preliterate peoples in Africa ritual demonstrations similar to those of the wake games usually form part of ceremonies directed towards ancestral spirits who had power over the luck and livelihood of the group. The women on these occasions often assume a dominant role and behave lewdly, and as part of this reversal or normal behaviour they wear men's clothes. Such rituals of rebellion, it is claimed, by canalizing social tensions, perpetuate the established systems of political organization.[1] We cannot expect to piece together the fragmentary evidences of Irish folk customs to make a coherent pattern, yet it is clear that the cathartic extravagances of the wakes not only served to dissipate overcharged tensions but were closely concerned with ancestral spirits and the perpetuation of the life of the community. Despite the emphasis on tobacco, which was, one supposes, a substitute for some forgotten magic substance, there are many hints of old custom in the names and rites of the wake games. Did the tobacco pipes, one wonders, take the place of offerings of potsherds when locally-made pottery ceased to be available? It is interesting to find that cheese is regarded as a necessary part of the food offered at wakes, for cheese is now rarely eaten by Irish countryfolk though we know that it was once an essential part of the summer diet.

Many superstitious customs pursued the corpse to the burying ground. The chairs on which the coffin rested were shaken in all directions before it was lifted off, and it was customary for those following the coffin to take some protective substance such as salt in the pocket, for 'there is never a funeral but the other people are at it, too, walking along behind'.[2] With the

[1]Max Gluckman, *Rituals of Rebellion in South-East Africa*, 24.
[2]C. M. Arensberg, *The Irish Countryman*, 216.

idea no doubt of deceiving the spirit of the dead the coffin was carried to the graveyard by the longest route, preferably a disused track, and the procession made a sunwise circle around some place or object on the way, a cross, a church-site, a lone thorn tree or a crossroads. In Connacht, stones were added to small cairns which stood at stopping places on the way. In many areas tradition tells that the coffin was carried three times around the ruined church that stands in many old graveyards. Dr. Browne's account of the procedure in the graveyard was written of Ballycroy, Co. Mayo: 'On reaching the cemetery the coffin is carried to the place where it is to be interred, and then the people all scatter to kneel and pray at the graves of their own relatives. After this, new pipes and tobacco are served out to those present, who sit down and smoke. After the pipes have been smoked, the weeds are cleared away and the grave is dug. It may be worthy of remark here that a grave is not dug on Monday if possible, and if for any reason a burial has to be made on that day, a sod is raised the day before. After the grave has been dug and the coffin lowered into it, a band of women gather round it and sing the *caione*, which here has not degenerated into mere discordant wailing . . . but is often really very musical and plaintive. When this has been done, the mourners are sprinkled with holy water and then engage in prayer: after which the grave is filled in, covered over with rough stones, often white in colour, and the unused pipes placed upon it.'[1] (Plate 14.) In Achill Island I have seen plates, which presumably once held food, left on the graves, and there are firm traditions of food and tools being placed in the coffin. 'Our neighbour John Ryan', wrote W. R. Le Fanu, 'put two pairs of shoes in the coffin of his wife—a strong one for bad weather, a light pair for ordinary wear.'[2] It was believed that the last person to be buried would be placed in charge of the other dead, and would have to carry water for them. This is the reason given for the fights which, it is said, sometimes broke out at the graveyard between rival funeral parties as to which corpse should be buried first, but it seems that fighting not infrequently occurred on the occasion of graveyard gatherings, and I have heard it justified

[1] C. R. Browne, *Ballycroy*.
[2] W. R. Le Fanu, *Seventy Years of Irish Life*, 36.

by the tradition that 'there must be blood spilt at a funeral'. In some parts of the country there were separate graveyards for men and women, and the prohibition against burying the wrong sex lasted into the present century in Inishmurray, Co. Sligo.

Many gruesome superstitions gather around old graveyards, yet it is to them that the old people wish to be taken, however neglected and overcrowded they may be. As one observer put it: 'The anxiety to be interred with their deceased relatives bestows even on death a feeling of social interest.'[1] I have referred to the Saints' Beds—small stone enclosures in very old graveyards which were perhaps oratories—and their power of curing barrenness. Bits of skulls, too, or scrapings of the moss growing on them, were sought as cures for various ailments, and the clay from the graves of priests was considered efficacious, with fine impartiality, for human sins and for the diseases of cattle. Such cures were apparently mixed with water and taken as medicine, and as part of the ritual the cloth in which they were removed was replaced on the grave. A potent love charm is said to have been worked by wrapping around the desired person, when sleeping, a long strip of skin removed from a corpse, and a dead man's hand, thrust into the milk, was, as a last resort, a sure way of getting the cream to rise.

[1]T. C. Croker, *Researches in the South of Ireland*, 167.

XXI

OLD PISHROGUES

AMONG the serious nineteenth-century students of Irish folk-life a Dublin surgeon, who is perhaps better known as the father of Oscar Wilde, deserves special mention. Sir William Wilde was not only a frequent contributor to the learned journals but he found time to compile a pioneer catalogue of the Irish antiquities now housed in the National Museum of Ireland. His very active life spanned the Great Famine, and the monumental report on the *Tables of Death* which appeared as Vol. I of Part 5 of the Census of 1851 was largely his work. In it he dwells on the shattering effects of those tragic years, 1845–47, on the immemorial customs and natural poetry of the Irish peasants: 'The closest ties of kinship were dissolved; the most ancient and long-cherished usages of the people were disregarded; the once proverbial gaiety and lightheartedness of the peasant people seemed to have vanished completely, and village merriment or marriage festival was no longer heard or seen throughout the regions desolated by the intensity and extent of the famine.'[1] Another observer noted that the traditions of hospitality were weakened greatly and that padlocks made their first appearance at this time.[2]

Wilde observed that the coming of the railway at about the same period was a contributory factor in the change because it worked to a time-table—more or less—and involved an artificial division of the day instead of an observance of the signs of nature changing with the seasons. Time was related to social activity and had different values at various seasons of the year.

[1] *Census of Ireland* (1851), I, Part 5 (1956), 242.
[2] A. M. Sullivan, *The New Ireland* (1877), 65.

The whistle of the 7.15 now replaced cock-crow. But if it were indeed true that peasant values had perished entirely and that the rural population was transformed into the moronic cattle-herders of Filson Young's *Ireland at the Cross-Roads*, then this book could not have been written. Luckily a mountain farmer will still relate time to nature and refer to a moment of summer twilight, in a memorable phrase quoted by Dr. James Delargy, as 'the time when the dew was thinking of falling'. The wonder is that so much lore and so many relics of pre-famine days have survived. Yet the term 'old pishrogues' which is applied to all varieties of witchcraft and fairy lore—even if sometimes used in awe rather than contempt—shows that these things are now regarded objectively and are no longer an accepted part of social life. Superstitious practices tend to be carried out in secret and to be resorted to only when more rational methods have been tried and found wanting. Many of the old customs, however, have had their life prolonged by children's games, the seasonal bonfires and May Queens becoming their amusements.

Most of the pishrogues relate to fairies and to trees, wells and stones; and that these elder faiths have their roots in a very remote pre-agricultural phase of human evolution is attested by their very general observance among primitive people. As an example we may take the South African Bushmen, one of the lowliest branches of the human family. In a recent report from G. P. van der Post's expedition to the Kalahari we read that in the heart of the Bushman country there are sacred hills which are regarded as the home of very ancient spirits. Van der Post was told that 'right on the top of the central hill there was a spring of water and beside it a tree which bore the fruit of knowledge, and close by the tree a rock with deep marks where the greatest spirit of all had knelt to pray'.[1] The sacred hill-tops, the ancestral spirits, the well of water, the 'gentle' tree and the cup-marked stone are familiar themes in Irish folk tradition. Throughout western Europe, from the fifth century Council of Arles onwards, churchmen denounced those 'who offer vows to trees, or wells, or stones'. The great religions have had to come to terms with such cults, in Monsoon Asia as

[1] *The Times* (14th December, 1955).

in Europe, and the emphasis on different elements of the complex naturally varies with regional circumstances and traditions. In Ireland the trees which the elder faiths had endowed with magic qualities were all small trees and shrubs—especially the rowan, holly, elderberry and whitethorn—and the evidence of archaeology and palaeobotany is that these plants first became common in the prehistoric landscape as weeds of cultivation following forest clearance by early cultivators. Thus they would have become symbols of the farming year, their white blossoms a sign of spring and the end of killing frosts, their red berries a token of the fulfilment of harvest and the promise of renewed life. At first sight one may wonder why the thorn tree should have been singled out for special attention, for it is ubiquitous in the lowland landscapes. The hedgerow thorns, of course, are newcomers, and they may be hacked with impunity, but woe betide the man who damages a fairy thorn, that is one not planted by man but growing on its own in the fields or on some ancient cairn or rath. They are to be found in every part of Ireland, but to see the fairy thorn in full majesty one should go to the naked hillsides where it stands in splendid isolation against the stone dykes and the bare hills (Fig. 89). As with the sacred groves of China, not even fallen dead branches which would serve as firewood should be removed. I have

Fig. 89. Fairy thorns. A cluster of 'gentle bushes' near Slieve Gullion, Co. Armagh: 'If you were in there on the hottest day it would starve you.'

297

known instances when a branch accidentally broken from a fairy thorn was carefully tied back in position.

The policy of the Church was to attach new myths to old rites, but only occasionally has the thorn tree been nominally won over to Christianity by dedication to local saints or by its association with sacred sites, with wells or Lammas celebrations, as for example the Criocan Thorn in the heart of Slieve Bloom.[1] On the other hand well-worship has had less stubborn roots, and 'holy water' has been more readily absorbed into Christian ritual. Nearly all the holy wells have close associations with the saints. Over 3,000 examples have been listed, most of them now half forgotten, others visited in secret and a declining number openly resorted to for cures. It is not difficult to understand the universal attraction of a spring of pure water. In the eyes of countryfolk a sense of mystery attaches to the upwelling of a spring well: it is considered lucky to have access to such a source of domestic water—a true 'well', not a hole bored in the ground—and one is invariably told that the local well yields the purest water for miles around, or even 'in all Ireland'. The attributes of purification, healing and fertility are natural concomitants of the magic welling of spring water, but besides possessing supernatural powers of this kind the holy wells are regarded as having had miraculous origins. The most famous sites where patterns are held have already been mentioned: the local holy well is rather an ever-present source of healing resorted to in need. One cannot but think of an ancient cult of waters springing from deep sources in primitive religion which was reinforced and adapted by successive intrusive cultures from the megalithic to the Christian (Pl. 16).

The ritual of 'paying rounds' at a well frequently involves associated stones and trees. A sunwise circuit of the well is made and the pilgrim, after taking a drink from the well, hangs a rag or a rosary on an adjacent bush. The ritual commonly includes also tracing with a pebble on a stone of the well-covering the mark of a cross which has been incised by countless other pebbles. This practice has a bearing on the mysterious cup-marked stones and basin-stones (bullauns) which are associated with numerous ritual sites, including wells, for I

[1]V. Cornish, *Historic Thorn Trees in the British Isles*, 53.

believe that many examples were ground out in much the same
way before the sign of the cross replaced that of the circle.
Cup-marked stones are commonly found in megalithic graves,
on standing stones and Bronze Age cists, both in the British
Isles and further afield. Some of the larger bullauns were certainly mortars, and very similar 'knocking stones' were used
until recent times for preparing barley meal by pounding the
grain with a beetle or maul (Fig. 90). To judge from the
frequency with which one finds a knocking stone in the ruins
of an old clachan it was one of the communal possessions of
such a settlement. Old specimens, more especially when the
basins are sunk in an outcrop of rock, are frequently found to
hold water, and they are then regarded as 'wells', the water
being held efficacious as a cure for warts. That such rock-basins
have magic powers is illustrated by the following reference to
a site in Scotland. On the Loch Avon side of Cairngorm is a
shelving rock bearing hand-made basins about a foot wide and
correspondingly deep: 'sitting on them is said to be efficacious
in cases of barrenness.'[1]

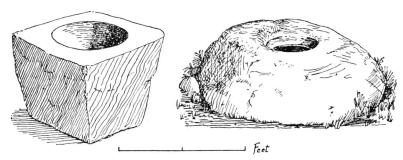

FIG. 90. Knocking stone and bullaun. Both Co. Antrim.

It is an interesting illustration of the pagan associations of
cup-marks, and of the success of the symbol of the cross, that
their use survived in folk practice only as cursing stones. Smooth
pebbles resting in certain stone basins are turned three times
against the sun. There are many examples in the west, some

[1] A. Mitchell, *The Past in the Present*, 265.

occurring on natural rock outcrops (Fig. 91), others ground into stone slabs resting on built-up foundations and termed altars, as at Inishmurray off the coast of Sligo. I have little doubt that they were the communal mortars of pre-Christian settlements. Their utilization as cursing stones continued into recent times. I was told of the example illustrated at Killinagh in Co. Cavan, that 'you would think twice before turning the stones, because the curse would come back on you unless the

FIG. 91. Cursing stones by Upper Lough Macnean at Killinagh, Co. Cavan. (For scale, the large central stone measures 15 in. by 12 in.)

cause was just'. At many holy wells curiously shaped stones were regarded as having curative powers, and they were borrowed for use by people too ill to visit the well. At St. Olan's Well, Dromatimore, Co. Cork, the rounds include visits to the saint's Cap and Stone. The former is an oval quartzite stone which rests on an ogham-inscribed monolith and which replaces one, removed by the parish priest a century ago, which was invested with magical properties. 'It was said to be an unfailing talisman, and was much sought after for various feminine ailments, particularly maternity cases. If worn on the head and carried three times round the church it was said to cure the most violent headaches and, in addition, it had the gift of locomotion in that, if removed to any distance, it unfailingly returned to its original position.'[1] St. Olan's Stone is a boulder bearing impressions which are regarded as being the imprint of the saint's feet. Many such marked stones, including some which are clearly artificial basin stones, have been regarded with superstitious awe up and down the country and were generally interpreted as the result of a saint's kneeling or standing on the spot. It is natural to suppose that these hagiological interpretations were substituted for another set of beliefs which attached the virtues of strength, healing and fertility to cup-marked stones.

Not infrequently cup-holes are found bored through thin slabs of stones, and these 'holed stones' are invested with aphrodisiac powers. We have referred to the ceremonies associated with the Ardmore stone in Chapter XIX, and the practice of erecting a stick or pole in similar stones at one of the major festivals is recorded from other localities. Wood-Martin wrote of the Hole Stone at Doagh, Co. Antrim: 'Marriage contracts are still ratified at this spot, as country couples go there to signify their betrothal by clasping hands through the hole.' Again, 'at the holed-stone of Clocnapeacaib, county Cork, women were in the habit of drawing some of their clothes through a hole, when their confinement was approaching, to secure a favourable result, and a similar practice is followed in many other localities of women similarly situated drawing clothes through the perforated arms of ancient Irish circular-headed stone crosses'[2] (Pl. 15, 1).

Before leaving this subject I should refer to certain cup-marks which have been utilized down to recent times for the purpose of making stone balls for the game of 'bullet-throwing'. Played along the country roads, and now prohibited in Northern Ireland because it endangers traffic, its main home is in Co. Cork, where it is known as bowling. One will occasionally surprise a game in progress in the Belfast hills or around Slieve Gullion in Co. Armagh, and it is here that stone bullets were manufactured within living memory. The 'bullet-holes', three to four inches in diameter and an inch or two deep, are worn in the flat tops of boulders in the process of hammering into a

[1]P. J. Hartnett, *Béaloideas*, 10 (1941), 103.
[2]Wood-Martin, *Elder Faiths*, 2, 239–42.

perfect sphere the rounded igneous pebbles which are selected for the purpose. One wonders whether some of the many cup-marked stones which turn up in the fields in certain districts—I have seen many in Inishowen in Donegal—were used for shaping stones, such as the sling-stones with which champion slingers, of whom the legendary Cuchulainn was one, performed their feats. The sling and the sling-rod were originally hunting weapons and probably instruments of war, and one of the last refuges of slinging as a pastime was the now vanished Claddagh, the fishing suburb of Galway, where a man was not reckoned a good shot until he could strike a shilling as far away as it could be seen.[1]

Where a holy well has dried up—the usual explanation is that it was desecrated and moved its position—the sanctity of the site may be transferred to a tree. The so-called pin-well at Arboe in Co. Tyrone is a beech tree, hirsute with pins and nails, growing in the burying ground on a Celtic monastic site. A rag-well at Clonmel is visited by mountain farmers who hang rag offerings on briars at lambing and calving times, and afterwards place more rags appropriate in number to the increase obtained.[2] There is on the island of Inishmurray a wind-well which has the power of controlling the wind, the ritual being to empty the well to produce a calm. Sticks and stones also figure in wind-raising ceremonies, and 'the rude stone image of Inniskea' (Inishkea in Co. Mayo), which was dressed up in flannel each New Year's Day, had powers of producing either storm or calm.[3] Powerful magic was worked by a wooden statue of St. Macdara, formerly kept in his chapel—an oratory of early type with projecting *antae*—on an island dedicated to the saint in the extreme south-western corner of Co. Galway. Sailors passing the island dipped their sails three times in honour of the image, but we are left to guess what superstitions were involved from the statement that about the year 1640 'the bishop of Tuam caused it to be buried for weighty reasons'.[4]

[1] *U.J.A.*, 2 (1854), 164.
[2] *Béaloideas*, 15 (1945), 284.
[3] C. Otway, *Erris and Tyrawly*, 107.
[4] C. R. Browne, *Carna and Mweenish*.

Old customs die hard in isolated islands and in the loneliness of ships at sea. Fishermen in the north to this day avoid direct mention of many words such as pig, priest and rat, and similar tabus are found among fishing communities as far away as Malaya, 'Formerly when starting on fishing expeditions the crews of Irish boats were very careful that their craft should leave the shore in a direction sunways, and even yet this superstition directs the course of many a fishing boat',[1] and, we may add, controls the casting of a net. A boat should always be entered on the right-hand side. In the kingdom of Mourne 'it was unlucky to be the third boat out on leaving harbour, and men would go to any lengths to avoid it, even tying two boats together so that there should be no third boat. On a Monday morning a fisherman will laughingly refuse to give you a light for your pipe, for he would be giving away his luck for the week. There were lucky and unlucky people to whom to sell fish, and it was the custom not to sell all the catch but to leave some fish in the boat. When a present of fish was made they were lifted backwards high over the head from the boat and not given straightforwardly. Nor would the old fishermen clean their boats until the end of the season, or even wipe the fish-scales from their boots. An unlucky boat would try to steal the luck of another boat by rubbing alongside it.'[2] The long-line fishermen of Carrickfergus would always spit on the first and last hook they baited, and in the mouth of the first fresh fish taken off the hook.[3] Superstitions attach also to fresh-water fish, especially to the sacred trout which, for the most part invisible, bring luck to pilgrims who catch a glimpse of them in certain holy wells.

Innumerable pishrogues concern the domesticated animals, and in particular cows and their milk and butter, which are peculiarly liable to supernatural influences. In the face of these unseen forces it is important that a new season or a new venture, or any operation carried out for the first time, should be begun with care and due ceremony, for special danger is attached to these occasions. Thus the first rich milk given by a

[1] Wood-Martin, *Elder Faiths*, 2, 52.
[2] E. E. Evans, *Mourne Country*, 196.
[3] S. McSkimin, *The History and Antiquities of Carrickfergus*, 260.

newly-calved cow should be milked on to a piece of metal placed in the pail. Offerings of the 'beastlings' were poured in the raths and at the roots of fairy thorns, to appease the fairies. When taking a drink out of doors, the old countryman will casually spill a portion of the draught on the earth as a complimentary libation to the good people. 'When a cow fell sick through fairy malice, it was formerly by no means an uncommon practice, in the west of Ireland, to devote the ailing animal to St. Martin. The ceremony was performed by letting a few drops of blood from the cow in honour of the saint.'[1] Cows which, for no apparent reason, are not thriving are said to be elf-shot. The elf-stones or fairy-darts which are supposed to have caused the mischief are prehistoric flint arrowheads such as can be picked up in the fields. One of the tricks of the cow-doctor who is called in, and who keeps a few arrowheads handy, is to produce one by sleight of hand from the flank of the ailing beast. Or counter-magic can be worked by means of a flint arrowhead which must not be allowed to touch the ground after it has been found. The cow-doctor uses sympathetic magic in curing calves believed to be suffering from intestinal knots by drawing apart over the animal's back the loose ends of a string tied in a complicated witch-knot or 'bat', of the type which comes undone when pulled. But as always he must work the magic correctly, for if the knot is not resolved another one is tied inside the calf.

Hanging in the byre one sometimes sees a flint pebble suspended on a string through a natural hole. It is a witch-stone, protecting the cows from milk-stealers, and it may owe its virtue to the flint or to its symbolic ever-watching eye. In the Ardenne a holed flint hung in the stable is believed to preserve the horses from nightmares,[2] and nearer home in the Yorkshire dales holed stones known as ring-stones protected the cows from the evil eye. 'Blessings on all that I can see' is the traditional formula to use when one enters a byre. An ill-disposed person could, merely by looking at it, 'blink' a cow so that its milk would yield no butter. The cow could be cured by burning under its nose a portion of the blinker's clothes

[1] Wood-Martin, *Elder Faiths*, 2, 6.
[2] H. H. Turney-High, *Château-Gérard* (1953), 232.

and a handful of thatch taken from above the door of his house. Butter-making must have been a chancy and critical business when each family had only one or two cows, ill-fed for a large part of the year, and there were fairies, witches and blinkers to contend with. The protective charms and prognostications connected with churning are legion. If you should enter an old-style mountain kitchen when churning is in progress you may well be invited to lend a hand, or at least to 'leave your weight on the staff,' just to show that your intentions are not evil. There must be no bad words during churning, no quarrels, no singing or drinking: to drink anything is presumably to dilute the milk. If the milk splashes the churner is fated to marry a drunken mate. When the butter at last breaks a small ball of it is traditionally taken and smeared on the wall or tossed on top of the dresser to bring luck to the house, perhaps originally as an offering to the fairies. And when the churning is finished the staff should be twisted round three times and placed across the mouth of the churn. There are many other precautions that may be taken: a horseshoe—preferably 'a shoe of one heating'—tied to the churn or nailed to the bottom; a nail from a horseshoe or from a coffin driven into churn or staff; a ring of salt placed on the lid; a twig of rowan tied round the churn. Or the plough coulter should be heated in the fire, and the churnstaff tied with a straw rope to the fire-crane: if the staff is made of rowan-wood so much the better. If despite all precautions the butter does not come there are ways of catching the thief. For instance, a cake is baked and stuck with pins and a bunch of yarrow placed in the churn. The thief will come crying to the door in pain, and he must not be allowed in but turned away.

Special precautions should also be taken to make the house safe at night from unwanted visitations. Before the fire is raked and 'smoored' (buried in peat-ash) a spark should be dropped into the foot-water, the water in which feet have been washed and to which many superstitions are attached. The carded flax should be placed under a weight, the band taken off the spinning wheel and the quern dismantled. Many stories are told of the risks involved in letting the fairies have access to these things. Finally the besom should be placed against the door: the besom's association with everyday tasks and with the fireside endows it with special power. Thrown after a departing match-maker or anyone going on an important errand, it brings luck to his mission.

For most people, needless to say, such things are now mean-ingless superstitions—old pishrogues. True, one still hears occasionally of cows being blinked, of a black cock buried alive as a cure for epilepsy, of a healthy woman pining away because a neighbour was sticking pins into a waxen image. These are stray survivals, doomed to disappear; but in a larger sense the past never wholly dies: it lives on buried in the minds of men and in the landscapes they have fashioned.

BIBLIOGRAPHY AND ABBREVIATIONS

A. B., *The Rosses in 1753:* An appendix to Walker, J. C., *Historical Memoirs of the Irish Bards,* Vol. 2 (2nd edition, 1818).

Advertisements for Ireland, 1623 (Edited by O'Brien, G., 1923).

Andrews, E., *Ulster Folklore* (1913).

Anon, A Tour in Ireland in 1672–74 (*J.C.H. and A. Soc.,* 10, 1904).

Anon, *A Tour Through Ireland in 1779* (1780).

Anon, *The Saxon in Ireland* (1851) (Author, W. Ashworth).

Antiquity, A Quarterly Review of Archaeology.

Arensberg, C. M., *The Irish Countryman* (1937).

Arensberg, C. M. and Kimball, S. T., *Family and Community in Ireland* (1940).

Aspects of Archaeology: Aspects of Archaeology in Britain and Beyond: Essays edited by Grimes, W. F. (1951).

Atthill, L., *Recollections of an Irish Doctor* (1911).

Barrow, J., *A Tour Round Ireland* (1836).

Béaloideas, The Journal of the Folklore of Ireland Society.

Berg, Gösta, *Sledges and Wheeled Vehicles* (1935).

Bichino, J. E., *Ireland and its Economy* (1830).

Binns, J., *Miseries and Beauties: The Miseries and Beauties of Ireland* (2 vols., 1837).

Boate, G., *Ireland's Natural History* (1652).

British Calendar Customs: Scotland, Vol. 1 (Banks, M.), 1937.

Browne, C. R., *Inishbofin and Inishshark:* The Ethnography of Inishbofin and Inishshark, Co. Galway, *P.R.I.A. 3* (1893–96), 317–70.

Browne, C. R., *The Mullet, Inishkea Islands, and Portacloy:* ibid. 587–649.

Browne, C. R., *Ballycroy: P.R.I.A. 4* (1896–98), 74–111.

Browne, C. R., *Clare Island and Inishturk: P.R.I.A. 5* (1898–1900), 40–72.

Browne, C. R., *Garumna and Lettermullen:* ibid., 223–68.

Browne, C. R., *Carna and Mweenish: P.R.I.A. 6* (1900–02), 503–34.

Browne, C. R. and Haddon, A. C., *The Aran Islands: P.R.I.A.* 2 (1891–93), 768–830.

Burdy, S., *The Life of Philip Skelton*, 1792 (1914 edition).

Bush, J., *Hibernia Curiosa* (1769).

C.S.P. (*I*): *Calendar of the State Papers relating to Ireland.*

Cable, M. and French, F., *The Gobi Desert* (1942).

Cambrensis, Giraldus, *Topography of Ireland* (Translated by J. J. O'Meara, 1951).

Cambridge Economic History of Europe, Vol. 1 (Edited by Clapham, J. H. and Power, E., 1941).

Campbell, Å., Irish Fields and Houses, *Béaloideas*, 5 (1935), 57–74.

Campbell, Å., Notes on the Irish House, *Folk-Liv*, 1937, 207–34; 1938, 173–96.

Campbell, T., *A Philosophical Survey: A Philosophical Survey of the South of Ireland* (1778).

Carew, Sir George, *Survey of Kerry and Desmond* (1617).

Carmichael, A., *Carmina Gadelica*, I (1928).

Census of Ireland for the Year 1851, part 5, Vol. 1.

Chapple, E. D. and Coon, C. S., *Anthropology: Principles of Anthropology* (1946).

Childe, V. G., *Skara Brae: Skara Brae, A Pictish Village in Orkney* (1931).

Co. Louth Arch. Journ.: County Louth Archaeological Journal.

Cole, Grenville, *Ireland the Outpost* (1919).

Connell, K. H., *The Population of Ireland*, 1750–1845 (1950).

Coote, Sir C., *Armagh: Statistical Survey of the County of Armagh* (1804).

Coote, Sir C., *Cavan: Statistical Survey of the County of Cavan* (1802).

Corkery, D., *The Hidden Ireland* (1925).

Cornish, V., *Historic Thorn Trees in the British Isles.* (N.D.)

Croker, T. C., *Researches in the South of Ireland* (1824).

Curwen, E. C., *Plough and Pasture* (1946).

Curwen, J. C., *Observations on the State of Ireland* (2 vols., 1818).

Custom is King: Essays presented to R. R. Marett (1936).

De Latocnaye, *A Frenchman's Walk through Ireland, 1796–97* (Translated by Stevenson, J., 1917).

Derricke, J., *The Image of Ireland* (1581).

Devon Commission: Digest of Evidence etc. Part I (1847), Part 2 (1848).

Dillon, Myles (editor), *Early Irish Society* (1954).

Dineley's Tour in Ireland, 1661. (Edited by Graves, J. 1870).

Dobbs, R., *County Antrim in 1683: Description of the County of Antrim* (1683) in Hill, G., *The McDonnells of Antrim* (1873).

Donaldson, J., *Upper Fews in 1838: A Historical and Statistical Account of the Barony of Upper Fews in the County of Armagh, 1838* (Reprinted 1923).

Doyle, J. B., *Tours in Ulster* (1854).

Drummond, J. C. and Wilbraham, A., *The Englishman's Food* (1939).

Dub. Univ. Mag.: The Dublin University Magazine.

Dubourdieu, J., *Statistical Survey of the County of Down* (1802).

Dubourdieu, J., *Statistical Survey of the County of Antrim*, 2 vols. (1812).

Dufferin, Lord, *Irish Emigration* (1867).

Duignan, M., Irish agriculture in Early Historic Times, *J.R.S.A.I.* 74 (1944), 124–45.

Dutton, H., *Clare: Statistical Survey of the County of Clare* (1808).

Economic History Review.

Edgeworth, R. L., *An Essay on the Construction of Roads and Carriages* (1813).

Evans, E. E., The Ecology of Peasant Life in Western Europe, in *Man's Role in Changing the Face of the Earth*, Ed. W. L. Thomas (1956).

Evans, E. E., *Irish Heritage* (1942).

Evans, E. E., *Mourne Country* (1951).

Fleure, H. J., *A Natural History of Man in Britain* (1951).

Flower, R., *The Western Isle* (1944).

Foster, T. C., *Letters: Letters on the Condition of the People of Ireland* (1846).

Freeman, T. W., *Ireland: Its Physical, Historical, Social and Economic Geography* (1950).

Gamble, J., *Views of Society and Manners in the North of Ireland* (1819).

Geography, Journal of the Geographical Association.

Gernon, Luke, *A Discourse of Ireland, Anno 1620* (in Falkiner, C. L., *Illustrations of Irish History*, 1904).

Gluckman, M., *Rituals of Rebellion in South-East Africa.* The Frazer Lecture, 1952 (1954).

Graham, H. C., *The Social Life of Scotland in the Eighteenth Century* (4th edition, 1937).

Gwerin, A Half-Yearly Journal of Folk Life.

Gwynn, S., *The Fair Hills of Ireland* (1906).

Haddon, A. C., *The Study of Man* (1898).

Haldane, A. R. B., *The Drove Roads of Scotland* (1952).

Hall, Mr. and Mrs. S. C., *Ireland—its Scenery, Character, etc.* (3 vols., 1841–43).

Hamilton, J., *Sixty Years' Experience: Sixty Years' Experience as an Irish Landlord* (1894).
Harris, W., *The Ancient and Present State of the County of Down* (1744).
Harris, W., *Hibernica* (1770).
Hennell, T., *Change in the Farm* (1934).
Hill, Lord George, *Gweedore: Facts from Gweedore* (1846) (5th edition, 1887).
Hornell, J., *British Coracles and Irish Curraghs* (1938).
Inglis, H. D., *Ireland in 1834: A Journey throughout Ireland during the Spring, Summer and Autumn of 1834* (2 vols., 1834).
J.C.H. and A. Soc.: Journal of the Cork Historical and Archaeological Society.
J.R.A.I.: Journal of the Royal Anthropological Institute of Great Britain and Ireland.
J.R.S.A.I.: Journal of the Royal Society of Antiquaries of Ireland.
Jones, W. Bence, *A Life's Work in Ireland* (1880).
Journal of the Galway Archaeological and Historical Society.
Joyce, P. W., *A Social History of Ancient Ireland* (1903).
Keating, G., *History of Ireland* (Irish Texts Society, I).
'Kinnfaela', *The Cliff Scenery of South-Western Donegal* (1867).
Knight, P., *Erris in the Irish Highlands* (1836).
Kohl, G., *Ireland* (1843).
Le Fanu, W. R., *Seventy Years of Irish Life* (1893).
Lever, C., *The Martins of Cro'Martin* (2 vols., 1864).
Loudan's Encyclopaedia of Agriculture, 1831.
Macalister, R. A. S., *The Archaeology of Ireland* (1949).
MacNeill, E., *Celtic Ireland* (1921).
Madden, Dr. S., *Reflections and Resolutions: Reflections and Resolutions proper for the Gentlemen of Ireland* (1738).
Man, A Monthly Record of Anthropological Science.
Martin, Martin, *The Western Isles: A Description of the Western Islands of Scotland, c. 1695* (1703), (Edition of 1934).
Mason, W. Shaw, *Parochial Survey: A Statistical Account or Parochial Survey of Ireland.* 3 vols. (1814–19).
Maxwell, C., *Country and Town in Ireland under the Georges* (1940).
Maxwell, W. H., *Wild Sports of the West* (1832). Every Irishman's Edition. N.D.
McClintock, H. F., *Old Irish and Highland Dress* (1943).
McLysaght, E., *Irish Life in the Seventeenth Century* (1939).
McParlan, J., *Statistical Survey of the County of Donegal* (1802).
McSkimin, S., *The History and Antiquities of Carrickfergus* (1811) (2nd Edition, 1823).
Miller, H., *My Schools and Schoolmasters* (1857).

Mitchell, A., *The Past in the Present* (1880).

M(offatt), W(illiam), *A Description of the Western Isle* (1724).

Mogey, J. M., *Rural Life in Northern Ireland* (1947).

Montgomery, W., *Description of Ardes Barony, in the County of Down,* 1683 (in Young, R. M., *Historical Notices of Old Belfast and its Vicinity,* 1896).

Montgomeryshire Collections, The: Collections Historical and Archaeological relating to Montgomeryshire and its Borders.

Morley, H., *Ireland under Elizabeth and James I* (1890).

Moryson, Fynes, *The Commonwealth of Ireland; The Itinerary.*

Moryson, Fynes, *The Manners and Customs of Ireland:* in Falkiner, C. L., *Illustrations of Irish History* (1904).

Muhlhausen, L., Contributions to the Study of the Tangible Material Culture of the Gaoltacht. *J.C.H. and A. Soc.* 38 (1933), 67–71; 39 (1934), 41–51.

Murphy, M., *At Slieve Gullion's Foot* (1940).

New Ireland Review, The.

North Munster Antiquarian Journal.

O'Brien, G., *The Economic History of Ireland in the Seventeenth Century* (1919).

O'Crohan, T., *The Islandman* (1934).

O'Flaherty, R., *H'Iar Connaught: A Chorographical Description of West or H'Iar Connaught* (1684). (Edited by Hardiman, J. 1846).

O'Grady, S., *Silva Gadelica* (1892).

O'Rahilly, T. F., *Early Irish History and Mythology* (1946).

Ordnance Survey: *Manuscript Memoirs,* 1834–38 (in Royal Irish Academy).

Ó Súilleabháin, *A Handbook of Irish Folklore* (1942).

Otway, C., *Sketches in Ireland* (1827).

Otway, C., *A Tour in Connaught* (1839).

Otway, C., *Sketches in Erris and Tyrawly* (1841).

P.R.I.A.: Proceedings of the Royal Irish Academy.

P.S.A.S.: Proceedings of the Society of Antiquaries of Scotland.

Parliamentary Gazetteer of Ireland, The (1844–46).

Peate, I. C., *The Welsh House* (1944).

Petty, Sir W., *The Political Anatomy of Ireland* (1691).

Piers, Sir H., *West-Meath: A Chorographical Description of the County of West-Meath* (1682) in Vallancey, C., *Collectanea de Rebus Hibernicis,* I (1770).

Pim, J., *The Condition and Prospects of Ireland* (1848).

Pococke's Tour, 1752: Pococke's Tour in Ireland in 1752 (Edited by Stokes, G. T., 1891).

311

Praeger, R. Ll., *The Way that I Went* (1937).

Report of the Royal Commission on the Land Law (Ireland) Act (1881).

Salaman, R. N., *The History and Social Influence of the Potato* (1949).

Sampson, G. V., *Statistical Survey of the County of Londonderry* (1802).

Sampson, G. V., *Memoir: A Memoir Explanatory of the Chart and Survey of the County of London-Derry* (1814).

Sauer, C. O., *Agricultural Origins and Dispersals* (1952).

Shand, A. I., *Letters from the West of Ireland* (1884).

Shaw, Rose, *Carleton's Country* (1930).

Sinclair, C., *Thatched Houses* (1953).

Spenser, E., *View of the State of Ireland* (1633).

Story, G., *An Impartial History of the Wars of Ireland*, 1691 (2nd edition, 1693).

Sullivan, A. M., *New Ireland* (1877).

Synge, J. M., *In Wicklow, West Kerry and Connemara* (1911).

Synge, J. M., *The Aran Islands* (1907); (1912 edition).

Thompson, R., *Meath: Statistical Survey of the County of Meath* (1802).

Tighe, W., *Kilkenny: Statistical Observations, County of Kilkenny* (1802).

Tuke, J. H., *A Visit to Donegal and Connaught in the Spring of 1880* (1888).

Turney-High, H. M., *Château-Gérard* (1953).

Twiss, R., *A Tour in Ireland in 1755* (1776).

Ulster Folklife: Journal of the Committee on Ulster Folklife and Traditions.

U.J.A.: Ulster Journal of Archaeology.

Ulster Medical Journal, The.

Wakefield, E., *An Account of Ireland, Statistical and Political* (2 vols., 1812).

Weld, I., *Roscommon: Statistical Survey of the County of Roscommon* (1832).

Wilde, Lady, *Ancient Legends, Mystic Charms and Superstitions of Ireland* (1888).

Wilde, Sir W., *A Descriptive Catalogue of the Antiquities in the Museum of the Royal Irish Academy.* 3 vols. (1857–62).

Williamson, K., *The Atlantic Islands* (1948).

Wood-Martin, W. G., *Elder Faiths: Traces of the Elder Faiths of Ireland* (2 vols., 1902).

Young, A., *Tour: A Tour in Ireland made in the years 1776, 1777, and 1778* (1780).

INDEX

(Page numbers in italics refer to the illustrations)

Calf shelter, *119*
California, 80, 124, 217, 268
Cambrensis, Giraldus, 4, *152*, 266
Campbell, A., 40, 46, 89, 115
Campbell, T., 46, 51, 189
Car, Irish, 165, *166*, 174–5, 196
—, slide, see Slide-car
Carew, Sir George, 4
Carlingford Lough, 221
Carmichael, A., 160, 276
Carrageen, 217, 219
Carrothers, E. N., 245
Caschrom, 131, 134
Cattle, 9, 35, 41, 255–9, 267, 272, 275
Cauldron, 75
Cavan, Co., 30, *55*, 65, 69, 70, 90, 110, *120*, 124, *125*, 129, 133, *135*, *142*, 146, *154*, 164, 194, *214*, *249*, 279, 286, *300*
Ceilidhe, 11, 32
Celtic Church, 7
— culture, 7, 68, 82
— language, see Gaelic
— overlords, 17, 39, 167
Central hearth, 62ff.
Chairs, *93*, *94*
Champ, 108
Changelings, 289
Chariots, 166
Charlesworth, J. K., 19
Cheese, 82, 289, 292
Childe, V. G., 62, 65
Chimneys, 55, 64–65
—, thatched, 54, *55*
China, 174, 210, 243, 249, 297
Christmas, 1, 151, 211, 223, 279–281
Churn, *2*, 93ff., *96*
—, harvest, 162–3
Clachans, 9, 11, 21, 23–26, *25*, 29, 40, 45, 106–7, 112
Claddagh, the, 302
Clapham, J. H., 3, 9, 134
Clare, Co., 29, 33, 46, 54, *61*, 80, *94*, 105, 131, 147

Clare, I., 41, 69, 170
Cleit, 125
Clews, 202
Clips, 149, *150*
Clochauns, 114ff, *116*, 125
Clod-slipe, 149
Clusters, *25*, 28, 30, 123. See Clachans
Coaring, 131
Cock-fighting, 262
Cocks, hay, 112, 153, *154*, 155, 164
Coghill nets, 247
Cole, Grenville, 5
Collar, horse, 69, *206*
Collins, A. E. P., 107
Collop, 36
Columbkille, 189, 270. See St. Columba
Congested Districts Board, 24
Cook, Captain, 243
Cooring, see Joining
Coote, Sir Charles, 134
Cork, Co., 29, 33, 46, 54, 76, *94*, 111, 130, 138, *154*, 201, 204, 216, 230, 264, 277
Corn, 140, see Oats
— kilns, see Kilns
Cornish, V., 298
Cornwall, 102, 118, 148, 155, 167
Cots, *239*, 242
Couples, 44, 50
Couvade, 289
Coves, 65, 118. See also Souterrains
Cow dung, 65, 100, 272
Cows, 23, 41, 45, 60, 66, 199, 255, 299. See also Cattle
Cow's grass, 29
Crab pots, *231*
Cradle, *93*
Crane, 66, 67
Crane, E. E., 126
Crannogs, 6
Crawford, O. G. S., 167

INDEX

Fairies, 30, 71, 103, 112, 272, 277, 280, 289, 296, 304–5
Fairs, 253ff.
Fairy thorns, 272, 297, 304
Famine, the Great, 5, 10–11, 20, 34, 40, 57, 97, 123, 131, 133, 282, 286, 295
Famine walls, 108
Fan-bellows, 63
Farls, 79
Faroe Is., 71
Farrows, 123
Fen peat, 14, 183, 185
Fences, 100ff. See Ditches
Fermanagh, Co., 49, 69, 80, 119, 128, 169, 178, 239, 263, 283, 287
Ferns, 216, 275
Fiddle design, 178, 179
Fiddle, sowing, 146, 147
Finland, 124, 174
Finlay, T. A., 60
Fir, bog, see Bog timber
— hatchet, 185, 198
— rooter, 185, 198
— ropes, 47, 52, 87, 203, 204, 241
— splits, 90, 185, 246
Fishing, 225ff., 233ff.
— floats, see Stookies
— frog, 225
Fitzgerald, E., 271
Flachter, 51, 138, 148, 188
Flags, 217, 226
Flail, 2, 213–16, 214, 246
Flake, 69
Flat roof, 119, 120
Flax, 26, 56, 157, 159
—, harvest knots of, 208, 209
Fleure, H. J., xvi
Flow peat, 188–9
Flower, Robin, 39
Foster, T. C., 26
France, 6, 91, 115, 118, 131, 148, 213
Frassing, 226

Freeman, T. W., 255
Friendship, 10
Funerals, 291ff.
Fynes Moryson, 62, 75, 82–83

Gaelic language, 2, 73, 200, 260
Gaeltacht, 3, 44
Gaits, 153, 158
Galway, Co., 26, 33, 42, 52, 55, 60, 69, 80, 108, 133–4, 169, 190, 198, 220, 239, 241–2, 251, 257–8, 268, 274, 302
Gardens, 29, 106, 141
Garland Sunday, 208, 275–6
Gates, 20ff., 22, 101, 102, 104
Gatherings, 218, 253ff.
Geddes, Sir Patrick, 148
Geese, 36
Gernon, Luke, 44
Giants' Graves, see Megaliths
Glacial period, see Ice Age
Glaiks, 98
Glassan, 226
Gluckman, Max, 292
Gneeve, 29
Goats, 11, 36, 267–9
Gobi, the, 210
Gold ornaments, 196
Good Friday, 142, 224, 271
Gorse, see Whins
Gort, see Gardens
Gowl-gob, 134, 135
Gracie, H. S., 174
Graddan bread, 81
Graffan, 132, 135
Graham, A., 44
—, H. G., 85
—, J. M., 34
Graves, J., 131
Green, E. R. R., 279
Griddle, 77
Gugger, 146. See Steeveen
Guy Fawkes, 277

Hack, 148
Haddon, A. C., 45, 174, 194

317

INDEX

Megaliths, 7, 17, 72, 103, 105, 114, 117
Melanesia, 268
Mell, 2, 148
Merryman, Bryan, 286
Mesopotamia, 174
Methers, 99, 196
Mexico, 268, 269
Michaelmas, 276
Milk, 35, 81, 95, 112, 118, 272, 294, 303
Miller, Hugh, 66
Mitchel, N. C., 244
Mitchell, A., 65, 79, 103, 115, 120, 299
Mitchell, G. F., 184–5
Moffatt, W., 40, 93, 197
Mogey, J. M., 172, 179
Mongols, 66, 86
Montgomery, W., 219
Morley, H., 54
Morocco, 197
Morrowing, 142
Mourne Mts., 16, 33, 35, 37, 62, 97, 108, 130, 222, 224
Mud houses, 46ff., 47
— turf, 194–5
Mulcaire, River, 245
Mummers, 1, 279, 287
Murphy, M., 103
Mussels, 224, 225
Myres, Sir John, 152

Neolithic period, 6, 8, 43, 73, 75–76, 117, 132, 186, 254
Nests, hens', see Hens
—, pigeons, 207
Nets, coghill, 247
—, draft, 250
—, seine, 250
—, trammel, 251
New Grange, 17
New Year's Day, 223, 280, 302
New Zealand, 81
Nigeria, 208
Nile, River, 240

Noggins, 74, 75
Norsemen, 7–8, 16, 237, 240
North America, 81–82, 127, 180, 198, 243, 247
Norway, 9, 27, 33, 35, 60, 82, 170, 241. See also Scandinavia
Nure, River, 242

Oak, 14, 49, 101, 186. See also Bog timber
Oatcakes, 77ff., 284–5
Oats, 8, 33, 56, 77, 81, 132, 140, 201
O'Brien, G., 109, 182
O'Brien, M., 233
O'Connor, Frank, 286
O'Crohan, T., 88, 224, 230
O'Donovan, J., 290
Offaly, 18. See also King's Co.
O'Flaherty, R., 34, 115, 149, 213
O'Grady, S., 236
O'Kelly, M. J., 76
Openfields, 9, 20–21, 29, 32, 36, 110, 149, 201
O'Rahilly, T. F., 18
Orangemen, 151, 212
O'Riordain, S. P., 107, 268
Orkney Is., 71, 93, 115
O'Sullivan, S., 215, 290
Otter, 248
Otway, C., 29, 83, 86, 107
Outfield, 9, 23, 32, 34, 56, 129, 132, 141, 147
Outshot, bed, see Cailleach
Oven-pot, 77

Pahvees, 258
Palaeolithic Age, 6
Pale, the, 9, 16, 78, 111, 143, 259
Pampooties, 213
Pardogs, 168, 169
Paring and burning, 121, 138, 147ff.
Pastoral nomadism, 3. See Booleying

320

Saints' beds, 294
Salaman, R. N., 11, 83
Sally (willow), 52, 54, 65, 95
Salmon, 233, 241–3, 250
— spears, 242, 245, 246
Salt, 284, 290–2
Sampson, G. V., 62, 103, 131, 144, 248
Sandeels, 224
Sandklef, A., 215
Sauer, C. O., 117
Sayce, R. U., 82, 112, 248
Scallops, 90, 224, 226
Scandinavia, 48, 74, 172, 183, 197, 202, 214–16
Scollops, 50–54, 55, 56
Scooches, 246
Scotland, 6ff., 79, 85, 89, 102, 117–18, 164, 168, 174ff., 181, 188, 213, 278, 280, 299
—, highlands of, 65, 78, 117, 148, 160, 257
Scots cart, 176–80, 177
Scott, Sir Walter, 261
Scraws, see Sods
Scutching, 123, 159
Scythe, 151, 156, 157, 221
— cradle, 156
Seaby, W. A., xv
Seals, 211, 231, 230, 237, 252
Seaweed, see Wrack
Settle-bed, 68, 87
Shannon, River, 17–18, 133, 233, 238, 242–7, 258
Shaw, Rose, 30
Sheaf, hooding, 153, 162, 164
—, last, 162–3, 270
Shearing, 203
— rope, 203
Sheep, 36, 60, 257
— -cock, 164
Shell sand, 34
Shetland Is., 81, 170
Sheugh, 105
Shovels, 128, 144
Shrove Tuesday, 271

Siam, 174
Sickles, 2, 56, 149, 151, 205, 221–2
Sieves, 212–13
Sinclair, Colin, 54
Skeagh, 69, 247
Skib, 212
Skiff, 240, 251
Skin, 143, 211–13, 237
— boats, see Curraghs
— shoes, see Pampooties
— windows, 49
Skiver, 247
Slane, 187–9, 190
Slater, G., 9
Sledges, 165, see Slipes
Slide-car, 155, 165–76, 173
—, plough, 130, 172
Slieve Bloom, 298
Slieve Croob, 276
Slieve Donard, 16
Slieve Gullion, 297, 301
Slievemore, 16, 60, 87, 91
Sligo, Co., 133, 289, 294, 300
Slipes, 155, 171, 172
Sloke, 59
Small, James, 129
Smith, F. T., 121
Smiths, 68, 134, 186, 190, 199, 200
Smokes, 59
Smooring, 71
Smuggling, 232
Snares, 205, 229, 243
Soot, 68
Soot houses, 114ff., 120
Sorrel, 36
Souterrains, 62, 118–19
Sowans, 277
Spades, 11, 127ff., 128, 136
—, turf. See Slane
Spain, 6, 9, 93, 115, 131, 134, 138, 168, 196, 210, 286
Spalpeens, 155, 259
Spears, fish, see Eel, Salmon
Spenser, Edmund, 34